BASIC
from the Ground Up

Hayden Computer Programming Series

BASIC

from the Ground Up

David E. Simon

HAYDEN BOOK COMPANY, INC.
Rochelle Park, New Jersey

To Edith Abbott

Library of Congress Cataloging in Publication Data

Simon, David E.
  Basic from the ground up.

  (Hayden computer programming series)
  Includes index.
  1. Basic (Computer program language)
I. Title.
QA76.73.B3S55   001.6'424   78-5392
ISBN 0-8104-5760-1 (trade)
ISBN 0-8104-5117-4 (text)

Printed in the United States of America

        2   3   4   5   6   7   8   9   PRINTING
    ───
     78 79 80 81 82 83 84 85 86   YEAR

PREFACE

In this book, we will study the BASIC computer language. We will assume that you know absolutely nothing about computers, and we will investigate everything from the very beginning. We will also assume that you know very little about mathematics, although you should know how to say, "Let x be the number of marbles in Norman's pocket," without flinching and also know some area formulas—that the area of a rectangle is base times height, for example. All of the examples and some of the problems in every chapter require only this much math, although there are more complex mathematical problems in later chapters to challenge math wizards.

In addition to BASIC, we'll peek at what is going on inside the computer when you write BASIC programs. Computers don't run by black magic, and knowing what's going on among the wires will help you both to write better BASIC programs and to learn further languages. We won't look at any wiring diagrams or circuitry, but we will consider how the possibilities and perversities of computer circuits can affect your programs.

New versions of BASIC continue to spring up like weeds, and so, of course, we can't consider all the different versions. On the other hand, we won't restrict our study to one particular version either; rather, we'll look at one form of each BASIC construction and then glance at some of the most common alternate forms. Afterwards, you'll have little trouble speaking your computer's dialect. A manual for your computer's version of BASIC will come in handy. It'll probably look completely meaningless to you now since it was written to describe the language concisely, not to teach you BASIC. As we progress, however, you'll begin to know what to look for, and the language will seem less formidable.

The examples and problems in Chaps. 2 through 4 assume that you know the material in previous chapters; therefore, you can't skip around too much. However, you needn't plod through reading every word on every page if that is not your style. You can read the first parts of each chapter until you get the general idea, try some of the problems, and then move on. This approach is rather sensible, since once you've read quickly as far as Sec. 3.2, you can work on more interesting programs while mastering details in the earlier chapters. All the information about each statement is contained in a single chapter for easy reference, but you needn't learn it all the first time through. A nodding acquaintance should suffice to guide you through subsequent chapters.

The sections of Chap. 5 are more or less independent of each other. They outline other useful BASIC features.

Chapter 6 presents six interesting problems for computer solution. Each presents the problem, outlines a method to try, and in some cases gives a solution. Each is intended as a jumping off place for you to try out your skills on larger, more complicated programs. They assume that you have read through Chap. 4; Section 6.3 also assumes that you have read Sec. 5.3. The mathematics you'll need for these sections is noted below. In Secs. 6.3 and 6.5, a little patience may substitute for a lack of proper knowledge.

Section	You Need to Know About:	It Might be Useful to Know About:
6.1	No special area	
6.2	Graphs of functions	
6.3		Points in a coordinate plane
6.4	Graphs of functions	
6.5		Elementary probability
6.6	Elementary physics	

Don't overlook the summary of BASIC in Appendix C. Not only is it a useful reference source, it also introduces you to the format which computer people often use in manuals to describe computer languages. You might read the introduction to that appendix as part of your computer education.

These people deserve thanks: David Lumsdaine, for moral support and occasional contributions; Henry Ledgard, for editing the manuscript; and all those students who became captive guinea pigs for early versions.

DAVID E. SIMON

CONTENTS

BASIC
from the Ground Up

1
BREAKING GROUND

1.1   What the Computer Hasn't Got—Brains

The IQ of a typical computer, to be blunt, is zero. Most of the behavior of a two-year-old child could not be emulated by even the most sophisticated of present-day machines.

Why, then, is the computer so widely used? Simply because it has one obvious redeeming social value: it is good at clerical work. A computer can do arithmetic calculations, do filing, search through files, and reorganize existing information at staggering speeds. Armies of office clerks could not match the speed and accuracy with which a computer calculates and prints monthly phone bills alone. The computer can look up all the calls, calculate the charges on each, add them up, figure tax, add that, and print the bill before a human clerk could even type the name. And the computer will figure bills all day without getting bored and without getting careless in the late afternoon.

The computer is obedient. It does exactly what it is told to do. If told that it should charge $1.75 for a phone call to New York, there is no danger of its forgetting. Unfortunately, the computer is obedient to a fault. If someone carelessly tells the computer to add $175 to a phone bill for a call to New York, the computer will do that as well. It will continue to add $175 to the bills of those calling New York until it is caught and told to stop. That probably won't happen until the phone company has acquired many irritated customers and the business manager has a splitting headache. For this is another outstanding feature of the computer: It can turn a small mistake into a gigantic snarl in several thousandths of a second; it can make more mistakes in a minute than a clerk can make in a lifetime.

The trouble with the computer is that it has no common sense whatsoever. A human clerk would look at a memo indicating that phone calls to New York now cost $175 and know that something was fishy. But such a memo doesn't bother a computer at all; it has never made long distance calls and has no

1

idea how much they should cost. The computer brings this irritating feature to the people who program it. If you ask a friend to add 588 and 439, he will do so and tell you the answer. If you ask a computer to perform the addition, it will do so, but unless you specifically ask it to print the answer, it won't. There is a temptation to holler at the computer (as one might at a smart-aleck friend who did the addition but didn't tell you the answer), "Do what I mean, not what I say!" This, unfortunately, would not be understood by the heap of electronics in front of you. It will act only on what you say.

A computer is a box filled with electrical circuits. Its operation consists of these circuits turning one another on and off. Circuits A and B turn on circuit 194, which turns off circuit Z3, and so on. Everything in the computer is represented by either a one (the electricity is on) or a zero (the electricity is off) and combinations of various circuits being on or off.

Remembering things is one of the principal occupations of the computer. It has an internal memory (often called *core*) which is divided up into a collection of pigeon holes (called *words*). Each word contains a collection of 1's and 0's, and each word can be used to store either a number (for calculating with) or the coded form for an instruction (telling the computer what calculations to make). Once inside the memory, numbers and instructions look quite similar. If the computer gets confused, disaster results.

The central processing unit (CPU) is the center of the computer. It can push things into the pigeon holes in memory, and it can look up the contents of any particular memory word. It can look up the instructions stored in memory and act on them. It can fish a number out of memory for use in a calculation. Typically, a CPU can add numbers, multiply, divide, negate (it can subtract by negating and then adding), check to see if a number is zero, positive, or negative, and check to see if the calculations it has performed have *overflowed*, that is, become larger than the computer can handle. To the CPU are attached the various input and output devices (as a group, called *I/O*). Extra memory is often treated as such a device, as well as things like line printers, teletypes, card readers, video display terminals, and so on.

How do you deal with an idiot savant who can do arithmetic at blinding speed, but who only understands a *machine code,* in which instructions are made out of strings of 1's and 0's? Isn't it tiresome to have to translate your thoughts into 10001010111. . . for the benefit of this hulk? Don't computer programmers go cross-eyed trying to find mistakes amid reams of this stuff? The answer is yes. Coping with computers can get very tiresome. Fortunately, it is seldom necessary to deal directly with 1's and 0's. Most computer programmers are privileged to go cross-eyed looking for mistakes in programs in so-called *high-level languages.*

These high-level languages are compromises between the 1's and 0's that the computer thinks in and the far more complicated ways that a human being thinks. It is unfortunately evident that the computer is far too dense to understand our language; all computer languages are *much* simpler than English. They are, however, miles above the mountains of 1's and 0's. The means by which a computer is made to appear to understand a more complicated language is a program running inside it that translates the language into 1's and 0's. Such a program is called a *compiler*, an *assembler*, or an *interpreter* depending on the type of language being used and the method that the program uses to process it into 1's and 0's. These programs also cope with sticky little problems which arise when you want to type your numbers in base ten, and the computer wants them translated into base two. A single instruction in BASIC or FORTRAN or COBOL typically translates into many instructions inside the computer.

The compiler makes the computer look at least a little more intelligent. The language that a compiler "understands" is far easier on human beings than the language that the computer understands. One must remember, though, that none of the previous faults of the computer are solved by changing the medium of communication. It still has no common sense, and it still does exactly what you tell it and nothing else.

The IQ of a typical compiler is also zero.

1.2   Nuts and Bolts of a Computer

Let us investigate the properties of several devices to discover the essential characteristics of a computer. Consider first one of those digital watches that lights up the time of day in little red lights when you push a button. Clearly, that button activates many miniature electrical circuits that determine the time and the numbers to light up on the display. It realizes by some process or other that after 8:59, the time will be 9:00, not 8:60 nor anything else. Some of them will even figure out ("keep track of" might be a more accurate description of their activities) the day and the date and light those up when you push a different button.

But however wondrous the digital watch is, it is not a computer. You can't instruct it to do a variety of things. No matter how you push its buttons, all it will ever do is tell you the time of day, and this behavior cannot be changed.

Consider next the hand calculator. You can punch in numbers and request that they be added, subtracted, multiplied, or divided. Some of these calculators perform a dozen additional operations, the purpose of which the user may or may not understand. Are these computers?

The calculator is certainly more computerlike than the digital watch. It might be used for the same sorts of purposes, and its innards bear a striking resemblance to those of a computer. However, the calculator is *not* a computer. There is no way to give it a *program*, that is, to give it a list of instructions to remember and then have it run through the whole list at once. It does certain things when certain keys are pressed, and that is it. Such an object is, in computer jargon, *hard-wired*. It behaves as it does, not because its user has given it instructions to perform, but because its manufacturer soldered the wires together in a certain way.

Now some of these hand calculators are so-called *programmable calculators*. They have some capacity for remembering a series of instructions and then executing them all when you push a button designated for that purpose. How does this differ from a "computer"? Besides the obvious differences in physical size, price, and the length and complexity of programs that the two will accept, there are two additional differences.

First, in a programmable calculator, there are two sorts of memory— one sort which remembers the program and one sort which remembers the numbers with which the machine is calculating. In a computer there is no such distinction. A single memory stores both the programs and the numbers.

Second, programmable calculators can seldom be rigged to use such *peripheral devices* as line printers, teletypes, extra memory, and the like. They are sold in sealed boxes. Computers can almost always be wired to peripherals.

A computer, then, is an electronic device that is capable of storing numbers and a sequence of instructions in a memory and of doing the entire list of instructions in the memory when asked to do so. The user of a computer is at liberty to change the numbers or the instructions in the memory, thereby changing the computer's behavior.

Certain aspects of a computer's work are, of course, hard-wired. For example, among other things, the computer is constructed to add, store numbers in memory, fetch them back, and check if they are equal to zero. It may or may not be wired to subtract. Some computers subtract with a little two-step program, that is, they first take the negative of the number to be subtracted and then add. The nuts and bolts and wires of the computer and the things that it can do without special instruction are called the *hardware*. *Programs*, which are sequences of instructions to be stored in the computer memory, are called *software*. The statements which make up a program are sometimes called *code*.

Computer Organization   The center of a large computer system is the central processing unit, or CPU (see Fig. 1.1). When somebody asks what kind of a computer system someone has, he will likely get a response such as "IBM 360" or "PDP 11." These both name the type of CPU that the system has. The duties of the CPU were described in the previous section.

Attached to the CPU and perhaps to be considered a part of it is the *central memory*. In this memory, the CPU stores anything that it is currently working on: the instructions that make up the program that it is executing and the numbers that the program is using. Typically, it takes the CPU about one millionth of a second to get a number out of memory or to put a number back into memory. Similarly, it takes about one millionth of a second to get the next instruction of the program out of the memory. This memory *cycle time* is usually the limiting factor on the speed of the computer. Computers that can get numbers and instructions out of the memory faster can usually operate faster.

Although central memory is speedy and convenient, two things limit the amount of central memory one can have. In the first place, it is expensive. In the second place, the CPU can keep track of only a certain size of memory without getting confused. Just as there is a limit on how large a card file one librarian can keep in order, there is a limit on the size of central memory one CPU can

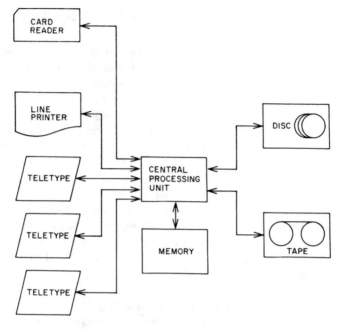

Fig. 1.1   Organization of a computer

handle. Although the central memory may store over 10,000 or even several million numbers or instructions, computer operators often want more than that. There are two types of auxiliary memory, and they are both comparatively slow. The first type is called *disc* memory. It operates more or less like a spinning record on a record player, although numbers are stored on it magnetically rather like music on a tape. Discs usually spin at sixty revolutions per second; hence it takes up to about one sixtieth of a second to get a number or instruction off the disc. A *tape drive* is even slower than disc. It works like a tape on a tape recorder, and the limiting factor on its speed is that if the computer wants to get a number stored at the far end of a 1000-foot reel of tape, it will take a while to rewind.

Also attached to the CPU are various I/O devices. A very common input device is the card. Each card may have up to eighty characters on it, and card readers can read cards at a speed of up to 20 per second. That's pretty brisk, but it is still not comparable to the one-millionth of a second cycle time. One of the most rapid output devices is the line printer. Large ones can grind out ten to thirty lines 132 letters long every second. That's fast, but the CPU can still swamp several line printers at once if it wants to. Then there are teletypes. Typing ten characters per second on one of these clunkers is well nigh impossible, although the computer might manage that speed on one. On video type terminals, a better speed might be attainable, but even so, twenty characters per second is a blazing typing speed for a human. Terminals are the slowpokes of the computer world.

Time Sharing   By comparing the speed at which the CPU operates and the speed at which a terminal runs, you can observe that it would be a gross waste of CPU time were it to pay attention to only one terminal user at a time. In the time that you can type one character on your terminal, the computer can execute tens of thousands of instructions. There is no point in having the CPU figuratively twiddling its thumbs while you are typing, so while it's waiting, the computer attends to other chores; for example, it reads a letter from another terminal; it reads someone else's entire program off a disc and runs it; it sends more lines to a line printer to be printed. This division of the computer's attention among several users is called *time sharing*, and it is a very common way of making one computer serve many people. What happens, you may object, if someone starts running a program on the computer that takes an hour and a half? Does everyone else have to wait until that program is run? No. On time-sharing systems there is always some limit on the amount of time that any one user can continuously use the computer. A tenth of a second might be the maximum. In that time, the computer does thirty or forty thousand instructions, and if that isn't enough to finish the program, the computer stops the program, saves it in half-finished form, and attends to its other users. A second or so later, it continues running that program from where it left off. The computer switches its attention from one task to another so rapidly that you will probably never be aware that it does anything besides run your own programs. If your computer is getting very heavy use, you might notice a lag of a second or two between your requests and the computer's responses.

Exercises

1. Which of the tasks on the following list would be easy to program the computer to do? Which would be difficult? Which impossible? If you think that a simplified version of one of the tasks would be significantly easier than the whole task, say so. If you think that a description of one of the tasks is vague, write down exactly what you think the computer can do.
    - (a)   Print payroll checks
    - (b)   Play tic tac toe
    - (c)   Play chess
    - (d)   Read handwritten addresses without zip codes and route mail
    - (e)   Read handwritten zip codes and route mail
    - (f)   Translate prose from English to German
    - (g)   Translate poetry from German to English
    - (h)   Keep track of General Motors' inventory
    - (i)   Write legal arguments
    - (j)   Listen to someone talking and write his words down
    - (k)   Recognize people by seeing them through a TV camera
    - (l)   Run a chemical factory
    - (m) Drive an automobile

Save your answer to this problem and look at it and revise it after you have read this book. Then keep your revised answer and take a look at it again ten years from now.

2. Find out how fast your computer system can output data when all of the teletypes, video display terminals, and printers are working. If they are all working at once, can the CPU keep up with them? Make the same investigation of input. Count card readers, paper tape readers, and teletypes. Assume that people can type at a rate of approximately seven characters per second.

1.3   Loaning Your Brain to the Computer (Flowcharting)

In order to deal with a computer, it is necessary to write explicit instructions. Instructions that are given to people are often incomplete and often assume a certain amount of savvy on the part of the recipient. With the computer no such assumption is possible.

An explicit set of instructions detailing the steps by which a problem is to be solved is called an *algorithm*.

To outline the necessary steps in solving a problem, one can use a *flowchart*. A flowchart is a diagram in which all the necessary steps are written out with arrows indicating the order in which they are to be performed. For example, a flowchart for taking the average of two numbers and writing the answer is shown in Fig. 1.2.

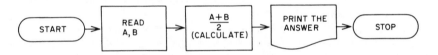

Fig. 1.2   Flowchart for taking the average of two numbers and writing the answer

Notice that the flowchart includes instructions to read two numbers, to calculate their average, and to print the answer. The square box is used for most instructions. A circle is used for a start or a stop statement. The funny shaped box (imagined by some prehistoric flowcharter to look like a piece of paper torn off a teletype) is used for instructions telling the computer to print something. The computer is to start its activity at the circle marked START and continue until it hits a box marked STOP, at which time it will terminate its activity. (See Fig. 1.3 for flowchart symbols.)

The next example is a flowchart for a computer program that checks out credit card accounts when a credit card is presented (see Fig. 1.4). The diamond-shaped box indicates an instruction which asks a computer to decide about something and to *branch* one way or the other depending on its decision.

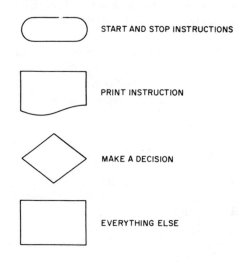

START AND STOP INSTRUCTIONS

PRINT INSTRUCTION

MAKE A DECISION

EVERYTHING ELSE

Fig. 1.3 Flowchart symbols

In this program, the computer reads the credit card number and checks whether such a number exists at all. If not, it follows the "no" branch from the diamond, prints its discovery, and stops. If there is such an account, the computer reads the amount to be charged. Then it checks that the credit limit is high enough to allow this charge. If not, it refuses credit; if so, it subtracts this charge from the remaining allowable credit and types "OK."

Flowcharts are useful for helping you clarify the logic of a complicated problem. It is necessary to have the solution organized exactly before you try to tell the computer how to do it since the computer has to be told precisely what the logic behind the problem is. As you begin to get some experience with programming, you will begin to see what sorts of things it is useful to include in flowcharts.

Phone Connection   Another example of flowcharting is the flowchart in Fig. 1.5 for the switching operation of a telephone exchange. Here are several simplifying assumptions that the flowchart presupposes:

1. This switching equipment deals with phone numbers whose prefixes are 439 (all numbers are 439-xxxx) in area code 707.
2. When you dial a 0, you get the operator right away.
3. You do *not* dial 1 for long distance in this region, but
4. All area codes have a 1 or a 0 as the second digit. Hence the machine can determine if a call is long distance by checking the second digit.
5. 411 is the number for local information.
6. 911 is the number for local emergencies.
7. There are long distance charges only if you are dialing out of the 707

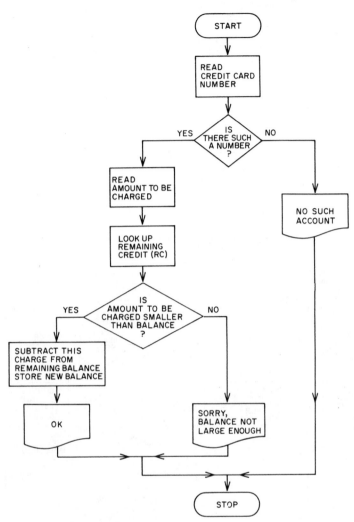

Fig. 1.4   Flowchart for credit card account checking procedure

area code. Furthermore, all calls to numbers in area code 800 are collect calls, and you are not charged.
8. If you dial your own area code, 707, you have made a mistake and should be enlightened immediately.

Exercises

Draw a flowchart describing how you would go about each of the following tasks. The short sentences following the tasks comprise partial lists of items to

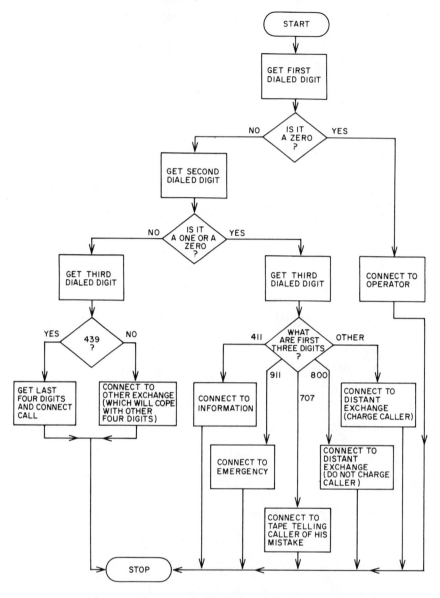

Fig. 1.5 Flowchart of telephone switching algorithm

put in the flowchart boxes. You should use the ones listed and add some of your own.

1. *Pay a visit to your least favorite aunt.* Did your car break down? Call to regret that your car has broken down. Refuse third cup of coffee. Is her coffee as bad as you

remembered it? Refuse second cup of coffee. Is it time to leave? Arrange dinner with a friend so that you can't stay for dinner.

2. *Get up in the morning.* Is it the weekend? Brush your teeth. Is it a holiday? Snooze for an extra hour. Fix breakfast. Has the morning paper arrived? Read the paper. Did you stay up til 3 in the morning? Go back to bed.

3. *Feed the cat.* Is the cat in evidence? Is there a half-empty can of food in the refrigerator? Find the can opener. Has the cat eaten yesterday's ration? Feed dry food today. Have you run out of cat food? Put cat food on the shopping list.

4. *Subtract one three-digit number from another.* Do you need to borrow? Subtract second digit of one from second digit of the other. Is number to subtract smaller than the number to be subtracted from? Can you borrow (or is next digit a zero)?

5. *Decide what opening bid to make if you are the dealer at bridge.* How many points do you have? Pass. Do you have a long suit? What is it? Open one heart. Can you preempt? Are you vulnerable? Open four clubs.

1.4   Coping with the Terminal

The great thing that a computer does is to remember a list of instructions and then act on it (very rapidly) when requested to do so. The ability of a computer to remember a list of instructions and execute them repeatedly is its greatest qualification as a clerk.

When you are "talking" to the computer on your terminal, there is a program already running in the computer. It is called the *monitor,* and one of its jobs is to make it as easy as possible for you to store a list of instructions (a *program*) in the computer and then have the computer *execute* (or *run*) the program. The monitor is also responsible for keeping order within the computer; it keeps track of who is using the computer; it makes sure that output intended for you is typed on your terminal and not somewhere else; it keeps track of your monthly bill. It does these other tasks without any fuss, and we will only be concerned with its assistance in writing and running programs.

Statements   To get an instruction stored in the computer's memory for later action, you use a *statement.* An example of one follows:

```
10 PRINT (5 + 6)
```

A statement starts with a *line number* (10, in this case), and then contains a BASIC instruction. The monitor will have the computer remember this instruction and that this is statement number 10. Nothing else will happen. No effort will be made by the computer to print the answer to the problem 5 + 6. In fact, no effort will be made even to figure out the answer. This will be done later when you ask the computer to run your program.

Every statement must have a line number. In the first place, the line number tells the monitor that you are typing a statement (rather than some other things, which will be discussed momentarily). In the second place, the line numbers tell the order for executing instructions. The computer does *not* execute instructions in the order you type them; it does them in order of line number, lowest numbers first.

It is customary and practical to number statements 10, 20, 30, and so on, rather than 1, 2, 3. It is not uncommon to want to go back and squeeze in some instructions, say between the second and third statements. If they are numbered 10, 20, 30, . . . there is no trouble since you simply number the new statements 21, 22, 23 or 24, 26, 28 or something similar. If your statements are numbered 1, 2, 3, . . . you will have great difficulty because statement numbers must be positive integers, and integers between 2 and 3 are in short supply; there are none.

There is some large number which is the largest allowable statement number. You can find it by playing on your terminal if you wish (or look in your system manual, where all this sort of information lurks).

Commands   When you have a program stored in the memory and you want the computer to execute it, you must give a *command* to the monitor. A command is an instruction to do something immediately (as opposed to a statement, which is stored now but executed later). A list of (more or less) important commands follows:

RUN   Commands the computer to execute all the statements you have put into memory, starting with the lowest numbered statement.

SCRATCH (can be abbreviated *SCR*)   Commands the computer to forget all the statements that are in memory. You should give this command when you first sit down at the terminal, since there may be a previous user's statements skulking in memory. Leftover statements are executed right along with yours when you give a RUN command, with predictably terrible results.

SAVE   Tells the computer to store your program on disc so that you can come back and use the program later without typing it in again. You will probably have to give your program a name; that may be a necessary part of the command. The rules for this procedure are in your manual.

LOAD   Tells the computer to recall some SAVEd program. Any statements currently in memory are erased when a new program is LOADed. You must tell the computer which SAVEd program you want, of course, and your manual will tell you how to do this. Often, there is also a single command to LOAD and RUN a program all in one swoop.

DAYTIME   Tells you the time of day.

BYE   Tells the computer that you are finished for the day. Subsequent to a BYE command, the computer will not respond to anything you type, except perhaps to type a message indicating that it is ignoring you. The people who run your computer system should have given you a method of regaining the computer's attention.

PRINT   Prints the value of the arithmetic expressions following the word PRINT; PRINT 5 + 6 has the computer type back 11. (Note that the mere lack of a line number changes this from a statement to a command.)

LIST   Lists all your statements presently in the computer memory in numerical order.

REN   Renumbers your statements. See your manual for details.

Errors   The monitor has one further duty: It tells you when it doesn't understand what you have typed. It does this by typing out an *error message*. This is a favorite computer trick; if something goes wrong, or if it doesn't understand what is going on, it assumes that *you* have made a mistake. It makes a feeble attempt to analyze the mistake you have supposedly made, and then it prints a message about its analysis. There is no doubt a list of error messages in your system manual.

Altering Programs   There are any number of reasons why you might want to make alterations in a program. Among them are the inability to write instructions that the computer can understand, the inability to type correctly all the time, or a disagreement between you and the computer about what constitutes proper usage of the BASIC language. (The computer always wins these arguments, unfortunately.) For these occasions, there are methods of "editing" programs. The following are useful tools:

1. If you wish to delete a line from your program, type its line number and a carriage return.
2. If you wish to change a line, retype it, line number and all. The old line will be replaced by the new one; the old one will be lost.
3. If you mistype a character in the middle of a line, delete the last one you have typed by hitting the rubout key or backspace key. (This works on most systems. Check your manual.) To go back two or more characters, hit the key twice or more. Each time you hit it, it will backspace and delete another character from the end of the line. (This happens inside the computer, not on the terminal; the terminal neither erases characters nor backspaces.) Then retype the rest of the line correctly. For example, if you have typed

        THIS IS AN EROR

you can hit the rubout, deleting the R, and then hit it again, deleting the O. Your line now looks like (inside the computer)

        THIS IS AN ER

and you type ROR. The result in the computer is

        THIS IS AN ERROR

(although on your paper, it may look like

        THIS IS AN EROR/←←/ROR

Don't worry. The computer can't read your paper.)

4. If you decide that the line you are typing is such a disaster that you would rather start over than try to correct it, hit the carriage return (which will get you an error message if your computer agrees that your line is a disaster), or hit the escape key, an act which may avoid the indignity of the error message. Some systems use a key other than the escape key for this purpose. Check with your manual.

Some systems offer a method by which you can modify an old line without retyping the entire thing. Such a method, if it exists, will be in the manual under the heading of *Editing* or *Editor*. These editing features can be helpful, but getting the hang of using an editor efficiently can be more bother than it's worth until you are writing long programs with lengthy statements.

1.5   Numbers and Their Idiosyncracies

Since the computer deals in numbers, you need to know something about how to communicate numbers to the computer in BASIC, and how the computer will type numbers back to you. If you wish to get to other topics, you need read only the first paragraph of what follows. You should, however, read the rest eventually. When you are at your terminal, keep the following rules in mind:

1. No commas are allowed. One thousand fifteen is written 1015. One million is written 1000000.
2. Decimal numbers are written as you would ordinarily write them, such as 1.17 or .00008 or 456.7.
3. Negative numbers have a negative sign in front of them: −9 or −.073.
4. There is a limit to the number of digits that a number can have. This varies from system to system; you can experiment to find out if you wish, or you can look it up.

If you come across numbers like 1.3E14* you have a choice: You can read the later section on numbers, or you can make your numbers a more reasonable size for the time being.

Numbers and Circuitry   Here is a number:

$$5782$$

It means 5 times a thosuand (10^3) plus 7 times a hundred (10^2) plus 8 times ten plus 2. The number ten is pivotal in our number system. It is the first number that we use more than one digit to express. There are ten digit symbols: 0, 1, 2, 3, 4, 5, 6, 7, 8, and 9. Place values are powers of ten. For these reasons, our method of expressing numbers is called *base ten*. Historically, other numbers

*Sneak preview: 1.3E14 means 1.3 × 10^{14}.

have been used as bases for number systems—12, 20, and 60, for example—and occasional inconvenient remnants of these systems are still in evidence: twelve inches in a foot; until recently, twenty shillings in a British pound; sixty minutes in an hour.

The computer uses none of these systems. Base ten has ten different symbols, the digits zero through nine, and the other number systems mentioned have even more or use a less convenient notation. The computer, however, has only two internal symbols. These signify that the circuit is on or that the circuit is off. Hence, the computer must express numbers using only these two symbols. It does so by representing a circuit that is on by a 1 and a circuit that is off by a 0 and by using the *base two* number system, which will be explained shortly. Although base two is good for computers, it is rather awkward for human beings, especially for those who are familiar only with base ten. For example, the number 500 becomes 111110100 in base two, a representation which is hard to read, tedious to write, and virtually impossible to express verbally. Hence, most computers are programmed to "understand" numbers in base ten by reading a number that the user types in (in base ten) and then translating it into base two for its own purposes. Answers that the computer has calculated (in base two) are converted back to base ten notation before they are printed.

The Workings of Base Two   When you write a number in base ten, the various digits have different significances depending on the positions they occupy in the number. For example, the two 5's in 573.45 mean radically different things, a phenomenon usually referred to as *place value*. The idea is that a number is broken into *places* surrounding the decimal point. The first digit to the left of the point occupies the *one's place*, and a digit there has exactly its face value. The 3 in the number above means three of something. The next place to the left is the *ten's place*; thus the 7 above means seven times ten, or seventy. The next place is the *hundred's place*. It becomes clear that the value of each place is a power of ten. There is the ten's place (10^1), then the hundred's place (10^2), then the thousand's place (10^3), and so on. To the right of the decimal point, the first place is the *tenth's place*; the 4 there represents four-tenths. In the next place to the right, the 5 represents five one-hundredths. Here the place values are reciprocals of powers often; one tenth ($1/10^1$), one one-hundredth ($1/10^2$), one one-thousandth ($1/10^3$), and so on.

In base two, different place values are used in order to express numbers using only the symbols 1 and 0. The first place to the left of the point is still the *one's place*, but the next place to the left is the *two's place*, the next is the *four's place*, then the *eight's*, then the *sixteen's*, and so on in powers of two instead of powers of ten.

For instance,

$$1011$$

in base two means one times eight, plus 0 times four, plus one times two, plus 1, which is eleven. Any integer can be expressed this way, as shown below.

Base 10	Base 2
1	1
2	10
3	11
4	100
5	101
6	110
7	111
8	1000
9	1001
10	1010
50	110010
100	1100100
103	1100111

To the right of the decimal point in base two, the first digit is the one-halves, then the one-fourths, then the one-eighths, and so on. For example, the number ¾ equals one-half plus one-fourth and would be written

.11

in base two. Any fraction can be written as a terminating or repeating number in base two. Any number you can write in base ten can also be written in base two.

Conversion The computer has been programmed to get numbers from you in base ten, translate them into base two, do its calculations in base two, and translate answers back into base ten for printing. As was mentioned in the introduction, the interpreter or compiler does this for you when you are writing BASIC. You can, therefore, almost forget about base two; you need not know about the technical details, about writing numbers in base two, or about translating numbers back and forth from base ten to base two. But there are some surprises in store that are comprehensible only if you have in the back of your mind that the computer is constantly translating your numbers into and out of base two.

As long as the computer does arithmetic only with integers, no surprises will come your way. There is a largest integer that you can use before the computer starts using scientific notation (to be discussed in a later unit), but since any integer can be written in the computer in base two with no inaccuracy, the computer's answers will be just what you expect.

With fractions, however, a difficulty arises. You have no doubt seen 1/3, expressed as a decimal, continuing forever across the page:

.333333333333333...

Write 3's until your pen runs dry and you will still not have the exact decimal representation of 1/3. Two-thirds is a similar row of sixes:

.666666666666666. . .

Now if you add 1/3 to 2/3, you should get 1, but if you add .3333. . . to .6666. . . you will get

$$.333333333333. . .$$
$$+ .666666666666. . .$$
$$.999999999999. . .$$

which is alarmingly different from

1.000000000000. . .

In base two this kind of problem arises more frequently than in base ten, and this will catch up with you from time to time. In base ten, the problem 1/10 + 9/10 becomes .1 + .9, which is 1. In base two, however, 1/10 is another never-ending fraction:

.000110011001100110011001100. . .

as is 9/10:

.1110011001100110011001100011. . .

If you add the two, you get

.1111111111111111111111111. . .

which is the base two equivalent of .9999. . . The computer may well print out

. 999999

instead of 1. Surprise!

Another, more practical problem crops up when you use numbers that are never-ending decimals. It arises from the limitations on the size of a computer. For example, when you type .1 into the computer, it gets translated into base two, and in theory the entire never-ending decimal should be stored in the computer. In practice, of course, the computer can be bothered to remember only a certain number of digits. Instead of

.0001100110011001100110011. . .

the computer stores

.000110011001100

This in itself is an inaccurate representation of 1/10, and when it is translated back to decimal, it may get back to the exact value, .1, or it may be .099999.

You can sometimes demonstrate this type of error with a pocket calculator with a square root key.* First find the square root of two (which is a never-ending decimal that starts out 1.41421356. . .), and then square the square

*Some clever calculator designs, the larger Texas Instrument models, for example, will not display the inaccuracy described in this paragraph.

root. You should get 2.0, but on some calculators you get something like 1.99999. The square root of two can only be expressed approximately in the machine; hence, all subsequent answers are also approximate. The same type of error occurs in the computer when it translates into base two and encounters never-ending decimals. The translation isn't exact, so after translation, some tiny error may have crept in.

These errors are very small. The difference between 1 and .999999 is miniscule, as is the difference between 2 and 1.99999. The machine's answers differ from the theoretical answers only in the machine's right-most digit. This is always the case, since what we are observing is the limitation of accuracy of the computer. It may seem heretical to the uninitiated to accuse the computer of numerical inaccuracy, but that is, indeed, the case. As the previous paragraphs have shown, both the base 10 system, which you use, and the base two numbers which the computer uses have certain intrinsic problems if you can write down only a limited number of digits. Your computer has been hard-wired and subsequently programmed to keep, say, accuracy up to fifteen digits (base two). (Some systems have more; some less. Some languages other than BASIC allow the user to choose how much accuracy he wants.) If the computer's calculations yield more digits than this, the machine rounds them off, and then the answers are no longer "exact." After the rounded results are translated back into base ten, the round-off error is difficult to predict and is alarming if you aren't expecting it. Calculating every last digit of mathematical exactitude is not practical, even with a computer.

Cleaning Up the Mess   Computer behavior is even more eccentric than has been suggested because computers often round numbers off after converting them to base ten. For example, a computer which prints out six digits, base ten, often does calculations with seven digits and then rounds off. Such a computer might, for example, get 1.999997 as an answer, but round it to 2 before printing it. It has been programmed this way to supress some of the behavior described above. For example, it might get 1/10 and 9/10 to add, calculate the answer .9999999 as above, but then round it off and print 1. This is highly satisfactory from the user's standpoint since it eliminates some of those interesting (but sometimes unwelcome) surprises.

But this system has its own hazards. For example, the computer might be adding 1/10 to itself repeatedly and print the following running totals:

```
. 1
. 2
. 3
. 4
. 5
. 599999
. 699999
. 799999
```

"Wait a minute!" you say. "Why did it revert to its old bad habits again at .6?"

Answer: The computer's calculations were inaccurate from the beginning, and they got a little bit more inaccurate with each calculation. However, rounding off the answers before they were printed covered up the mess that the computer was making for the first five answers. After that, though, the inaccuracy got too big to be swept under the carpet.

BCD   Computer manufacturers can, incidentally, absolutely eradicate the inaccuracy involved in adding 1/10 to itself. By using *binary coded decimal* (BCD), they can make the computer behave as though it were operating entirely in base ten. Computers using BCD, however, are slow compared to those using base two, and therefore if you are doing a large number of calculations, BCD is a hindrance. It is almost universally used for pocket calculators, however, since the number of calculations to be performed with them is relatively small, and translating to base two is so much greater a hassle than translating to BCD that the loss of efficiency can be ignored. Besides, even in BCD a pocket calculator can calculate faster than its user can push its buttons. On a computer doing several millions of calculations, however, efficiency may be vital. Thus BCD is less frequently used in larger machines doing longer processes.*

Conclusion   Computer systems are programmed differently to cope with the problems of base ten and base two and with the inaccuracies inherent in all calculations with numbers that are only approximate on paper or in the computer. Getting a computer to behave respectably in this area is an art. Certain balances must be made among accuracy, cosmetics, and efficiency, and every system programmer will have his own opinions. BCD is appropriate in some situations, for example, but not in others. More accuracy is pleasant to have, but it takes its toll in time consumed in the computer. Rounding off the printout takes up computer time and hides some of the accuracy that the computer does have in order to beautify the output.

    This section has shown you some of the things that lurk inside of the computer in the guise of numbers. When one of them jumps out and bites you, you will know it for what it is and need not become superstitious about little green men inside the computer.

---

*The upshot of the material in this paragraph is that if you add .1 to itself many times on a pocket calculator, the answer will always come out exactly correct, unlike on most computers. The problem of inaccurate square roots still remains.

2
THE CORNER STONE
OF BASIC

2.1   Moving Numbers Around Inside the Computer (LET statement)

As mentioned earlier, the computer has a memory filled with pigeon holes in which it can store numbers. It numbers these pigeon holes, but the BASIC language gives them names. A BASIC name is either a single letter (A, B, C, ... Z) or a single letter followed (with *no* space) by a single digit (A0, A1, A2, A3, ... , A9, B0, B1, B2, B3, ... , B9, C0, C1, C2, ... , Z9). We call these names *variables* since they take on whatever value is stored in the pigeon hole designated by the name.

Any time that you need the computer to remember some value, you give that value a variable name and store the number there. If your program needs to remember your weekly allowance, you may store that in A6. Later you may want to put the size of the national debt in O9, the sheriff's home phone number in N8, and the wholesale price of popcorn in P7. You need to keep in mind which variable represents which quantity. Write that down somewhere for your own use.

LET Statement   One of the most useful instructions in the BASIC language is the LET statement. Consider

$$44 \ \text{LET} \ U4 \ = \ 2.83$$

The number 44, of course, is the line number. This statement announces to the computer: "I am going to use a variable called U4. When my program is run and you get to this instruction, put the number 2.83 in the pigeon hole labeled U4. If there is another value in the space reserved for U4, erase it."

In a LET statement, the computer evaluates the expression on the right-hand side of the equal sign and puts the result in the designated memory space. Let us analyze the effect of this series of statements:

20

```
10 LET X = 5
20 LET X = 3 - 2
30 LET Y = X
40 LET Y = Y + 2
```

Statement 10 sets up a memory space to store the value of X and puts the number 5 in that space. Statement 20 erases the 5 in space X and writes in 1 (the result of 3 − 2) instead. Statement 30 sets up a memory space for Y; the value of X is to be stored there. Thus the computer looks up the value of X, which is now 1, and stores this 1 in memory space Y. Now both memory spaces contain the number 1. Statement 40 looks a little confusing, but the computer's point of view is this: Figure out what is on the right-hand side of the equal sign and put the result into memory space Y. Thus the computer looks up the value of Y, which is 1, adds the 2, and gets 3. Then it erases whatever value is in Y (1) and puts 3 there. The mathematical ridiculousness of the sequence doesn't bother the computer. The values of the variables are summarized in Fig. 2.1.

Statement	X	Y
10	5	?
20	1	?
30	1	1
40	1	3

Fig. 2.1   Values of variables in program fragment

A slight change in the order of the statements makes a big difference in the result:

```
10 LET X = 5
20 LET Y = X
30 LET X = 3 - 2
40 LET Y = Y + 2
```

What happens? X is set to 5 by statement 10. Then Y is set to 5 by statement 20. Then X is changed to 1. This does *not* change Y. Statement 20 has already been executed, and its effect was to make Y equal to X *at that time*. If X subsequently changes, Y is not affected. Statement 40 changes the value of Y to 7. The results of this program fragment are shown in Fig. 2.2.

Statement	X	Y
10	5	?
20	5	5
30	1	5
40	1	7

Fig. 2.2   Values of variables in altered program fragment

Omitting the "LET"   On some computers it is permissible to omit the word LET. A statement such as

$$15 \ X \ = \ 17$$

has exactly the same effect as

$$15 \ LET \ X \ = \ 17$$

Using this convention, one occasionally writes ridiculous things like:

$$25 \ P \ = \ P \ - \ 8$$

Mathematically absurd, of course, but eminently sensible to the computer. (Find the value of P, subtract 8, and store the result in memory space P. The old value of P is lost.)

Even if your computer allows you to omit it, however, you should insert the LET in your program statements. Although it may take 15 percent longer to type such statements, they are subsequently 100 percent easier for other people to understand. The statement,

$$25 \ P \ = \ P \ - \ 8$$

is, after all, confusing even after it has been explained. The statement,

$$25 \ LET \ P \ = \ P \ - \ 8$$

is far better. Do not delude yourself that programs are written only for computer consumption. People often read programs to find out how to change or improve them or to find and eliminate *bugs* (errors).

END Statement   In order to avoid the predicament of the sorcerer's apprentice, who couldn't stop his slaves from working, there is the END statement. It looks like this:

$$50 \ END$$

(whatever line number is appropriate, of course). When the computer is running your program and encounters an END statement, it knows that it should stop. The computer responds by typing

$$*READY$$

to indicate that it has found an END statement and is finished running your program.

Some systems insist that the highest numbered statement in any program be an END statement to tell the computer that there are no more statements. Further, in some of these systems, no statement other than the highest numbered statement may be an END statement. This restriction may come back to haunt you later. This text assumes that an END statement can appear anywhere in a program that the computer should stop, whether or not it is the highest numbered statement, but your computer may not be that easy-going.

Exercises

For each of the following program segments, figure out the final value of each variable.

```
1.    10 LET Z = 3
      20 LET Y = 3 + 7
      30 LET Z = 8
      40 LET X = Z


2.    10 LET M = 3
      20 LET Q = M + M
      30 LET M = Q
      40 LET Q = M + M


3.    10 LET A = 1
      20 LET B = 2
      30 LET C = A + B
      40 LET D = A + B + C


4.    10 LET S = 5
      20 LET S = S + S + S + S
      30 LET S = S - 5
      40 LET S = 5 + S


5.    10 LET A3 = 4
      20 LET A4 = 3
      30 LET A4 = A3
      40 LET A3 = A4
```

2.2   Getting Numbers Out (PRINT Statement)

The computer's great calculating ability would be worthless if it didn't print the answers. Filling this gap is the PRINT statement, which tells the computer to type something on the terminal. A PRINT statement looks up (or calculates) the value it has been asked to print and then prints it. For example, consider

```
10 LET Q = 6
20 PRINT Q
30 PRINT Q + 3
40 PRINT 64 + 98
50 END
```

Statement 10 stores the number 6 in memory space Q. Statement 20 looks up the value of Q, which is 6, and prints

```
6
```

Statement 30 looks up the value of Q, adds 3, and prints the answer:

```
9
```

Statement 40 adds 64 and 98 and prints

162

Therefore, the output looks like

6
9
162

*READY

(The *READY indicates that the computer has found the END statement. This will be deleted in what follows.)

Instead of printing the value of something, a PRINT statement can be made to print a message simply by putting the message in quotes. Look at this program:

```
10 LET Q = 6
20 PRINT "WHO ARE YOU?"
30 PRINT "Q"
40 PRINT Q
50 END
```

The output would be

WHO ARE YOU?	(The result of statement 20)
Q	(Statement 30 says to print the letter Q)
6	(Statement 40 says to look up the value of the variable Q and print that)

Use of the Colon to Mean PRINT Some systems allow you to use a colon (:) in place of the word PRINT. On such systems,

```
20 PRINT Q
```

and

```
20 :Q
```

are identical in effect. You should know about this abbreviation, but you should use the word PRINT. Few people can look at a colon and comprehend it quickly, whereas the meaning of the word PRINT is quite clear. Remember that people read programs. The people likely to read your programs include you, your teachers, your bosses, and your clients. You want to make life simple for yourself, and you want to impress all those others with your clearly written programs; hence, "PRINT" is far better than a colon. Don't worry. Your fingers will soon learn to type "PRINT" rapidly.

Frills (Use of the Comma and Semicolon to Make the Output Neat) Unless specific action is taken, each PRINT statement starts a new line on the terminal. This is usually a clumsy way of presenting the results. A program to make a table of squares and square roots, for example, prints a more legible table if the number, its square, and its square root are all on one line.

A line on the terminal is divided into five *teletype zones*. They are (usually) 16 spaces long, and they begin in spaces 1, 17, 33, 49, and 65. They act like tap stops on a typewriter in that the terminal will automatically space to the beginning of one of these zones.*

A comma placed in a PRINT statement between the items to be printed tells the machine to print the next item on the same line but in the next teletype zone. Examine the following program:

```
10 LET Q = 6
20 PRINT Q,Q + 3,64 + 98,"WHO ARE YOU?"
30 PRINT Q - 1,Q
40 END
```

It produces the output:

```
6              9              162            WHO ARE YOU?
5              6
```

Since there is no comma after WHO ARE YOU?, the computer starts the next printed item on a new line. The columns of numbers are lined up neatly. As long as there are commas between items to be printed and until it runs out of zones, the computer prints each item in the next zone. When it runs out of zones on one line, or if it finds no comma between items, it starts on a new line.

Normally a PRINT statement starts a new line, but a comma ending the previous PRINT statement can prevent this, making this PRINT statement continue on the same line. The following program, therefore, has the same output as the one above:

```
10 LET Q = 6
20 PRINT Q,
30 PRINT Q + 3,
40 PRINT 64 + 98,
50 PRINT "WHO ARE YOU?"
60 PRINT Q - 1,
70 PRINT Q
80 END
```

(Note the lack of a comma after "WHO ARE YOU?" Hence statement 60 starts on a new line.)

Another way of prettying output is to use a semicolon (;). If a semicolon appears between items to be printed, the second item is printed starting in the next space (without tabulating to the next zone as a comma would make it do). As with the comma, a semicolon at the end of a PRINT statement affects the following PRINT statement.

---

*These zones are nothing mechanical in the teletype. They are a creation of the BASIC system. In addition to translating BASIC into a computer-understood language, the compiler or interpreter takes care of this tab stop.

Two identical programs are shown below:

```
10 LET Q = -8              10 LET Q = -8
20 PRINT "Q ="; Q,         20 PRINT "Q =";
30 LET Q = 8               30 PRINT Q,
40 PRINT "Q ="; Q          40 LET Q = 8
50 END                     50 PRINT "Q =";
                           60 PRINT Q
                           70 END
```

The output from both programs is

$$Q =-8$$

and

$$Q = 8$$

Note that the -8 starts immediately after the $Q =$. The computer left a space before the positive 8, because it always leaves a space for a sign but doesn't bother to print a plus sign. All the output is on one line, because of the comma in line 20 in the first program and in line 30 in the second. (See Fig. 2.3.)

Blank Lines   One technique is worth mentioning: The computer is often called upon to print long columns of numbers. These are far easier to read if a line is skipped occasionally, say every third or every fifth line. This can easily be done, since the statement

```
80 PRINT
```

prints a blank line. If the previous PRINT statement ends with a comma or a semicolon, you will need to use two of these statements back-to-back; the first one finishes the line that you were supposed to continue, and the second one prints the next line blank.

Example   Look at the following jumble of numbers:

```
11
121
1331
12
144
1728
13
169
2197
```

Then look at these same numbers reorganized as follows:

NUMBER	SQUARE	CUBE
11	121	1331
12	144	1728
13	169	2197

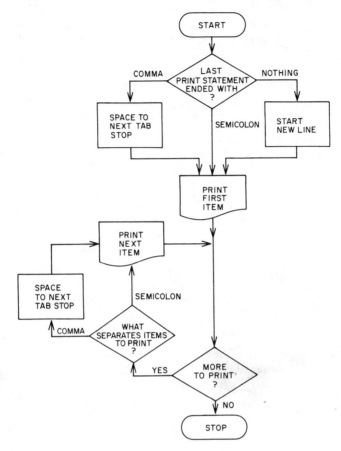

Fig. 2.3   Flowchart for the PRINT statement

The latter presentation is a distinct improvement because the numbers form a logical arrangement on the page. The following program generates the improved output:

```
10 PRINT "NUMBER","SQUARE","CUBE"
20 PRINT
30 PRINT 11,11↑2,11↑3
40 PRINT
50 PRINT 12,12↑2,12↑3
60 PRINT
70 PRINT 13,13↑2,13↑3
80 END
```

(Since ↑ means "to the power" in BASIC, 11 ↑ 3 represents 11^3.) Statements 20, 40, and 60 print the blank lines between the entries. The commas in statements 30, 50, and 70 line the numbers up neatly in the columns. The commas in statement 10 serve to line the headings up over their respective columns.

Up to five columns in a table are possible using the comma. The following program extends the previous one to the maximum number of columns:

```
10 PRINT "NUMBER", "SQUARE", "CUBE", "FOURTH", "FIFTH"
20 PRINT
30 PRINT 11, 11↑2, 11↑3, 11↑4, 11↑5
40 PRINT
50 PRINT 12, 12↑2, 12↑3, 12↑4, 12↑5
60 PRINT
70 PRINT 13, 13↑2, 13↑3, 13↑4, 13↑5
80 END
```

The output would be as follows:

NUMBER	SQUARE	CUBE	FOURTH	FIFTH
11	121	1331	14641	161051
12	144	1728	20736	248832
13	169	2197	28561	371293

Six columns won't work because five columns use up the entire line. The statement,

```
10 PRINT 1, 2, 3, 4, 5, 6
```

gives the output,

1	2	3	4	5
6				

Note that the 6 lands in the first column of the new line.

Example   Consider the output of this program:

```
10 PRINT "I AM THE";
20 PRINT "HUNGRY COMPUTER"
30 PRINT "FEED",
40 PRINT "ME"
50 END
```

The semicolon at the end of line 10 makes the PRINT statement on line 20 start printing in the next space on the same line. The PRINT statement of line 30 starts a new line, however, because there is nothing to keep it from doing so. The PRINT statement on line 20 ends with no punctuation mark. Line 40 starts printing at column 17 because of the comma in line 30. So we get the following:

```
I AM THEHUNGRY COMPUTER
FEED            ME
```

Obviously, statement 10 should be revised to

```
10 PRINT "I AM THE ";
```

Note the space after THE.

An Experiment for the Ambitious to Try   Try the following program on your computer just to see what it does:

```
10 LET D = 12345
20 LET E = -12345
30 PRINT "XXX";D;"XXX"
40 PRINT "XXX";E;"XXX"
50 END
```

You might expect the output to be

```
XXX12345XXX
XXX-12345XXX
```

but don't be surprised if it turns out differently. Many BASIC systems print spaces as part of every number, perhaps a space before and a space after, as follows:

```
XXX 12345 XXX
XXX -12345 XXX
```

These spaces are shoveled in automatically whenever you ask the computer to print a number. This computer habit is annoying because just when you think that your output is going to be nicely lined up, one of these spaces sneaks in to foul you up.

Another Useful Technique   Sometimes the following technique is useful:

```
10 PRINT " "," ","HELLO"
```

This prints a space, then goes to the second teletype zone, where it prints another space, and then goes on to the third teletype zone. The output:

```
HELLO
```

Using this technique beats typing

```
10 PRINT "                         HELLO"
```

On some machines you can even get away with

```
10 PRINT ,,"HELLO"
```

which has the same effect.

Exercises

1. Write BASIC programs from the following flowcharts:

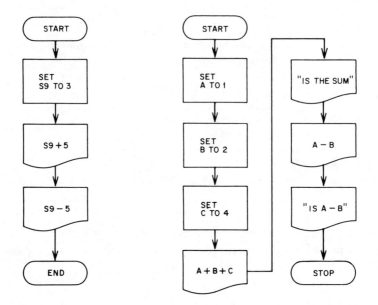

2. Set K1 to 1, K2 to 2, K3 to 3, K4 to 4, and K5 to 5. Write a program which produces each of the following output:

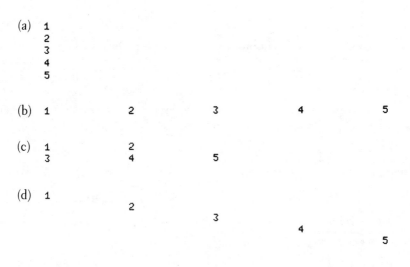

(a) 1
    2
    3
    4
    5

(b) 1   2   3   4   5

(c) 1   2
    3   4   5

(d) 1
        2
            3
                4
                    5

(e) 12345

2.3   Doing Arithmetic

Since the computer is good at arithmetic, it stands to reason that we ask it to do many arithmetical things. Getting a computer to do arithmetic in BASIC is relatively simple since arithmetic expressions in BASIC resemble those used in algebra.

The computer uses the symbols +, −, *, /, and ↑ to mean add, subtract, multiply, divide, and exponentiate, respectively (some systems use ** instead of ↑ for exponentiation). Consequently,

$$3 + 2 \text{ produces 5 in the computer}$$
$$3 - 2 \text{ produces 1}$$
$$3 * 2 \text{ produces 6}$$
$$3 / 2 \text{ produces 1.5}$$
$$3 ↑ 2 \text{ produces } 3^2 \text{ or 9.}$$

Variables may be used in arithmetic expressions. For example:

```
10 LET X = Y + Z
```

means that the computer is to look up the values of Y and Z, add the two numbers, and put the result in memory space X.

Order of Operation   When several arithmetic operations occur in one statement, the computer does them in a special order similar to the order you would do them in arithmetic. To begin with, it does additions and subtractions from left to right: $X - 4 + 5$ subtracts 4 from the value of X and then adds 5, just as you would do in arithmetic. (Note that if you do the addition of 4 and 5 first, the result is different.) Slightly more troublesome are multiplication and division, also done from left to right: $X / 4 * 5$ means to divide X by 4 and then multiply the result by 5 (*not* to multiply the 4 by the 5 and then divide X by the resultant 20).

The computer does all multiplication and division before it does addition and subtraction. In algebra, $x + yz$ means to multiply y and z together and then to add the result to x. Similarly, if the computer encounters $X + Y * Z$, it does the multiplication *first* and the addition afterwards.

Exponentiation has precedence over multiplication and division (and hence also over addition and subtraction). In algebra, ab^c means to raise b to the cth power and then multiply the result by a. The computer does the same thing when it encounters $A * B ↑ C$. It raises B to the Cth power, and then multiplies by A. Similarly, $5 * 2 ↑ 2$ means 5 * 4, or 20 (rather than $10 ↑ 2$, or 100).

The computer treats parentheses just as you do in algebra. Expressions in parentheses are evaluated first, and then the rest of the arithmetic is done. The expression $5 * (3 + 7)$ means to add 3 and 7 and then to multiply the result by 5. If there were no parentheses, the multiplication would be done first, and the result would be different.

Let us look through the same program fragment below and see the result of each statement.

```
10 LET X = 10
20 LET Y = 4 + 8 - X
30 LET Z = Y↑3
40 LET X = 3 * (X↑2 + 5)
50 LET Z = Z - X
60 PRINT (334 + Z)/27  - 18
70 LET M = 48 + X + W
```

Statement 10 stores the number 10 in space X. Statement 20 adds 4 and 8, subtracts the value of X, which is 10, and stores the result in Y. Line 30 cubes Y and stores the result in Z. Line 40 starts by evaluating the expression in parentheses: it first squares X; then it adds 5 to the result; lastly, the result is multiplied by 3. Then the old value of X is erased, and the result of this calculation is entered. Statement 50 looks up the values of Z and X and does the subtraction. Statement 60 calculates 334 + Z, divides the result by 27, subtracts 18, and prints the answer. Statement 70 attempts to find the value of W with which to do the calculation. Since we haven't given W a value, the computer gives out an error message and stops. (On some systems, W is automatically given the value zero and calculation continues.)

Figure 2.4 contains a table of the values of all the variables as they occur through the program. Check with the previous paragraph to see if you agree with these values.

Statement	X	Y	Z	W	M	Output
10	10	?	?	?	?	
20	10	2	?	?	?	
30	10	2	8	?	?	
40	315	2	8	?	?	
50	315	2	-307	?	?	
60	315	2	-307	?	?	-17
70	tries to find the value of W, which is unknown, so an error message is printed.					

Fig. 2.4 Values of variables in example program

Add a few extra parentheses when needed to make your program clearer. Expressions such as 1/A*B are ambiguous at best and downright misleading at worst, but the meaning of (1/A)*B is self-evident. The computer doesn't care which you use, but you will thank yourself for such program clarity if later you want to make corrections. Especially when using expressions such as

$$1+X+X↑2/2+X↑3/6+X↑4/24$$

a few parentheses can save a lot of grief:

$$1 + X + (X\uparrow2 /2) + (X\uparrow3 /6) + (X\uparrow4 /24)$$

Although both expressions evaluate to the same result, the latter statement is far easier to read.

Common Mistakes   Most of the time, if you have written a correct algebraic expression, you can translate it directly into BASIC and the result will work. There are several cases, however, when this is not possible. A relatively simple error is that of leaving out the multiplication sign. Expressions like 5(x + y) or xy + z are common in algebra, and the multiplication is assumed. The computer does not make this assumption, and when these two expressions are translated into BASIC arithmetic expressions, the asterisk must be inserted: 5 * (X + Y) and X * Y + Z. If you leave out the asterisk, the computer will give you an error message.

There are two rather more insidious errors possible, both of which result from conventions of algebraic notation. The first is the following: in algebra, $\frac{2+4}{2+1}$ is the same as $\frac{6}{3}$ or 2. If you translate this directly, you get: 2 + 4 / 2 + 1. The computer does the division first, gets 2 + 2 + 1, and then does the addition and gets 5. The problem is that the line in $\frac{2+4}{2+1}$ not only indicates division, but also acts as parentheses, telling you to evaluate the numerator and the denominator first and *then* divide. Correct translation into BASIC requires that you insert these implied parentheses: you get (2 + 4)/(2 + 1), which evaluates correctly in the computer. The most annoying thing about this kind of error is that the computer blunders right ahead and does the calculating, getting the wrong answer.

A second mistake is rather similar. It involves translating an expression such as a^{bc}. This algebraic expression says to multiply the b and the c together and then raise a to that power; that is, there are implied parentheses: $a^{(bc)}$. These must be inserted when you translate into BASIC: a^{bc} becomes A $\uparrow$ (B * C). A $\uparrow$ B * C means $a^b c$ (which is different) because the computer does exponentiation first, and then multiplication.

To keep your programs error-free, there are three things you can do. First, write out algebraic expressions very carefully before translating them into BASIC. Second, keep the above errors in mind. Third, when in doubt, add extra parentheses. The effect of extra parentheses is to make your program take microseconds longer to run in the computer. A program which runs slowly but correctly is inifinitely preferable to one which runs faster but gives the wrong answer.

Exercises

1. Remember that PRINT can be used as a command. Use the computer to calculate each of the following:

    (a) $579 + 386$
    (b) $5 \cdot 6^3$
    (c) $\frac{217 + 8}{25}$
    (d) 2^{3+2}
    (e) $417 - (46 + 12)$
    (f) $\frac{63}{8 \cdot 3}$
    (g) $(5 + 8)(2 + 7)$

2. Translate each of the following into BASIC. Use parentheses where necessary to make the order of operation clear.
    (a) $a + bc$
    (b) xyz
    (c) $(x + y)z^3$
    (d) $(xy)^4$
    (e) $7x + 3y^3$
    (f) $\frac{s + y}{tw}$
    (g) $\left(\frac{ab^3}{4}\right)^c$

3. The formula for the area of a trapezoid (a diagram of which is shown below) is $\frac{1}{2}(b_1 + b_2)h$. Write a program to calculate the areas of each of the following trapezoids:
    (a) $b_1 = 3$ $b_2 = 8$ $h = 10$
    (b) $b_1 = 4$ $b_2 = 9$ $h = 16$
    (c) $b_1 = 7$ $b_2 = 12$ $h = 390$

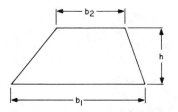

2.4 Getting Numbers In (INPUT Statement)

    Frequently, you will want to write a program before data become available. For example, if you want to write a vote-tallying computer program, you had better write it *before* election night, leaving only the actual numbers to be typed in. Election night will probably be hectic enough without having to write a computer program.

    To get a program to accept data while it is running, you use the INPUT statement. To demonstrate the power of the INPUT statement, let us suppose that we wanted to know the areas of several rectangles. If the first rectangle had sides 43 and 76, we could write the program as follows:

```
10 LET B = 43
20 LET H = 76
30 LET A = B * H
40 PRINT A
50 END
```

To find the area of the next rectangle, we would have to alter lines 10 and 20, which borders on being a public nuisance. The INPUT statement comes to the rescue. We would then write the program as follows:

```
10 INPUT B
20 INPUT H
30 LET A = B * H
40 PRINT A
50 END
```

write in print statements for each question.

When the computer comes to step 10 in this program, it types a question mark, indicating that it is waiting for a number to be typed in, and then it waits for you to type a number and a carriage return. (The carriage return tells the computer that you have finished typing your number.) The computer puts your number in memory space B. When it comes to step 20, it types another question mark and waits for another number. When the user types in a number (and a carriage return), the computer puts this number in space H and then continues to the end of the program. If you need the areas of several different rectangles, you need type only "RUN," the base, and the height, and out comes the answer for each rectangle.

Prompts   Before rushing off to use the INPUT statement, consider the severe shortcoming of the revised program above: it doesn't tell the user what he should type in. Remember that the person who types in the data for the INPUT statement may not be the programmer himself. When the INPUT statement types a question mark, this other person may be completely in the dark. Should he type in the height of the rectangle?, the length of its diagonal?, the time of day?, the speed of light? He doesn't know. You should help him out by having the computer print out *prompts*, short messages indicating what the computer expects of the user. The same revised program as above but with prompts added is shown below, along with a sample of the interaction between program and user. In this program, whenever the user should type something, the computer tells him what it wants to know. Notice also that the output is now labeled so that the user knows what it represents.

```
 5 PRINT "WHAT IS THE LENGTH OF THE BASE";
10 INPUT B
15 PRINT "WHAT IS THE HEIGHT";
20 INPUT H
30 LET A = B * H
40 PRINT "THE AREA OF THE RECTANGLE IS ";A;". "
50 END
```

semicolin puts
? on same line

Notice that the INPUT statements print the questions marks on the ends of the questions. A run of the program might look like this:

```
WHAT IS THE LENGTH OF THE BASE?221
WHAT IS THE HEIGHT?475
THE AREA OF THE RECTANGLE IS 104975.
```

Prompts are particularly important if the user must input many different data items or if he must use some special format. The second program below contains a prompt explaining to the user how to type in three numbers. The instructions make it easy for him to use the program without assistance from the programmer.

Commas in INPUT Statements   The two programs below calculate the area of a trapezoid after the user types in the dimensions:

```
10 PRINT "THE LENGTH OF THE FIRST BASE IS";
20 INPUT B1
30 PRINT "THE LENGTH OF THE SECOND BASE IS";
40 INPUT B2
50 PRINT "THE HEIGHT IS";
60 INPUT H
70 PRINT .5 * (B1 + B2) * H
80 END
```

```
10 PRINT "TYPE THE LENGTHS OF THE TWO BASES"
11 PRINT "AND THE HEIGHT OF THE TRAPEZOID."
12 PRINT "SEPARATE THE NUMBERS WITH COMMAS"
13 PRINT "AND HIT A .CARRIAGE RETURN AT THE END."
20 INPUT B1,B2,H
30 PRINT "THE AREA OF THE TRAPEZOID IS ";
40 PRINT .5 * (B1 + B2) * H; "."
50 END
```

The difference between the two programs is minor. In the first one, the computer reads B1, types another question mark, and waits for B2. It receives the value of B2 and types yet another question mark. The second program types one question mark, and then it waits for three numbers. The user must type in all three numbers separated by commas (some systems also allow separation with carriage returns) and a carriage return (to indicate the end of the last number). For example, the second program would type:

```
TYPE THE LENGTHS OF THE TWO BASES
AND THE HEIGHT OF THE TRAPEZOID.
SEPARATE THE NUMBERS WITH COMMAS
AND HIT A CARRIAGE RETURN AT THE END.
?
```

and the user might type

`14, 6, 10`

(and a carriage return) and then the computer would type the answer:

`THE AREA OF THE TRAZEZOID IS 100.`

Notice that the computer assumes that the first number typed in is B1; the second, B2; the third, H. The prompt tells the user in what order to type the numbers.

Note that if you were to type fewer than three numbers, the computer would not know the values of one or more of the variables. Computer reactions to this situation vary. Some type another question mark or two to indicate to the user that the computer's greed for data is as yet unsatiated; some just sit and sulk until more data is typed in; some immediately terminate the program with an error message (for example, INSUFFICIENT DATA).

Exercises

1. Write a program which reads the speed and the distance to your destination and tells you how long it will take to get there.
2. Write a program which reads your mileage and how many gallons of gas you use and prints back the miles per gallon average that you are getting.
3. Write a program that reads the number of widgets you are buying and the price per widget. Have it print these two numbers back, then figure the total cost and print that. Have the computer label the output neatly.
4. Add to your program in exercise 3 so that after it prints the total, it calculates 10 percent tax (ghastly), prints it, and then prints a grand total.
5. Improve your program in exercise 4 so that you can type in numbers and prices of both widgets and widget wrenches. Make the output look like this:

```
XX WIDGETS AT $YY              ZZ
QQ WIDGET WRENCHES AT $RR      SSS

             TOTAL             MMM

               TAX             TT

       GRAND TOTAL             GGG
```

6. Write a program which inputs two numbers and then prints (appropriately labeled) their sum, product, and average.

3
ELEMENTARY
ARCHITECTURE

3.1   Going Around in Circles (GOTO Statement)

At the beginning of the book, we considered the computer's great ability
to do repetetive work, but so far no tools for doing repetetive work have been
discussed. A program to do something three times has to be written out with the
instruction sequence copied over three times.

The first method of getting the computer to repeat a sequence of statements is the GOTO statement. A GOTO statement consists of a line number,
the expression GOTO (or GO TO), and a number. When the computer encounters a GOTO statement, it does not continue to execute statements in numerical
order. Instead, it executes next the statement whose number is the number in the
GOTO statement and continues from there. Consider the following example (a
rather stupid one):

```
10 LET A = 1
20 LET B = 2
30 PRINT A
40 PRINT B
50 GOTO 30
60 END
```

The statements 10 through 40 print the numbers 1 and 2. When the computer
gets to statement 50, it goes back to statement 30. It will again print a 1. Then it
continues on from statement 30 to statement 40 and prints a 2. Then it comes to
statement 50, which sends it back to 30 again. It again prints a 1. Then it prints a
2. Then it will go back to statement 30. . . . (See the flowchart in Fig. 3.1.)

The ESCAPE Key   The program above certainly succeeds in getting the
computer to repeat a set of instructions. The computer is busy printing:

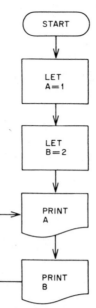

Fig. 3.1   Flowchart of a loop

```
1
2
1
2
1
2
1
2
.
.
.
```

In fact, this program is a little too successful; the computer will continue to type 1's and 2's until the next power failure or the end of the world, whichever comes first. Such a situation is called an *infinite loop*. To prevent the over-zealous machine from inundating the county with 1's and 2's, there is the ESCAPE key. The ESCAPE key is a cease and desist order to the computer. Pressing it stops your program and returns control to the monitor. In the case given, the computer would immediately stop printing 1's and 2's, and you would be able to alter the program or give commands.

Examples   A more reasonable example is a program to calculate the areas of several different rectangles without stopping. We previously had the program:

```
 5  PRINT "WHAT IS THE LENGTH OF THE BASE";
10  INPUT B
15  PRINT "WHAT IS THE HEIGHT";
20  INPUT H
30  LET A = B * H
40  PRINT "THE AREA OF THE RECTANGLE IS ";A;"."
50  END
```

If you wanted to know the areas of several rectangles, you would have to type RUN for every area, because the program stops after calculating each one. One slight improvement in the program is shown below:

```
 5  PRINT "WHAT IS THE LENGTH OF THE BASE";
10  INPUT B
15  PRINT "WHAT IS THE HEIGHT";
20  INPUT H
30  LET A = B * H
40  PRINT "THE AREA OF THE RECTANGLE IS ";A;" "
50  PRINT
60  GOTO 5
70  END
```

Now after executing statements 10 through 30 and calculating the area of the first rectangle, the computer goes back to statement 10 and waits for the dimensions of a new rectangle. The user can continue to input dimensions of rectangles until he is finished, whereupon he will hit the ESCAPE key and the program will end.

The PRINT statement at statement 30 serves to separate data for one rectangle from that for another, thereby improving the looks of the output.

Here is another example (stupid looking, but useful):

```
10  LET N = 1
20  PRINT N
30  LET N = N + 1
40  GOTO 20
50  END
```

At statement 20, the computer prints 1. Statement 30 sets N equal to 2; then statement 40 sends the computer back to 20, and the computer prints the new value of N, that is, 2. Now statement 30 sets N equal to 3. When the computer gets back to statement 20, it prints 3. So the computer prints

$$1$$
$$2$$
$$3$$
$$4$$
$$5$$
.
.
.

until the ESCAPE is pressed. We will use this example later.

Another Example—Tables Revisited   We can improve the example of the PRINT section to print out the squares and cubes of the integers starting at 11 and going on up. In the PRINT section we had a lengthy program that did little. With the GOTO statement and a little work we can make the program do a lot:

```
10 PRINT "NUMBER", "SQUARE", "CUBE"
20 LET N = 11
30 PRINT
40 PRINT N, N↑2, N↑3
50 LET N = N + 1
60 GOTO 30
70 END
```

When this program first gets to statement 40, $N = 11$ and the computer prints out 11, 11^2, and 11^3. Then, statement 50 increases N to 12. Statement 60 sends the computer back to line 30. The computer prints a blank line and then goes on to line 40, which prints 12, 12^2, and 12^3. Statement 50 sets N to 13, and the process continues, giving us the squares and cubes of ever larger numbers for as long as we care to watch it. The output is as follows:

NUMBER	SQUARE	CUBE
11	121	1331
12	144	1728
13	169	2197
14	196	2744
15	225	3375

In this example, as in the previous ones, the use of variables serves us well in a GOTO loop. We can reuse statement 40 of the previous program again and again, and whenever the value of N changes, the result of the PRINT statement also changes. Since statement 50 changes the value of N each time through, something different happens each time at statement 40. It is common to use statements that the computer executes repeatedly but which do slightly different things each time because the variables have changed.

A Warning (partly tongue in cheek)   The GOTO statement can also be used to confuse the computer programmer (although not the computer):

```
10 PRINT "THE ";
20 GOTO 70
30 PRINT "CAT ";
40 END
50 PRINT "IN THE ";
60 GOTO 30
70 PRINT "HAT" ;
80 GOTO 50
```

prints

THE HAT IN THE CAT

When a program begins to bristle with GOTO's in this manner, it is time to do some rewriting.

Exercises

1. What do the following programs do?

(a)
```
10 LET N = 1
20 PRINT N
30 LET N = N + 2
40 GOTO 10
50 END
```

(b)
```
10 LET N = 3
20 PRINT N
30 LET N = N + 10
40 GOTO 20
50 END
```

(c)
```
10 LET N = 1
20 PRINT N
30 LET N = N + 0
40 GOTO 30
50 END
```

(d)
```
10 LET M = 1
20 PRINT M
30 PRINT M + 1
40 PRINT "BUCKLE MY SHOE"
50 LET M = M + 2
60 GOTO 20
70 END
```

2. (a) Write a program to get the computer to print 1, 3, 9, 27, 81, . . .
   (b) Write a program to get the computer to print 0, 8, 10, 18, 20, 28, 30, 38, 40, . . .
3. (a) Write a program which inputs a number, prints it, inputs another number and prints the sum of the two numbers, inputs another number, adds it to the previous sum and prints the new total, and so on until the user ESCAPEs.
   (b) Change the program in (a) so that the computer only starts to print totals after the third number has been typed in.
4. A Fibonacci series is 1, 1, 2, 3, 5, 8, 13, 21, . . . where the first two numbers in the series are 1, and each succeeding number is found by adding the two previous numbers in the sequence: $2 = 1 + 1$, $3 = 1 + 2$, $5 = 2 + 3$, and so on. The next number in the series shown would be 34, the sum of 13 and 21. Write a program which prints out this Fibonacci sequence.

5. Is this program ever a mess! Find out what it does and write another to do the same thing using no more than six statements.

```
10 GOTO 110
20 LET N = 1
30 GOTO 40
40 LET N = N + 9
50 GOTO 130
60 PRINT "WHAT A MESS!"
70 GOTO 150
80 LET N = N + 1
90 PRINT
100 GOTO 40
110 INPUT N
120 GOTO 20
130 PRINT N;
140 GOTO 80
150 END
```

6. Write a program to make a table of the squares and cubes of the negative integers, starting at -1 and continuing down.

3.2   Making Decisions (IF-THEN Statement)

Numerous clerical jobs involve using very simple criteria to decide certain things about a large number of cases. For example, a clerk at a bank might compare the amount of each incoming check with the corresponding checking account balance and decide on the basis of the comparison whether to pay or to return the check. Another clerk might sort a large pile of tax returns, choosing for audit those showing either a gross income of over $40,000 or itemized deductions of over $10,000. Yet a third might check a person's age and seniority on the job and decide whether or not he qualifies for a pension. These jobs are not difficult; you merely look at each case, apply the rules, and make a yes or no decision. This is the sort of thing that computers ought to be doing.

The BASIC instruction which allows us to have the computer make a decision is the IF-THEN statement. The IF-THEN statement consists of a line number, the word IF, a condition that the computer must decide whether or not is true, the word THEN, and another line number.

What kind of conditions can the computer decide about? Since the computer deals with numbers, it can cope with conditions involving numbers. For example, if you have been using a variable called X, the computer can decide the truth of any of the following assertions:

```
X = 0
X - 3 = 57
X > 2
2*X - X < X + 3
X <> 3
X >= 17
X <= 35
```

Let us look at a possible IF-THEN statement:

```
40 IF X > 2 THEN 70
```

When the computer comes to this statement, it must first decide whether or not X is greater than 2. If X is not greater than 2, the computer simply goes on to the next statement in the program, but if X is greater than 2, the computer will GO TO 70. When the condition is true, the IF-THEN acts like a GO TO statement.

Using IF-THEN to Stop an Infinite Loop   Let us use the IF-THEN statement to improve on the program of the last section that typed the numbers 1, 2, 3, 4, 5, ... The program below does the same thing except that it stops automatically after printing the number 3.

```
10 LET N = 1
20 PRINT N
30 IF N = 3 THEN 60
40 LET N = N + 1
50 GOTO 20
60 END
```

This program prints a 1 at statement 20. When it gets to statement 30, N is not equal to 3; thus it goes on to statement 40. N is set to 2, and we go back and print the 2. At statement 30, N is still not equal to 3; thus we continue to 40; N is set to 3, and the 3 is printed. Now at statement 30 the condition (N = 3) is true. Therefore, the program goes to statement 60 and ends. A flowchart for this program is shown in Fig. 3.2(A).

Let us modify the last program to print three 1's:

```
10 LET N = 1
20 PRINT 1
30 IF N = 3 THEN 60
40 LET N = N + 1
50 GOTO 20
60 END
```

The only purpose of the variable N is to count the number of times that the computer has gone through the process. This is a common trick, one which will be refined in a future chapter. Note also that with this sort of program, it would be as easy to have the computer type five-hundred 1's as to have it type three; you need only change statement 30 slightly.

Another Example   Here is another possible use of the IF-THEN statement. We will write a program which inputs a series of numbers that the user types in. When the user types in the number 0, the computer prints out the sum of the numbers he has typed in.

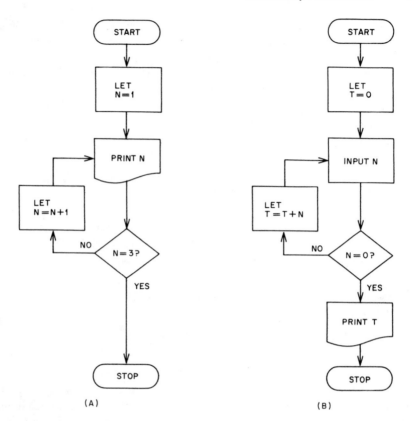

Fig. 3.2 Loops with ways to stop looping: (A) Flowchart of program to print 1, 2, 3, and stop, and (B) flowchart of a program to keep a running total and print it when a zero is input

```
10 LET T = 0
20 INPUT N
30 IF N = 0 THEN 60
40 LET T = T + N
50 GOTO 20
60 PRINT T
70 END
```

T is the running total of the numbers typed in so far. N stores the last number that the user has typed in. Whenever the user types in a nonzero number, we pass statement 30 (since the condition is false), add the number to the running total at 40, and await a new number at 20. If the user types in a 0, then the condition at statement 30 will be true, and the computer goes to statement 60, prints the total, and stops.

A flowchart for this program is shown in Fig. 3.2(B).

Example   Although getting the computer to write original English prose is an exercise on the fringes of modern research, here is a program to write the first sentence of a sports page news report. A rather uninteresting first sentence, by the way. It inputs the Warrior's score, W, and the Laker's score, L, and prints an appropriate sentence based on who won and by how much.

```
10 INPUT W,L
20 PRINT
30 PRINT "THE LAKERS ";
40 IF L < W THEN 200
50 LET D = L - W
60 PRINT "BEAT THE WARRIORS BY A ";D;" POINT MARGIN IN LAST"
70 PRINT "NIGHT'S NBA GAME IN LOS ANGELES."
80 END
200 LET D = W - L
210 IF D > 10 THEN 250
220 PRINT "LOST TO THE WARRIORS IN A ";
230 GOTO 260
250 PRINT "WERE BEATEN DECISIVELY BY THE WARRIORS IN A ";
260 PRINT W;" TO ";L;
270 IF D > 15 THEN 300
280 PRINT " GAME IN LOS ANGELES LAST NIGHT."
290 END
300 PRINT " ROUT IN LAST NIGHT'S LOS ANGELES ENCOUNTER.  A BRAWL"
310 PRINT "FOLLOWED."
320 END
```

Statement 40 decides who won. If the Lakers won, then L is greater than W and the computer goes on to statements 50 to 80 which print appropriate messages. If the Warriors won, then W is greater than L and the program goes to statement 200, skipping statements 50 to 80. Depending on the winning margin, the computer continues the sentence as LOST TO or WERE BEATEN DECISIVELY. The computer then gets to statement 260 where it prints the score of the contest. At 270, it decides whether or not the margin was more than 15 points, and if it was, the game is designated as a ROUT rather than just a GAME, and the ancillary comment about the brawl is added.

This example illustrates not only the use of the IF-THEN statement to decide which clauses are appropriate, but also the trick of printing a sentence one piece at a time. The computer prints the first two words of the sentence

THE LAKERS

before deciding anything about who won and by how much. Later, it adds BEAT or LOST TO or WERE BEATEN DECISIVELY BY, depending upon the facts. The sentence may be typed in as many as four parts:

```
THE LAKERS WERE BEATEN DECISIVELY BY THE WARRIORS IN A
```

            1   2

```
112 TO 101  GAME IN LOS ANGELES LAST NIGHT.
```

      3   4

Part one is printed by statement 30. Part two is printed by statement 250. The third part comes from statement 260. Statement 280 creates part four.

Example Suppose that you are good friends with the British hardware distributor, Nuts 'n' Bolts, Ltd., and that Nuts 'n' Bolts offers you a 25 percent discount whenever you order from them. Suppose also that your uncle is president of Threads, Inc., but that he is so stingy that he allows only a 10 percent discount. Since he doesn't have to ship your orders overseas, however, he subtracts $5 from your bill after the discount. Which is cheaper overall?

The mathematically inclined might see how to solve this problem quickly with pencil and paper, but it lends itself to computer solution. Let us investigate two cases first. Suppose that you want to order $20 worth of hardware. The British dealer will give you that 25 percent discount, and the cost will be $15. Uncle Threads will give you only a 10 percent discount, charging $18, but then he will subtract that $5, leaving a bill of $13. Your uncle isn't such a bad guy after all.

Suppose, though, that you are ordering $100 worth of goods. Britain charges you $75. Threads gives you that 10 percent, leaving $90, and then subtracts $5, leaving $85. Order from Britain.

Since it is the size of your order that determines the matter, let us write a program which inputs the dollar amount of your order into space X and then figures out from which company to order. To do this, the computer must figure out what each firm will charge; thus we must give the computer formulas for figuring these charges. Now since Nuts 'n' Bolts gives you a 25 percent discount, you pay them 75 percent of the cost of the order; N&B's charge will thus be $.75*X$. Threads takes off 10 percent of the cost, leaving you 90 percent of the cost, and then subtracts $5; the formula is thus $.90*X-5$. The program is shown below and the flowchart in Fig. 3.3.

```
10 INPUT X
20 LET N = .75*X
30 LET T = .90*X - 5
40 PRINT "NUTS 'N' BOLTS CHARGES ";N
50 PRINT "THREADS CHARGES ";T
60 IF T <> N THEN 90
70 PRINT "IT DOESN'T MATTER WHICH COMPANY YOU ORDER FROM."
80 END
90 IF T < N THEN 120
100 PRINT "YOU SHOULD ORDER FROM NUTS 'N' BOLTS."
110 END
120 PRINT "THREADS IS OFFERING THE BETTER DEAL."
130 END
```

First this program calculates T and N, the charges that the two companies will levy. It prints out these charges in statements 40 and 50. Although not necessary, this allows you to check whether or not the program has correctly calculated the costs. At statement 60, the computer skips down to 90 if T is not equal to N. If it doesn't skip down to 90, it is because T is equal to N, in which case it doesn't

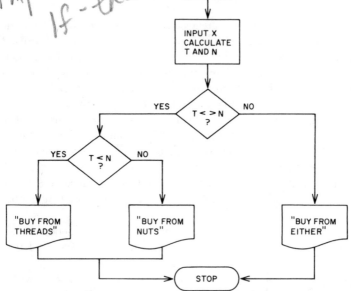

Improved If-then

Fig. 3.3 Flowchart for the hardware problem

matter from which company you buy. If T is not equal to N, the machine jumps to 90 and checks if T is less than N. If T is less than N, you should buy from Threads. Therefore, at 120, the machine prints a message to that effect. At statement 90, if T is not less than N, then T must be greater than N. Therefore, the computer tells you to order from the overseas firm.

Improved IF-THEN   Although the previous program example is perhaps somewhat clumsy, it is the best you can do on some BASIC systems. Other systems, however, allow a rather more convenient form of the IF-THEN statement. You can't do anything with this form that you couldn't do anyway, but you can do things more easily. This other form is the same as the first except that *any statement* can follow the word THEN. The statement is executed if the condition is true. Whether or not the statement is executed, the computer then continues to the next statement in the program. Consider, for example:

```
15 IF T = N THEN PRINT "IT DOESN'T MATTER WHICH COMPANY. "
```

If T equals N, the message is printed. If T is not equal to N, the PRINT statement is skipped. In either case, the program continues to the next statement. Here are two other examples of the same thing:

```
23 IF X > Y THEN LET P = 1
97 IF L + 5 <> K * 3 THEN END
```

Statement 23 sets P to 1 if X is greater than Y. If X is not greater than Y, the LET statement is skipped. Statement 97 ends the program if the condition is true. If the condition is false, the program continues with the statement following statement 97.

With this kind of IF-THEN statement we can rewrite the Nuts "n" Threads program in the more comprehensible form shown below:

```
10 INPUT X
20 LET N = .75*X
30 LET T = .90*X - 5
40 PRINT "NUTS 'N' BOLTS CHARGES ";N
50 PRINT "THREADS CHARGES ";T
60 IF T = N THEN PRINT "BOTH FIRMS CHARGE THE SAME."
70 IF T > N THEN PRINT "BUY FROM NUTS, LTD."
80 IF T < N THEN PRINT "THREADS IS A BETTER DEAL."
90 END
```

If your system allows this, it can be very helpful.

Warning   One extremely annoying thing about computers is that their ideas about when two numbers are equal may not coincide with yours. For example, consider the program below:

```
10 LET T = .1
20 PRINT T
30 IF T > .95 THEN 60
40 LET T = T + .1
50 GOTO 20
60 END
```

The programmer intended the computer to print the numbers .1, .2, .3, . . . 1 and then stop, but because the computer converts numbers to binary, as discussed earlier, T may never equal exactly one. The output of this program might turn out to be that shown below:

```
              .1
              .2
              .3
              .4
              .5
              .599999
              .699999
              .799999
              .899999
              .999999
             1.09999
             1.19999
             1.29999

              .
              .
              .
```

Since T is never exactly equal to one, the smart-alecky computer goes right on printing numbers into eternity.

The moral of this example is: Avoid the use of the equals sign in IF-THEN statements except in integer arithmetic (which is exact, even on un-cooperative machines). Usually, you can replace the equals sign with greater-than, less-than, greater-than-or-equal-to, or less-than-or-equal-to signs. The above program, for example, could be rewritten as shown below:

```
10 LET T = .1
20 PRINT T
30 IF T = 1 THEN 60
40 LET T = T + .1
50 GOTO 20
60 END
```

Exercises

1. Write a program which types out 21, 31, 41, 51, ... , 101 and then stops.
2. Write a program which inputs a number. If the number is bigger than 3, it types back "YOU HAVE TYPED A LARGE NUMBER." If the number is less than 3, it types back "YOU HAVE TYPED A SMALL NUMBER." Then it waits for a new number. If you type a 0, it stops the program.
3. (a) Write a program which inputs numbers from the terminal until the user types a 0. Then the computer types back the largest of the numbers that the user typed. (Hint: The computer need only remember the largest number typed in so far.)
   (b) Write a program which inputs numbers from the teletype until the user types a −1. Then the computer types out the mean (the average) of the numbers typed in (not including the −1).
4. Write a program which reads X, Y, and Z and then decides whether or not

$$X^2 + Y^2 = Z^2$$

Have it print its findings.
5. Write a program which inputs two integers and then types the integers between the two, starting with the first one and going to the second one. If the first one is smaller than the second, the numbers will be in ascending order. If the first one is bigger than the second, then the numbers will be in descending order. (You may have to write two little programs to take care of these two cases and then use an IF-THEN statement to decide which of the two the computer should execute.)
6. Use the statement

```
10 LET N = INT(500*RND(0))+1
```

to have the computer pick a number from 1 to 500 and store it in N. You try to guess the number, and after each guess, the computer tells you whether your guess was high, low, or just right. The game ends when you guess the computer's number. (If after playing several times, you notice that the computer picks the same number every time, insert the statement

```
5 RANDOMIZE
```

in your program. If this doesn't do the trick, look in your manual for a statement which scrambles the random numbers.)

7. Write a program which inputs first the original balance in a savings account and then a second number which will represent a deposit if it is positive and a withdrawal if it is negative. The computer should print whichever of the following statements is appropriate:

```
WE HAVE PROCESSED A DEPOSIT TO YOUR ACCOUNT IN THE
AMOUNT OF $---.--.   YOUR NEW BALANCE IS $---.--.

WE HAVE PROCESSED A WITHDRAWL FROM YOUR ACCOUNT IN THE
AMOUNT OF $---.--.   YOUR NEW BALANCE IS $---.--.

WE HAVE PROCESSED A WITHDRAWL FROM YOUR ACCOUNT IN THE
AMOUNT OF $---.--.   YOUR ACCOUNT IS OVERDRAWN IN THE
AMOUNT OF $---.--.
```

Naturally, your program should print "WE HAVE PROCESSED A" before it does anything else. Then it should decide about the other things.

8. Write a program which types out the first 25 terms of a Fibonacci series, then stops.
9. N factorial, written N!, equals $1*2*3*4*\ldots*(N-1)*N$. Thus 4! equals $1*2*3*4$, which is 24. Write a program which types out a table of these factorials. It should start a line, type N, then type N! on the same line. Have your program print a table of factorials for values of N from 1 to 8.

3.3   Telling It Like It Is (REM Statement)

When you write a program, it may be clear to you what the program is supposed to do and what each variable stands for. To others, however, it may be clear as mud. For instance, consider the following program:

```
10 INPUT X
20 LET N = 2
30 IF N = X THEN 70
40 IF N > X THEN 90
50 LET N = N * 2
60 GOTO 30
70 PRINT "!"
80 GOTO 10
90 PRINT "?"
100 GOTO 10
110 END
```

What this program does, and what X and N are supposed to represent are not self-evident. Some kind of commentary is needed, and it would be ideal if

$RE M$

this commentary were included in the listing of the program itself for all to read. However, were you to write in your program the following:

```
5 THIS PROGRAM DECIDES WHETHER X IS A POWER OF TWO.
6 IT PRINTS A "!" IF IT IS AND A "?" IF IT IS NOT.
```

you would be bombarded with error messages.

In BASIC, the solution is the REMARK or REM statement. It consists of a line number and the letters REM followed by anything. Since the computer will placidly ignore the entire line, any gibberish you care to write is fine. A REM statement is strictly for human consumption; hence, more latitude of expression is allowed. For example, the following would be acceptable:

```
5 REM THIS PROGRAM DECIDES WHETHER X IS A POWER OF TWO.
```

A REM statement is not executed, but it will be printed if you give the LIST command asking for a listing of your program.

If you wish to write a remark that takes up several lines, you must put "REM" at the beginning of each line. Otherwise, the computer will conclude that the lines after the first one are statements which it doesn't understand. As usual, it then responds with error messages. You might, for example, write:

```
5 REM THIS PROGRAM DECIDES IF X IS A POWER OF TWO.
6 REM IT TYPES A "!" IF IT IS.
7 REM IT TYPES A "?" IF IT IS NOT.
```

A remark statement can be used to indicate what a program does; it can be used to tell you what a variable stands for and what values it is expected to take on (these remarks are often the most useful); it can tell you what parts of a program are doing what facets of the work. Remark statements are informative to other people who are looking at your program and trying to improve it; they are useful to you if you come back to your program after a lapse of time and wish to make some changes in the way it works; they are useful if you have to leave your program half-finished overnight and come back to it in the morning (unless your memory is phenomenal).

Study the three programs on the next two pages to see how the REM statement may be used to improve readability. Notice in particular the use of indentation to improve readability even more.

A second, less obvious use of the REM statement is as a separator between logical sections of the program. By grouping several REM statements together, you can create a blank space in the listing of your program which helps the reader see that the statements above the space serve a different purpose from those below. Consider the listing in Program 1. It is the hardware program of the last section, but it is easier to understand due to the addition of a few blank lines.

A Suggestion   From here on, the example programs contain not only the blank lines suggested in the above paragraph, but also blank spaces within

PROGRAM 1

```
4 REM ***********************************************************
5 REM *** THIS PROGRAM DECIDES WHOSE HARDWARE TO BUY. ***
6 REM ***********************************************************
7 REM
8 REM *** CALCULATE WHAT EACH COMPANY CHARGES. ***
9 REM
10 INPUT X
20 LET N = .75*X
30 LET T = .90*X - 5
40 PRINT "NUTS 'N' BOLTS CHARGES ";N
50 PRINT "THREADS CHARGES ";T
55 REM
56 REM
57 REM
58 REM *** DECIDE WHICH CHARGE IS GREATER ***
59 REM
60 IF T <> N THEN 90
70 PRINT "IT DOESN'T MATTER WHICH COMPANY YOU ORDER FROM. "
80 END
85 REM
86 REM
90 IF T < N THEN 120
100 PRINT "YOU SHOULD ORDER FROM NUTS 'N' BOLTS. "
110 END
120 PRINT "THREADS IS OFFERING THE BETTER DEAL. "
130 END
```

PROGRAM 2

```
4    REM ***********************************************************
5    REM *** THIS PROGRAM DECIDES WHOSE HARDWARE TO BUY ***
6    REM ***********************************************************
7    REM
8    REM *** CALCULATE WHAT EACH COMPANY CHARGES ***
9    REM
10   INPUT X
20   LET N = .75*X
30   LET T = .90*X - 5
40   PRINT "NUTS 'N' BOLTS CHARGES ";N
50   PRINT "THREADS CHARGES ";T
55   REM
56   REM
57   REM
58   REM *** DECIDE WHICH CHARGE IS GREATER ***
59   REM
60   IF T <> N THEN 90
70      PRINT "IT DOESN'T MATTER WHICH COMPANY YOU ORDER FROM. "
80      END
90   REM
95      IF T < N THEN 120
100        PRINT "YOU SHOULD ORDER FROM NUTS 'N' BOLTS. "
110        END
120     REM
125        PRINT "THREADS IS OFFERING THE BETTER DEAL. "
130        END
```

PROGRAM 3

```
10   REM  ************************************************************
11   REM  *** THIS PROGRAM PRINTS A TABLE OF SUMS OF POWERS ***
12   REM  ************************************************************
13   REM
14   REM
100  REM *** INITIALIZE VARIABLES AND PRINT HEADINGS ***
101  REM
110  LET P1 = 0
120  LET P2 = 0
130  LET P3 = 0
140  LET N = 1
150  PRINT "NUMBER","SUM OF NUMBERS","SUM OF SQUARES","SUM OF CUBES"
160  PRINT " ",       "SO FAR",        "SO FAR",        "SO FAR"
170  PRINT
180  REM
185  REM  ************************************************************
190  REM
199  REM *** LOOP THAT PRINTS THE TABLE ***
200  REM
210     LET P1 = P1 + N
210     LET P2 = P2 + N↑2
230     LET P3 = P3 + N↑3
240     PRINT N,P1,P2,P3
250     PRINT
260     LET N = N + 1
270     IF N > 10 THEN 300
280  GOTO 200
290  REM
295  REM  ************************************************************
296  REM
300  END
```

statements to make their meanings clear. By including such spaces and by indenting certain sections of code, we can clarify the logic behind the program for those subsequently reading it. Unfortunately, many BASIC systems automatically remove all extraneous spaces (extraneous, that is, from the computer's point of view) from your statements, so that you may not be able to take advantage of this technique. Do so if you can, however. Program 2 is an improved version of Program 1. Program 3 shows some of the possibilities of the method; note how easy it is to discern the extent of the loop in that program.

3.4   Blessed Is He Who Expects the Worst

There will be days when the computer types out beautiful results on the first try. There will be days when no amount of coaxing seems to produce reasonable results from the machine. These are the days when the computer blithely informs you that phone calls to New York cost $175, that the average annual wheat crop of the United States is five bushels, and that tomorrow's weather in Denver will include a 230 degree high and 40 feet of rain.

More seriously, there will also be days when minor changes in your program will put the computer's version of the world back into proper perspective, and there will be days when you will be convinced that *this* time it *must* be the computer's fault because you can *clearly* see that there *aren't* any mistakes in the program.

The bad days require special patience if you are to preserve your sanity. One of the best solutions is to think at the computer's level. To demonstrate the method, here is an example. The following program is supposed to input M, the monthly service charge on a telephone, calculate T, the 10 percent tax on this, input L, the long distance charges, add 10 percent of L to T to get the total tax, and then add tax, monthly charge, and long distance together to get B, the bill. Then it repeats the process for the next customer.

```
10 LET T = 0
20 INPUT M
30 LET T = T + .1*M
40 INPUT L
50 LET T = T + .1*L
60 LET B = M + L + T
70 PRINT B
80 GOTO 20
90 END
```

An eager-beaver telephone company employee decides that he had better check the computer's results since some of them look suspicious. He concludes that the first bill is correct, that the second is a little too large, that the tenth is twice as big as it should be, and that the hundredth is about ten times as big as it should be. What is wrong?

Well, to begin with, whoever wrote this particular piece of computer code should be taken out and shot. This is not because the program isn't working, but because it is so complicated. Several far simpler alternatives should spring to mind. For example:

```
10 INPUT M, L
20 PRINT 1.1 * (M + L)
30 GOTO 10
40 END
```

This is not only easier to understand but also takes less computer time to run. Be that as it may. Patching up an existing program is usually easier than writing a new one, and besides, morbid curiosity may lead you to want to know why the present one isn't working.

On good days you will see the problem right away, but there will be days when you don't. If this is a bad day, pretend you are the computer. To do so, you need two pieces of paper, one with a listing (remember the LIST command) of the program, and the other blank. On the blank page make a column for each of the variables, M, L, T, and B. In each column keep track of what number is stored in that memory space. Put a question mark initially in each, since you don't yet know what any of the variables are. Now place your thumb on statement 10. Just as the computer would do, erase, cross out, or otherwise obliterate the question mark in column T and replace it with 0. Move your thumb to statement 20. Suppose M is typed in as 4 (dollars, presumably). Cross out the question mark in the column for M and put in a 4. Move your thumb to statement 30. Perform the indicated calculation and replace whatever is in T with the result of the calculation. As a result, the number .4 lands in T. Suppose that L is typed in as 6. Continue on.

When you come to statement 70, the scratch sheet should look like this:

T	M	L	B
~~?~~	~~?~~	~~?~~	~~?~~
~~.4~~	4	6	11
1			

A little calculation indicates that this is indeed correct; taxes, monthly charge, long distance, and total bill are all as they should be. So continue. Statement 80 says to go to 20, so move your thumb back to 20 and continue. Suppose that this time M is input as 6 and L is input as 8. When you get to statement 70 the second time, the scratch sheet should look like this:

T	M	L	B
~~?~~	~~?~~	~~?~~	~~?~~
~~.4~~	~~4~~	~~6~~	~~11~~
~~1~~	6	8	16.4
~~1.6~~			
2.4			

You have a problem. The bill should be

Monthly charge: $6
Long distance: $8
Subtotal: $14
10% Tax: $1.4
Total: $15.4

The scratch sheet indicates that the computer has calculated the tax wrongly as $2.40 instead of as $1.40. Thinking back about the process shows that what has happened is that when the computer started to figure out the bill for the second customer, T was already equal to 1 (from the tax to the first customer). Statements 30 and 50 added the correct tax for the second customer, but nowhere was the $1 tax to the first customer disposed of. It was added to the second customer's bill.

Knowing this, fixing the program is not too difficult. Probably the fastest way is to change statement 80 to GO TO 10. If you do this, then T will be reset to 0 before the calculation of the second bill begins. This should solve the problem.

Call this process playing computer.

Exercises

Play computer on each of the following programs. On programs with INPUT statements, try several different supposed inputs.

```
A)   10 LET X = 1
     15 LET Y = 3
     20 LET X = X + Y
     30 PRINT X, Y
     40 GOTO 10
     50 END
```

```
B)   10 LET Q = 5
     20 LET R = 3
     30 LET Q = Q + 2
     40 LET R = R + 2
     50 PRINT Q, R
     60 GOTO 20
     70 END
```

```
C)   10 GOTO 40
     20 PRINT "E";
     30 GOTO 70
     40 PRINT "A";
     50 PRINT "T";
     60 GOTO 20
     70 END
```

```
D)   10 INPUT T, U
     20 REM *** LOOP ***
     30    PRINT T + U
     40    PRINT T + U + U
     50    LET T = T + U
     60 GOTO 20
     70 END
```

```
E)   10 LET X = 26
     20 LET Y = 7
     30 REM *** LOOP ***
     40    IF X < 0 THEN 90
     50    LET X = X - Y
     60    LET Y = Y - 1
     70    PRINT "S",
     80 GOTO 30
     90 END
```

```
F)   10 INPUT M, N
     15 LET X = M
     20 REM *** LOOP ***
     25    IF X > N THEN 60
     30    IF X = N THEN 80
     40    LET X = X + M
     50 GOTO 20
     60 PRINT "NO"
     70 END
     80 PRINT "YES"
     90 END
```

3.5   More Circles (FOR-NEXT Statement)

Getting the computer to repeat a sequence of steps is big business. The FOR-NEXT *loop* is a way of doing more conveniently something that we can do anyway. Consider the following program:

```
10   LET N = 0
20   REM *** LOOP ***
30      IF (N + 1) > 10 THEN 110
40      LET N = N + 1
..      .......
..      .......
..      .......
..      .......
100  GOTO 20
110  END
```

The computer does the steps of interest ten times, the variable N perhaps serving no purpose but to count the number of times the computer has done the process. The following program does *exactly* the same thing.

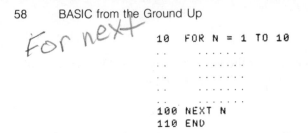

```
        10    FOR N = 1 TO 10
        . .        . . . . . . .
        . .        . . . . . . .
        . .        . . . . . . .
        . .        . . . . . . .
        100 NEXT N
        110 END
```

This program sets the variable N to 1, performs the steps of interest, increments N to 2, repeats the steps, and so on until N is greater than 10, when the process stops. See Fig. 3.4 for two flowcharts for this program.

The format of the FOR-NEXT loop is as follows. The word FOR is followed by the name of any legal variable, an equal sign, an arithmetic expression, the word TO, and another arithmetic expression. The variable named in a FOR statement is often called an *iteration variable,* since it counts the number of iterations, or repetitions, that the computer has made. The iteration variable is set to the value of the first arithmetic expression; the computer does the arithmetic and puts the result in the memory space reserved for the iteration variable. Every time the computer executes the series of statements in the loop, it adds one to, or *increments,* the iteration variable, and when the iteration variable exceeds the value of the second arithmetic expression in the FOR statement, the computer jumps to the statement in the program immediately following the repeated steps.

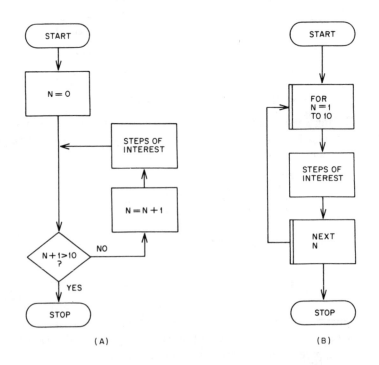

Fig. 3.4 Flowcharts for program loops

The NEXT statement consists of the word NEXT followed by the iteration variable name (which must be the same as the name in the FOR statement or else the computer will give you an error message). The sole purpose of the NEXT statement is to tell the computer where the sequence of statements to be repeated ends.

The following program prints a table of squares of the numbers 50 to 60. Note that the iteration variable can be used inside the FOR-NEXT loop.

```
10 PRINT "NUMBER","ITS SQUARE"
20 FOR N = 50 TO 60
30    PRINT N,
40    PRINT N↑2
50 NEXT N
60 END
```

N is set to 50, and statements 30 and 40 print 50 and 50^2. Then N is incremented to 51, and statements 30 and 40 print 51 and 51^2. This continues until 60 and 60^2 are printed, when the program ends. The output of this program is as follows:

```
NUMBER          ITS SQUARE
50              2500
51              2601
52              2704
53              2809
54              2916
55              3025
56              3136
57              3249
58              3364
59              3481
60              3600
```

Following is a program that lets the user type in a number N and then types out a table of cubes of the number N and of the next ten numbers:

```
10 INPUT N
20 FOR I = N TO N + 10
30    PRINT I, I↑3
40 NEXT I
50 END
```

The computer evaluates N and N + 10 when it comes to statement 20. For example, if the user types in 44, then statement 20 is the same as

```
20 FOR I = 44 TO 54
```

I is the iteration variable in this case.

Example   A pensioner has $40,000 in the bank drawing 5 percent interest every year. At the end of each year, after the interest is payed, he withdraws $4000 to augment his other income. How much can he expect to have left in the bank at the end of each of the next ten years?

The program below keeps the balance of his bank account in the variable B. At the end of each year, it calculates I, the interest, adds that to B, subtracts $4000, and prints the remaining balance. It repeats this ten times.

```
10 PRINT "YEAR","REMAINING BALANCE"
20 LET B = 40000
25 REM
30 FOR Y = 1 TO 10
40    LET I = .05*B
50    LET B = B + I - 4000
60    PRINT Y,B
70 NEXT Y
75 REM
80 END
```

The program initializes the balance to $40,000. In the loop from statements 30 to 70, Y is set to 1, and the interest and then the new balance are calculated. Then Y is set to 2, and the process is repeated on the new balance. This continues until Y is equal to 10. The output is as follows:

YEAR	REMAINING BALANCE
1	38000
2	35900
3	33695
4	31379.75
5	28948.74
6	26396.17
7	23715.98
8	20901.78
9	17946.87
10	14844.21

The STEP Option   Suppose that we slightly change the problem about printing a table of cubes. We now want to type in a number and get a table of cubes of that number and of nine numbers greater than it in one-tenth increments. That is, if we type in 7, we want the cubes of 7, 7.1, 7.2, 7.3, ... up to 7.9. It would be possible, of course, to do the gymnastics of the last section, using IF-THEN and GOTO statements, to set up our own iteration variable to take on the values 7, 7.1, and so on. It would also be possible to write a FOR-NEXT loop in which the iteration variable was multiplied by .1 to get the correct numbers to cube. But this is all unnecessary because of the STEP option on FOR-NEXT loops.

The STEP option works like this: Unless prompted to do otherwise, the FOR-NEXT loop increments its iteration variable by one each time through the loop. In our problem, however, we want the iteration variable to be incremented by .1. The computer can be asked to add the word STEP and the number .1 at the end of the FOR statement. Then, instead of adding 1 to the iteration variable, the computer will add .1 to it.

The following program will do what we asked:

```
10 PRINT "NUMBER","ITS CUBE"
20 INPUT X
30 FOR J = X TO (X + .9) STEP .1
40    PRINT J, J↑3
50 NEXT J
60 END
```

If X is input as 7, J starts as 7. After statement 40 prints 7 and 7³, J is set to 7.1. Then J becomes 7.2 and so on until J is 7.9, when the program ends. The output is shown below.

NUMBER	ITS CUBE
7	343
7.1	357.911
7.2	373.248
7.3	389.017
7.4	405.224
7.5	421.875
7.6	438.976
7.7	456.533
7.8	474.522
7.9	493.039

It is permissible to have a negative number as your STEP, but a few changes must be made. Since the iteration variable will be decreasing, you must start it at a higher number and end it at a lower. For example:

```
80 FOR X = 29 TO 5 STEP -4
```

sets X to 29, 25, 21, and so on until X is *less* than or equal to 5, when the loop ends. The following program does the obvious:

```
10 FOR Q = 10 TO 0 STEP -1
20    PRINT Q
30 NEXT Q
40 PRINT "BLAST OFF"
50 END
```

Nesting FOR-NEXT Loops   Suppose that you wish to find two integers X and Y such that $X^2 + Y^2 = 317$. Not knowing any good formula to find such an X and Y, let us do it by trial and error. Since the computer can't figure out what good guesses to try, let us have the computer try all possible pairs of integers X and Y.

Since 20^2 is 400, X and Y must both be less than 20. We set X equal to 1; then we let Y run from 1 to 20 (using a FOR-NEXT loop, of course). Then we set X to 2 and let Y run through from 1 to 20, set X to 3, and so on. Since we let X run from 1 to 20 also, we put X in a FOR-NEXT loop which goes around the outside of the FOR-NEXT loop of Y:

```
10   FOR X = 1 TO 20
20      FOR Y = 1 TO 20
 . .        . . . . . . .
 . .        . . . . . . .
 . .        . . . . . . .
 . .        . . . . . . .
 . .        . . . . . . .
 . .        . . . . . . .
 . .        . . . . . . .
100    NEXT Y
110 NEXT X
120 END
```

This program sets X equal to 1. Then it executes the FOR-NEXT loop of statements 20 to 100, setting Y equal to all the numbers from 1 to 20 in turn. When it finishes with this loop, it comes to statement 110, sets X to 2, and goes back to statement 20. Then it goes through the whole list of Y's again. X becomes 3, and so on. In this way, all the pairs of X and Y will be checked. The whole program might look like the one below:

```
10 FOR X = 1 TO 20
20    FOR Y = 1 TO 20
30       IF  X↑2 + Y↑2 <> 317   THEN 50
40          PRINT "X ";X, "Y ";Y
50    NEXT Y
60 NEXT X
70 END
```

Note in passing the use of a comma and semicolons in statement 40 to make the output neat. Note also that this program makes a lot of stupid guesses. To let X = 1 and Y = 1 is a guess that you would never waste your time with, since it obviously will not work. However, the computer has no common sense.

There are several ways of improving this program. One is the following: You know that either X or Y is bigger than the other. The above program finds two pairs of numbers: X = 14, Y = 11 and X = 11, Y = 14. These are the same answer for most purposes, and having the computer figure and print both is a waste of time. To avoid the repetition, assume that Y is the bigger of the two. Then whatever X is, check only the bigger Y's. The following program does this:

```
10 FOR X = 1 TO 20
20    FOR Y = X TO 20
30       IF  X↑2 + Y↑2 <> 317   THEN 50
40          PRINT "X ";X, "Y ";Y
50    NEXT Y
60 NEXT X
70 END
```

Each time we come to statement 20, we start with Y equal to X, and then check only those Y's that are between X and 20. The first time we go through, with X equal to 1, Y goes all the way from 1 to 20, but the second time,

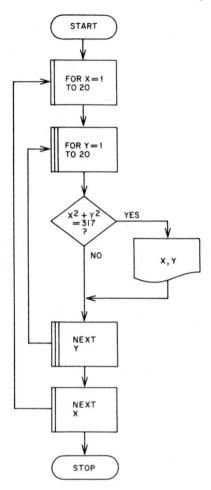

Fig. 3.5   Flowchart of nested FOR-NEXT loops

with X equal to 2, Y goes only from 2 to 20, and so on. In this way, the number of Y's to be checked is considerably cut down. When X is 17, for example, the only Y's to check are 17, 18, 19, and 20. This method obviously consumes far less computer time than checking all 20 possible Y's from 1 to 20. A flowchart for this program is shown in Fig. 3.5.

The Harmonic Series (An Example of Nested Loops)   The series of numbers

$$1 + 1/2 + 1/3 + 1/4 + 1/5 + 1/6 + \dots$$

is called the *harmonic series*. Although the numbers 1/2, 1/3, 1/4, ... get smaller and smaller, the series can add up to as large a number as one wishes simply by adding enough terms. For example, the sum will be greater than six if one adds up the terms through 1/227:

$$1 + 1/2 + 1/3 + \ldots + 1/226 + 1/227 > 6$$

A proof that the sum will get as large as you like is not our purpose, but we can investigate the sums using a computer program. The first possible program might be the following:

```
10 LET T = 0
20 FOR I = 1 TO 100
30    LET T = T + 1/I
40    PRINT T,
50 NEXT I
60 END
```

This prints first the number 1, then $1 + 1/2$, then $1 + 1/2 + 1/3$, and so on, as each fraction is successively added to T. Each of the sums up to and including

$$1 + 1/2 + 1/3 + \ldots + 1/99 + 1/100$$

is printed. For reasons to be discussed in a moment, consider the following program, which does the same thing:

```
10 LET T = 0
15 LET K = 0
20 FOR I = 1 TO 100
25    LET K = K + 1
30    LET T = T + 1/K
40    PRINT T,
50 NEXT I
60 END
```

The only change is the introduction of the variable K. Since K starts out with the value 0 and increases by 1 each time through the FOR-NEXT loop, K is always equal to I. Hence this program does rather less efficiently the same thing as the previous program.

Now suppose that you want to know only every twentieth such sum. That is, you want to know:

$$1 + 1/2 + 1/3 + \ldots + 1/19 + 1/20$$
$$1 + 1/2 + 1/3 + \ldots + 1/39 + 1/40$$
$$1 + 1/2 + 1/3 + \ldots + 1/59 + 1/60$$

.
.
.

and so on up to

$$1 + 1/2 + 1/3 + \ldots + 1/499 + 1/500$$

You could simply change the previous program so that it executes the loop 500 times, and among the 500 sums that it would print would be the ones that you want. This is a feeble-minded method. A better way is to add the first twenty numbers, print out that sum, add on twenty more numbers, print a second sum, add another twenty numbers, and so on. The following program does this:

```
10 LET T = 0
20 LET K = 0
30 FOR I = 1 TO 25
40    FOR J = 1 TO 20
50       LET K = K + 1
60       LET T = T + 1/K
70    NEXT J
80    PRINT T,
90 NEXT I
99 END
```

The FOR-NEXT loop in which J goes from 1 to 20 (statements 40 through 70) is the same as the FOR-NEXT loop in the previous program except that it is missing the PRINT statement. This FOR-NEXT loop adds up the first twenty fractions of the sum before anything is printed. J and K will then each equal 20, and T will equal

$$1 + 1/2 + 1/3 + \ldots + 1/19 + 1/20$$

Now the program gets to statement 80 and prints the sum of the first twenty fractions, which is stored in T. At statement 90, $I = 1$, and we go back to statement 40. J is set back to 1, but K continues, starting at 21, and we go through the loop from 40 to 70 twenty more times, adding

$$1/21 + 1/22 + 1/23 + \ldots + 1/39 + 1/40$$

to the previous sum. Note that K is not reset to 1, as is J. J couldn't be used to add the new fractions to the sum because it doesn't run from 1 to 500 but is reset every twentieth number when the sum is printed. A table of the values of I, J, and K for successive times through the inner loop from 40 to 70 is shown below:

Time through inner loop:	I	J	K
1	1	1	1
2	1	2	2
3	1	3	3
.	.	.	.
.	.	.	.
.	.	.	.
19	1	19	19
20	1	20	20
21	2	1	21
22	2	2	22
23	2	3	23

.	.	.	.
.	.	.	.
.	.	.	.
39	2	19	39
40	2	20	40
41	3	1	41
.	.	.	.
.	.	.	.
.	.	.	.
499	25	19	499
500	25	20	500

An alternative way to write the program is as follows:

```
10 LET T = 0
20 FOR I = 0 TO 24
30    FOR J = 1 TO 20
40        LET T = T + 1/(J + 20*I)
50    NEXT J
60    PRINT T,
70 NEXT I
80 END
```

How does it work?

Exercises

1. Write a program to print a table of factorials of the numbers from 1 to 10.
2. Write a program which inputs two integers, a smaller integer A, and a larger integer B, and then prints a table of squares and cubes of the integers from A to B.
3. Another way to improve the method of finding X and Y with $X^2 + Y^2 = 317$ is to note that one of them must be even and one must be odd. (Why?) Write a program that lets X be the odds from 1 to 19 and Y the even's from 2 to 20. (Remember STEP?)
4. Newton's algorithm for finding the square root of N is as follows. First, take a guess G at the square root. (The computer can take the number 1 as its first guess.) Calculate N/G and take the average of G and N/G as your new guess, G1. Divide N by G1 and take the average of G1 and N/G1 to get yet a third guess. Repeat this process twenty times, and your guesses will get closer and closer to the square root. Write a program which finds square roots of inputted numbers by Newton's algorithm. You might have it type out its intermediate guesses. About how many guesses does it take before the guesses are very close to the square root?
5. Pythagorean triples are triples of integers X, Y, and Z such that $X^2 + Y^2 = Z^2$. Write a program which finds all the Pythagorean triples in which Z is less than or equal to 30 and X is less than Y.
6. Write a program whose output is as follows:

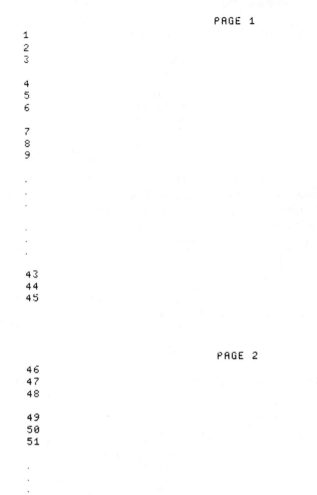

7. A printer is supposed to set the number $a^b c^a$ in type, where a, b, and c are integers less than 10. Instead, he sets the number abca (a is the thousands place, b is the hundreds place, and so on). Lo and behold, it turns out that abca $= a^b c^a$. Write a program which tries all possible a, b, and c to find the number which the printer set.

8. Use FOR-NEXT loops to have the computer print out a multiplication table of the numbers from 1 to 5.

9. (a) Have the computer input two integers X and Y and print a block of asterisks whose dimensions are X by Y. (b) Have the computer input three integers X, Y, and Z and print a block of asterisks whose dimensions are X by Y surrounded by a frame of 0's whose width is Z. For example, if X, Y, and Z are input as 5, 7, and 2, respectively, then the output from this program should be:

```
000000000
000000000
00*****00
00*****00
00*****00
00*****00
00*****00
00*****00
00*****00
000000000
000000000
```

10. Rewrite the example in the text that uses the STEP option to print the table of cubes from 7 to 7.9 two ways: (a) Write it without a FOR-NEXT loop, and (b) write it with a FOR-NEXT loop but without a STEP. These two programs will illustrate the power of the STEP option.

11. Consider the FOR-NEXT loop in this program:

```
10 INPUT A
20 INPUT B
30 FOR I = A TO B
40    PRINT I
50 NEXT I
60 PRINT I
70 END
```

Here are three methods of rewriting the program without a FOR-NEXT loop.

```
A)    10 LET I = A - 1
      20 REM *** LOOP ***
      30    IF (I + 1) > B THEN 70
      40    LET I = I + 1
      50    PRINT I
      60 GOTO 20
      70 PRINT I
```

```
B)    10 LET I = A
      20 REM *** LOOP ***
      30    IF I > B THEN 70
      40    PRINT I
      50    LET I = I + 1
      60 GOTO 20
      70 PRINT I
```

```
C)    10 LET I = A
      20 REM *** LOOP ***
      30    PRINT I
      40    IF I >=B THEN 70
      50    LET I = I + 1
      60 GOTO 20
      70 PRINT I
```

When the computer encounters a FOR-NEXT loop, it must translate it to one of the above. What are the differences among the above methods? Which do you think is best?

12. Don't fall off the deep end. FOR-NEXT loops are useful, but situations exist where they work badly. Consider this problem: Add the numbers $1 + 2 + 3 + 4 + \ldots$ until the sum is greater than 1000; then print the last number added, the sum, and a row of asterisks. Here are two efforts to solve this problem using a FOR-NEXT loop to do the sum:

```
A )    10   LET T = 0
       20   FOR I = 1 TO 100
       30     LET T = T + I
       40     IF T >= 1000 THEN 60
       50   NEXT I
       60   PRINT I, T
       70   FOR I = 1 TO 70
       80     PRINT "*";
       90   NEXT I
      100   END
```

```
B )    10   LET T = 0
       20   FOR I = 1 TO 100
       30     LET T = T + I
       40    ·IF T < 1000 THEN 70
       50       LET I1 = I
       60       LET I = 100
       70   NEXT I
       80   PRINT I1, T
       90   FOR I = 1 TO 70
      100     PRINT "*";
      110   NEXT I
      130   END
```

Criticize each program. One of them will probably break down and give an error message. Which? Write a better program to solve the problem without a FOR-NEXT loop. Why doesn't this problem lend itself to the use of FOR-NEXT loops?

4
BUILDING
UPWARDS

4.1 Packages (Functions)

Suppose that you are writing a program that uses the square roots of several numbers. You would have several unattractive alternatives: you could have the computer stop every time it needed a square root while you looked it up in a table and typed it in, or you could type a whole table of square roots into the machine before your program starts, or you could write a (probably long and messy) program fragment that figures out square roots. You need pick none of these choices, however, because the computer system has a library of *functions* to take care of these occasions. For your program involving square roots, you could borrow the square root function from the library to solve your problems. The function is called SQR. If the computer sees

```
10 LET R = SQR(.3)
```

it finds the square root of .3 and stores the result in R.

When the computer finds the name of one of the functions followed by an arithmetic expression in parentheses (called the *argument*), it figures out the value of the argument and then applies the function to it. For example, if the computer sees

```
20 LET S = SQR(5 + A*B)
```

it first gets busy figuring out the value of the argument, $5 + A*B$. Then it takes the square root of whatever number $5 + A*B$ turns out to be. A function is said to *return* a result. Thus SQR(4) *returns* the value 2. A function can be part of an arithmetic expression, as in

```
30 LET X = 8 + SQR(5)
```

In the order of operations, functions have priority over everything. For example, SQR(3 + 6)*3 means to find the value of SQR(3 + 6) and then to multiply by 3:

70

$$SQR(3 + 6)*3 = SQR(9)*3 = 3*3 = 9$$

Every computer has its own list of library functions, and your system manual will have a complete description of each one. Some of the most common are discussed below. One warning is in order: these library functions use up unbelievable amounts of computer time—fifty times the length of time that it takes to do an addition is not out of line. Therefore, if you need the result of one of these functions more than once, use the function the first time and store the result in a variable so that the value can subsequently be used without recalculating it.

List of Common Functions   For those people doing trigonometry, computers almost always provide the following functions, in which X is assumed to be expressed in *radians* (if you have an angle in degrees, convert it):

SIN(X)
COS(X)
TAN(X)
ASN(X)
ACS(X)
ATN(X)

The last three functions are the arcsine, the arccosine, and the arctangent, respectively.

One might imagine that the computer has a gigantic trig table hidden in it, but this is not the case. The computer calculates the values of these functions by using a Taylor series. For example, sine x is approximately equal to

$$x - \frac{x^3}{6} + \frac{x^5}{120} - \frac{x^7}{5040} + \frac{x^9}{362880}$$

You can see that the calculation will take a while.

Usually, computers also provide a logarithm function. Some logarithm functions return natural logarithms (base e) and some return common logarithms (base 10). Some computers provide both functions, calling one of them LOG(X) and the other LN(X). Check your manual to see what you have. The function EXP(X) is often available as well; it returns the value e^x.

Five other functions often found in system libraries are the following:

1. INT(X) returns the integer part of X, that is, the largest integer that is less than or equal to X. (On some systems, the largest integer strictly less than X is returned instead.) Thus, INT(4.9) is 4 and INT(-3.4) is -4.
2. RND(X) returns a random number between 0 and 1. Usually, the value of the argument is simply ignored. The care and feeding of random number functions varies greatly, and you are advised to check your manual.
3. ABS(X) returns the absolute value of the number X. Thus, ABS(5) equals 5, for example, and ABS(-2.2) equals 2.2.

4. SGN(X) decides whether X is positive, zero, or negative. If X is positive, then SGN(X) equals 1. If X equals zero, then SGN(X) equals zero. If X is negative, then SGN(X) equals −1.
5. TAB(X) is used only with a PRINT statement. For example,

```
20 PRINT TAB(23);
```

spaces the teletype over to the column 23 spaces from the left margin. If the teletype is already past this point because of previous PRINT statements, then the statement has no effect. If the argument of the TAB function is not an integer, it is fed to the INT function first. Thus,

```
20 PRINT TAB(23.89);
```

has the same effect as the above statement. Note that a semicolon is necessary if this statement is to do any good, for if there is no semicolon, the teletype will start the next PRINT statement on the next line (in the first space by the left-hand margin) instead of staying in column 23.

The INT Function Used to Check Divisibility   The INT function has interesting mathematical uses because it can be used to check whether or not one number is divisible by another. The method is this: C is divisible by D if and only if C/D is an integer. C/D is an integer if and only if C/D = INT(C/D). Therefore, C is divisible by D if and only if C/D = INT(C/D). (Here it is presumed that your INT function works by returning the least integer less than or equal to your number. If your INT function returns the least integer *strictly* less than your number, then C/D is an integer if and only if C/D = INT(C/D) + 1.)

This feature can be used to check if an integer is prime. You need only see that the integer is not divisible by any integer smaller than it other than 1.

Using the INT Function to Separate Digits   A number of interesting problems demand that you separate numbers into digits. Suppose that the computer needs to know the value of the digit just to the right of the decimal point in 456.789. To do this, it can use the following procedure (assuming INT(X) returns the greatest integer less than or equal to X). Assume that the number is stored in W and that we want to end up with the tenths place stored in W. First arrange to get rid of the 456 by using the statement,

```
10 LET W = W - INT(W)
```

Since INT(W) is 456, W − INT(W) is 0.789. Now use the statement,

```
20 LET W = 10 * W
```

W contains 7.89. To get rid of the .89, use the statement,

```
30 LET W = INT(W)
```

At last W contains 7, which is what we wanted.

If you want some digit besides the tenths digit, you can get it by first multiplying or dividing W by the power of ten, which puts the digit of interest in the place immediately to the right of the decimal point, and then performing the same procedure.

If your system is one of those in which INT is strictly less than the argument, you must be careful to take care of certain troublesome situations, such as finding the tenths digit of something like 5.00 or 5.10. Check the program suggested above and note that it doesn't work for these two numbers. A program segment which will work is shown below:

```
10  IF W <> INT(W) + 1 THEN 40
20      LET W = 0
30      GOTO 90
40  REM
50      LET W = W - INT(W)
60      LET W = W * 10
70      IF W = INT(W) + 1 THEN 90
80          LET W = INT(W)
90  REM *** PROGRAM CONTINUES FROM HERE ***
```

Note that in statement 20, W is an integer so that the tenths place is 0, and that in statement 60, if W is now an integer, it must be the tenths place that we wanted.

Exercises

1. The following are very short exercises:
    (a) Write a program which prints out a table of square roots of the numbers from 1 to 10.
    (b) Use the quadratic formula to write a program which inputs the coefficients of a quadratic equation and prints the real solutions. (You had better check to make sure that you do not try to take the square root of a negative number.)
    (c) Write a program which rolls a pair of dice. It should print two random integers from 1 to 6.
    (d) Write a statement that rounds a number off to the *nearest* integer. (This is easy using the INT function, but there is a trick to it.)
    (e) Write a program that allows the user to type in the coordinates of two points in the coordinate plane and then types back the distance between them. The formula for distance, remember, is

$$d = \sqrt{(x_2 - x_1)^2 + (y_2 - y_1)^2}$$

    (f) Write a program that prints a diagonal row of stars. (Use the TAB function.)
2. Write a program to find the greatest common factor and the lowest common multiple of two numbers which the user types in. The greatest common factor is

the biggest number which goes evenly into both numbers. The lowest common multiple is the smallest number which is a multiple of both.

3. Prime numbers:
   (a) Write a program which inputs a number and decides if it is prime.
   (b) Using part (a) as part of your program, have the computer find and print a list of the prime numbers less than 100.
   (c) To check the primeness of a number, it is only necessary to make sure that it had no factors which are less than its square root. (Why?) Improve your programs by incorporating this fact in your algorithm.

4. Write a program to find the perfect numbers less than 1000. A *perfect number* is one which is equal to the sum of all its factors (including 1). For example, the number 6 is perfect because its factors—1, 2, and 3—add up to 6: $1 + 2 + 3 = 6$. The number 8 is not perfect because $1 + 2 + 4 \neq 8$.

5. Digits problems:
   (a) Write a program which finds the numbers from 1 to 1000 which are equal to the sum of the cubes of their digits.
   (b) Write a program to find out if any three-digit numbers equal the square of the product of their digits.

6. Use the random number function to write a program which flips a coin 100 times and then reports how many heads and tails it generated. You must figure out how to make the random number function simulate a tossed coin.

7. Write a program which solves right triangle ABC (right angle at C). The program should ask the user for the lengths of $\overline{AB}$, $\overline{BC}$, and $\overline{AC}$ and for the measure of angle B. The user inputs values for two of these numbers and inputs zeros for the other two. The computer then solves the triangle and prints out the lengths of $\overline{AB}$, $\overline{BC}$, and $\overline{AC}$ and the measures of angles A and B. If the user inputs more than two zeros, the computer should warn him that he has input insufficient data and let him try again.

8. Write a program to solve a triangle given two sides and the included angle. (Use the law of cosines to find the third side and the law of sines to find the other two angles.)

9. SGN and ABS:
   (a) Consider the statement

   ```
   10 LET Y = ABS(X)
   ```

   If there were no ABS function, you would have to write a sequence of statements that did the same thing. Write that sequence of statements.
   (b) Write a sequence of statements to take the place of

   ```
   20 LET Y = SGN(X)
   ```

   supposing that the SGN function isn't on your computer.
   (c) How do you think the computer evaluates SGN and ABS?

4.2   Packaging (User-Defined Functions)

Suppose that you have written a program that inputs the temperatures of certain gasses and does various calculations with these temperatures. Suppose that when you wrote the program, you expected temperatures to be input to the nearest degree Centrigrade, but you find, to your horror, that the users are typing in the temperatures in Fahrenheit. To avoid having everything go completely to pot, the computer must convert each temperature from Fahrenheit to the nearest degree Centigrade. The formula for the conversion from Fahrenheit degrees (F) to Centigrade degrees (C) is

$$C = 5/9*(F - 32)$$

The value for C may or may not turn out to be a whole number of degrees; to round it off to the nearest degree, you must add .5 and then take INT:

$$C = INT(5/9*(F - 32) + .5)$$

You must grind each input temperature through this formula. Thus, for example, if you have

```
345 INPUT T
```

where T will be a temperature in Fahrenheit, you must add the statement,

```
346 LET T = INT(5/9*(T - 32) + .5)
```

The result of this statement is that the temperature T is expressed in degrees Centigrade to the nearest degree. You must add such a statement at each place where a temperature is to be input.

Now, you might have a dozen input statements at various places in your program, and typing

```
784 LET X = INT(5/9*(X - 32) + .5)
```

more than twice could get to be a chore. Although you cannot save yourself from having to insert a statement after every input statement to do the conversion (admit it: this situation is a fiasco), you can ease your typing job with *user-defined functions*. These functions allow you to type that beastly expression once, give it a name, and subsequently refer to it by name. To do this, you need the following statement somewhere early in your program:

```
3 DEF  FNC(F) = INT(5/9*(F - 32) + .5)
```

This *function definition statement* informs the computer of your intentions. In this case, it tells the computer that you intend to use the letters FNC to mean INT(5/9*(F - 32) + .5). Subsequently, instead of writing

```
346 LET T = INT(5/9*(T - 32) + .5)
```

you can write

```
346 LET T = FNC(T)
```

Consider the two program segments below. Which looks easier to type? Which is easier to read?

```
3    DEF  FNC(F) = INT(5/9*(F - 32) + .5)
.    . . . . . . .
.    . . . . . . .
.    . . . . . . .
345  INPUT T
346  LET T = FNC(T)
. . .  . . . . . . .
. . .  . . . . . . .
. . .  . . . . . . .
499  INPUT M
500  LET M = FNC(M)
. . .  . . . . . . .
. . .  . . . . . . .
. . .  . . . . . . .
708  INPUT Q
709  LET Q = FNC(Q)
. . .  . . . . . . .
. . .  . . . . . . .
. . .  . . . . . . .


. . .  . . . . . . .
. . .  . . . . . . .
. . .  . . . . . . .
345  INPUT T
346  LET T = INT(5/9*(T - 32) + .5)
. . .  . . . . . . .
. . .  . . . . . . .
. . .  . . . . . . .
499  INPUT M
500  LET M = INT(5/9*(M - 32) + .5)
. . .  . . . . . . .
. . .  . . . . . . .
. . .  . . . . . . .
708  INPUT Q
709  LET Q = INT(5/9*(Q - 32) + .5)
. . .  . . . . . . .
. . .  . . . . . . .
. . .  . . . . . . .
```

The power of the user-defined function is that it allows you to type some expression once, name it, and afterwards treat it just like one of the system functions such as SQR or RND or SIN. These functions can save you typing and reading horrid arithmetic expressions over and over again.

Rules   The *function definition statement* (statement 3 in the example) consists of a statement number, the letters DEF, a space, the name of the function, which must be the letters FN and a third letter, the name of a simple variable enclosed in parentheses, an equals sign, and a numerical expression. The variable can be any of A, B, C, . . . , Z or of A1, A2, . . . , Z9.

The numerical expression following the equals sign can be anything that the computer can evaluate. It can include the variable in parentheses on the left-hand side of the statement (although it need not), and it can include any other variables. Any of the following are acceptable:

```
50 DEF FNP(X) = X + 58 + SQR(X)
60 DEF FNQ(Y) = Z + 28*Y
70 DEF FNR(W) = X + Y + Z
```

The user can define up to twenty-six different functions, naming them FNA, FNB, FNC, and so on.

Subsequent to definition, these functions behave like library functions such as SQR and can be used anywhere in an algebraic expression. We have already seen the following:

```
346 LET T = FNC(T)
```

We could also write

```
90 LET P = FNC(R) + FNC(S)
```

if we wished. Or even

```
1010 IF FNA(17) = 48*FNQ(R - 7) THEN 80
```

In all these cases, the computer finds the value of the numerical expression inside the parentheses (just as with a library function), looks up the definition of the function, and calculates the result. Consider the statements below:

```
7    DEF FNH(Y) = 48*Y + 6
8    DEF FNC(X) = 5 * X
9    DEF FNQ(X) = 17*(X + 1) + 6
88   LET R = 8
89   LET S = 17
90   LET P = FNC(R) + FNC(X)
1010 IF FNH(17) = 48*FNQ(R - 7) THEN 80
```

When the computer gets to statement 90, it first looks up the value of R, which is 8, pretends that X is 8, and sends back the value 40. Then, since S equals 17, the computer pretends that X is 17, multiplies it by 5, and returns the value 85. It adds 40 and 85, getting 125, and stores the result in P. In statement 1010, if R is still equal to 8, the computer calculates 8 − 7, then looks up the definition of FNQ to find FNQ(1). It compares 48 times this value with the value of FNA(17) to decide whether to jump to statement 80.

The previous paragraph insisted that the computer "pretend" that a variable has a certain value, a terminology that needs clarification. Examine the following program fragment, which does nothing in particular:

```
10 DEF FNN(X) = 3*X + 12
20 LET X = 9
30 LET P = 11
40 PRINT FNN(P)
50 PRINT X
```

On most systems, when the computer gets to statement 40, it takes the value of P, which is 11, and finds $3*11 + 12$. That is, it pretends that X equals 11. Now X really equals 9 as a result of statement 20. What happens to the 9? *Nothing.* It stays right there, and a 9 is printed when we come to statement 50. What happens is that the computer reserves an extra, special pigeon hole in memory for the variable X in statement 10. When you are evaluating FNN, the variable name X refers to this new pigeon hole. At any other time in the program, X refers to the old pigeon hole. The numbers stored in these two different places do not affect one another, and X can refer to either, depending on whether or not you are figuring out FNN. At statement 40, when the computer finds FNN(P), or FNN(11), it puts the 11 in the new, special pigeon hole in order to calculate FNN. The 9 is stored in the old pigeon hole and is thus unchanged.*

Putting Function Definitions Up Front   Although most BASIC systems are not fussy about where your function definition statements appear, it is bad practice to put them anywhere besides at the very beginning of your program. First, you may forget from time to time what your functions mean and have to look up the definitions. If they are buried in a morass of other statements, finding them could be a highly frustrating endeavor. Second, when someone else reads your program, he reads from the beginning to the end, and he wants to know what the functions mean before he finds them used in the program. Third, a number of other languages and even some BASIC systems insist that function definitions come first in the program because the computer wants to know what the functions mean before it finds them used in the program.

Some BASIC systems allow you to redefine functions in the middle of a program. You can define FNC to mean one thing at the beginning of the program, redefine it to mean something else later on, and the computer will use the most recent definition. To take advantage of this feature is absolutely criminal. Although it will be clear to the computer which definition it is using at any given time, it will *not* be clear to you. Consider the program that follows. Is Q equal to 3 times X or to 5 times X? What about R? What if statement 30 were changed to GOTO 500; how would things change?

```
10   DEF FNC(Y) = 5*Y
20   INPUT X
30   GOTO 510
40   LET R = FNC(X)
. .   . . . . . . .
. .   . . . . . . .
. .   . . . . . . .
500  DEF FNC(Y) = 3*Y
510  LET Q = FNC(X)
520  GOTO 40
. . .  . . . . . . .
. . .  . . . . . . .
. . .  . . . . . . .
```

Using One Function to Define Another   Suppose that you want to write a program to calculate pay checks. Assume that workers are paid $5 per hour and that the amount of time that each works is typed in hours and minutes in such a way that

2. 43

represents two hours and forty-three minutes and that

7. 04

represents seven hours and four minutes. Let's call this type of number an *hours-minutes number.* The computer can't simply multiply the hours-minutes number by the $5 rate because, for example, a man who has worked an hour and a half deserves $7.50, whereas his time would be input as 1.30 (an hour and thirty minutes), and multiplying 1.30 by 5 yields $6.50. One way around this problem is to convert the amounts of time to fractions of hours. For example, 7.30, which is seven hours and thirty minutes, is seven hours and a half and could be converted to 7.5. Similarly, 3.06 is three hours and six minutes, or three and one-tenth hours, or 3.1. These numbers of hours can be multiplied by the hourly rate because they are ordinary decimal numbers.

Let us write the functions to turn the hours-minutes number into a fractional number of hours. The number of hours equals the integer part of the hours-minutes number plus one sixtieth of the number of minutes. We could write the function immediately if we had another function which took the hours-minutes number and returned the number of minutes.

We will define the function FNM to find the minutes in an hours-minutes number. We want FNM(3.15) to equal 15, the number of minutes represented. We want FNM(4.20) to equal 20. To get 15 out of 3.15, the computer must subtract the 3 (which is the integer part of 3.15), getting .15, then multiply the result by 100:

```
9 DEF FNM(X) = (X - INT(X))*100
```

Let us try this function on 4.20:

$$X = 4.20$$

so that

$$INT(X) = 4$$
$$X - INT(X) = .20$$
$$(X - INT(X))*100 = 20$$

which is what we wanted.

*Be forewarned that there are a few extremely annoying systems on which the 9 would be erased and an 11 printed at statement 50. With luck, you will never have to use such a system. Also note that if we had the statement 45 PRINT FNN(X), the machine would look up the value of the old X (9), stick the 9 in the new space for X, and calculate FNN.

With this function, which extracts the number of minutes from the hours-minutes number, we can define the function which finds the total number of hours. As noted before, the number of hours is the integer part (the hours part) of the hours-minutes number plus one-sixtieth of the number of minutes (which is what FNM finds for us). Therefore:

```
10 DEF FNH(X) = INT(X) + FNM(X)/60
```

When we ask the computer to find, say, FNH(3.15), the computer puts 3.15 in its special pigeon hole for X. INT(X) is therefore 3. Since the definition of FNH calls upon the computer to figure out FNM(3.15), the computer placidly sticks 3.15 in the special pigeon hole that it has reserved for X in the definition of FNM (separate from the other two pigeon holes called X), and, as we have already seen, gets back the number 15. Thus in figuring the number of hours that 3.15 represents, the computer now has

$$FNH(3.15) = 3 + 15/60$$

which is

$$3 + .25$$

which is

$$3.25$$

or 3 1/4, which is three hours and fifteen minutes.

This example illustrates that while the computer is figuring out the value of one function (FNH), it is capable of interrupting its work to find the value of another function (FNM). This operation doesn't bother it a bit. In fact, the computer is very patient about looking up a second function in order to figure out a first. It will put up with things like this:

```
10 DEF FND(X) = X + 5*FNC(X)
20 DEF FNC(X) = FNB(X) - FNA(X + 2)
30 DEF FNB(X) = INT(X) + SQR(X) + 499*FNA(X)
40 DEF FNA(X) = X↑4 - 23 + RND(0)
```

If the computer is asked to find out FND(84), it finds out in the process that it needs to know FNC(84), which it will start to do. To figure FNC(84), it needs both FNB(84) and FNA(86), and it takes time out to find both of those. To find FNB(84), it needs to know FNA(84). It does all these calculations and eventually finds FND(84) without getting the slightest bit confused.

The computer's largess does not extend to things like the following, however:

```
10 DEF FNX(Q) = 27 + FNY(Q - 4)
20 DEF FNY(Q) = 489/FNX(2*Q)
```

The computer, when it is asked to figure FNX(7), finds that it needs to know FNY(3). For this, it needs to know FNX(6). For FNX(6), it needs to know

FNY(2). For FNY(2), it needs FNX(4). For FNX(4), it needs FNY(0). And so on. The BASIC system is not programmed to be so dumb as to do this for long before accusing you with an error message of trying to make a fool of it.

Using Several Variables in One Function   A few BASIC systems allow you to define a function with many variables:

```
28 DEF FNQ(X,Y,Z,W) =
```

which equals any gobbledygook with liberal helpings of X, Y, Z, and W thrown in. Many BASIC systems, however, permit only one variable in parentheses after the name of the function:

```
29 DEF FNQ(X) = . . .
```

Although this is the best that is allowed, it shouldn't stop you from using functions with more than one variable, despite the fact that the official restriction to one variable makes it a little less convenient.

Suppose that you have a program that needs random integers from time to time, but in which the desired range of the random integers changes. Sometimes you need numbers from 1 to 10, sometimes from 50 to 80, sometimes from 100 to 200. An expression which will yield such random numbers is the following:

$$\text{INT}((Y + 1)^* \text{RND}(0)) + X$$

This returns random numbers from X to X + Y. If X = 5 and Y = 8, this expression returns a random number from 5 to 13. Now there is nothing to keep you from writing

```
22 DEF FNR(X) = INT((Y + 1)*RND(0)) + X
```

if you want to. You have to remember to set Y to the correct value before you call FNR. If you want a random number between 5 and 13 inclusive, you write

```
505 LET Y = 8
506 LET M = FNR(5)
```

The computer will pretend that X is equal to 5, and Y is really equal to 8. Therefore, M ends up as a random number between 5 and 13.

This technique, in which one part of your program (statement 505) tells another part of your program (the function FNR) how to do something by setting the value of some variable (Y), is called *parameter passing*. The variable Y is called a *parameter*. The computer does something of that nature itself when it executes

```
506 LET M = FNR(5)
```

It automatically sets the value of Y to 5. All BASIC systems pass this one parameter to user-defined functions for you. If you want more parameters—the random function above needs two—then you must pass the extra ones yourself with statements such as 505. BASIC systems which allow the multivariable functions

```
8 DEF FNC( S, T, U, V, W, X, Y, Z, A, B, C )
```

are simply offering to pass more parameters for you. When you write

```
27 LET P = FNC( 1, 2, 3, 4, 5, 6, 7, 8, 9, 10, 11 )
```

the computer automatically sets S = 1, T = 2, U = 3, and so on. If your BASIC system doesn't do this for you, you must write the LET statements in yourself. We will meet parameter passing again in the section on subroutines.

Exercises

Use at least one user-defined function for each of the problems below.

1. Write a program into which you can input a time of day T, which is an integer number of hours either A.M. or P.M., such as 6 P.M. or 11 A.M., and then input any integer number of hours N, and the computer will tell you what time of day it will be N hours after T. The interaction between computer and user might be:

```
STARTING TIME?9
A.  M.  ( TYPE 0 ) OR P.  M.  ( TYPE 1 )?1
LENGTH OF INTERVAL?8

8 HOURS AFTER 9 P.  M.  THE TIME WILL BE 5 A.  M.
```

2. Combine exercise 1 with the hours-minutes numbers example in the text so that you can input any time of day, such as 4:35 A.M., and any amount of time elapsed. Also allow yourself to input a number of time intervals. An example of the interaction of computer and user might be:

```
STARTING TIME?8. 11
A.  M.  ( TYPE 0 ) OR P.  M.  ( TYPE 1 )?1
LENGTH OF INTERVAL?. 55
NUMBER OF INTERVALS?5

THE ENDING TIMES OF 0 HOUR,  55 MINUTE INTERVALS
.STARTING AT 8:11 P.  M.  WILL BE
9:06 P.  M.
10:01 P.  M.
10:56 P.  M.
11:51 P.  M.
12:46 A.  M.
```

3. Write the program which inputs the hourly wage rate for a worker and the number of hours and minutes that he worked in a week and then outputs his paycheck.

4. Write a program in which you input any number between 1 and 10 and an integer from 1 to 6, and the computer rounds the first number to the number of decimal places indicated by the second number. For example, if you input 3.14159 and 3, the computer should output 3.142.

5. A drawback to solving exercise 2 by converting everything to hours is that during the conversion you must divide the number of minutes by 60, thereby opening a path for round-off errors. It might be a better idea to convert everything to minutes instead. If you wrote the program in exercise 2 with user-defined functions, then making this change shouldn't be difficult. You simply write some new functions to replace the old ones.

6. Improve problem number five so that the program will handle *hours-minutes-seconds numbers*. Hours-minutes-seconds numbers use the third and fourth decimal places to represent seconds. For example: 3.0634 means 3 hours, 6 minutes, 34 seconds.

4.3 More Idiosyncracies (Scientific Notation)

The distance from here to the sun is about

$$150,000,000,000 \text{ meters}$$

The number of molecules in a liter of air is about

$$26,900,000,000,000,000,000,000$$

The weight of a water molecule is about

$$0.0000000000000000000000299 \text{ grams}$$

Scientists have long since become tired of writing out such numbers and invented *scientific notation*. Scientific notation for a number consists of expressing the number as the product of a number between one and ten and a power of ten. The above three numbers come out, respectively, as

$$1.5 \times 10^{11}$$
$$2.69 \times 10^{22}$$
$$2.99 \times 10^{-23}$$

In BASIC, the above three numbers come out as

```
1. 5E+11
2. 69E+22
2. 99E-23
```

The E stands for "times 10 to the power." On most systems the power of ten has a sign before it even if it is positive, and on some systems it is always two digits long. Thus, 5×10^6 would be

```
5E+06
```

The computer prints numbers in this manner, and you can write this kind of number into your program statements. For example,

```
10 LET P = 3. 68E-11
20 LET Q = P + 14. 89E-12
30 IF Q < 8E-12 THEN 90
```

You can also use scientific notation to input numbers.

Inside the Computer   The reason why the computer uses scientific notation is that if numbers such as 26,900,000,000,000,000,000,000 are not changed into scientific notation, they obviously will use up as much space in the computer as they do on paper. The monster above, translated into base two, takes 75 digits, the last 20 of which are zeros. A lot of that circuitry simply indicates that this number is very large, a fact that can be stored in fewer than 75 digits. The computer can instead remember the two relatively reasonable numbers, 2.69 and 22, and with them, using fewer than thirty digits, can reconstruct the number above through scientific notation:

$$2.69 \times 10^{22}$$

Numbers are stored in the little pigeon holes, called *words*, in the computer's memory, and the manufacturer wired the computer with a certain number of bits in each word. Word sizes are usually multiples of eight, ranging between 8 and 48. For the sake of illustration, suppose that your computer has 24-bit words. Integers stored in base two, in 24-bit words, can be only so large. The largest number that you can store (or write) in 24 digits, base ten, is

$$999999999999999999999999$$

The largest number that you can store in 24 digits, base two, is

$$111111111111111111111111$$

In base ten, this number is

$$16777215$$

Since one bit, the *sign bit*, is usually used to indicate whether the number is positive or negative, only 23 bits are left for the size of the number. The largest number that can then be stored in 24 bits is thus

$$8388607$$

This number, needless to say, is a great deal smaller than

$$26900000000000000000000$$

Even if your computer accommodates 32-bit words, the largest storeable number (if one bit is used as a sign bit) is

$$2147483647$$

Scientific notation uses up considerably less space. To keep 6 decimal digits of accuracy (base ten) requires 20 bits, plus a sign bit. If we use 23 or 24 bits, we can keep 7 decimal digits of accuracy and do some rounding off. An exponent requires perhaps 7 bits, including a sign bit. Note that although this method of storing numbers uses fewer than 32 bits, we can now store much larger numbers. We allowed six bits for the size of the exponent; therefore, the exponent can be as large as 63. Our numbers can therefore be a little larger than 10^{63}. Numbers this large are rare. We have traded off some accuracy in exchange for this increase in the size of our numbers. With a thirty-two bit word and no scientific notation we could distinguish between 33167789 and 33167770. With scientific notation, both of these become

$$3.31678 \times 10^7$$

The above allocation of the bits in a word is common. Frequently, all numbers are kept in scientific notation and are printed in scientific notation only if they cannot be printed conveniently without it. The advantage of this is that only one kind of number inhabits the computer. The disadvantage is that if you never use numbers large enough to need scientific notation but want more than six digits of accuracy, you are out of luck. Some languages allow you to choose among various methods of storing numbers, allowing you to have some of several kinds if you wish. This option, however, forces the compiler (and usually the user) to keep the various kinds of numbers carefully segregated. Each kind of number is, after all, only a pattern of ones and zeros in the memory, and the computer must know how to interpret each pattern if it is to do its arithmetic correctly. See Fig. 4.1 for tables giving the limitations on number sizes.

The following table shows the largest number that can be stored in the given number of bits without scientific notation.

Number of bits	Largest number possible (no sign bit)	Largest number possible (with a sign bit)
8	255	127
16	65535	32767
24	16777215	8388607
32	4294967295	2147483647
40	1099511627775	549755813887
48	281474976710655	140737488355327

The following table shows how many bits are needed to store numbers of given sizes as integers. All these numbers can be squeezed into 32 bits in scientific notation.

Number to store	Number of bits needed (including a sign bit)
10	5
100	8
1000	11
one million	21
one billion	31
one trillion	41
6.02×10^{23} *	80
8×10^{44} †	151

*Avagadro's number
†Approximate mass of the galaxy in grams

Fig. 4.1   Tables of limitation on number sizes

4.4   Collections of Numbers (Arrays)

Earlier in the book we discussed the problem of finding the largest or the average of a series of input numbers. These programs do not require that the computer remember the numbers typed in. To find the largest number, you need only remember the largest number input so far, forgetting all the rest. To find the average, the running total and the number of numbers typed are all that need be remembered.

Unfortunately, some programs require keeping many pieces of data in memory. For example, to input a series of names, sort them alphabetically, and print them out, the computer must remember the names. The computer that figures your phone bill also cannot get by with recalling only the total but must remember each long distance call for later printing on your bill. A program to find the median of a series of input numbers (that is, the number in the middle, with half the numbers larger and half smaller) has to remember all the numbers.

Let's work on the following program. We input 25 numbers for the computer to remember. Then, as we type more numbers in one at a time, the the original list of 25 numbers in memory storage spaces A, B, C, . . . , X, Y. The number to be checked we store in Z. Our program might look like that shown below.

```
5      REM  ****************************************************
6      REM  *** THIS PROGRAM INPUTS 25 NUMBERS AND THEN CHECKS   ***
7      REM  *** TO SEE IF OTHER INPUT NUMBERS ARE AMONG THE 25   ***
8      REM  ****************************************************
9      REM
10     INPUT A, B, C, D, E
20     INPUT F, G, H, I, J
30     INPUT K, L, M, N, O
40     INPUT P, Q, R, S, T
50     INPUT U, V, W, X, Y
53     REM
54     REM
55     REM *** LOOP TO INPUT AND COMPARE THE OTHER NUMBERS ***
58     REM
60        INPUT Z
70        IF Z = A THEN 1000
80        IF Z = B THEN 1000
90        IF Z = C THEN 1000
100       IF Z = D THEN 1000
...       .......
...       .......
...       .......
310       IF Z = Y THEN 1000
330          PRINT Z; " IS NOT ON THE LIST. "
340          GOTO 1020
1000      REM
1010         PRINT Z; " IS ON THE LIST. "
1020   GOTO 55
1030   END
```

Looking at this program with all its repeated steps should make you sick. Suppose that the list, instead of being only 25 entries long, were 250 entries long? Or 2500? For a pretty simple-minded operation, you would be typing steps like statement 90 for the rest of your life.

Before looking for a way out of this situation, let us observe that this sort of program is by no means rare. Computers are used, for example, to keep lists of people passing bad checks. A user types in your name, and the computer searches its memory list to see if you are one of the lucky entries. To make this problem even more difficult, the computer must be prepared to add names to or delete names from the list. Since the list will be useful only if it is fairly complete, and hence fairly large, the above program (which will obviously become impossibly unwieldy) must be improved.

An *array* is a series of memory spaces in the computer. A super-variable, it is arranged so that problems such as the above retire into FOR-NEXT loops, where they belong. An array is always designated by a single letter, such as A, B, or G, but since the array contains a series of numbers, there must be a way to tell the computer which one you mean. This is done with a "subscript" following the array name; it consists of an integer in parentheses. For example, $U(8)$ refers to the eighth number stored in the array U. Most BASIC systems allow the subscript to be anything from zero to some large number, often 256. Each piece of the array variable, called an *element*, acts just like a regular variable. The elements $U(8)$ and $O(67)$ behave no differently from M and N and R5. Thus,

```
10 LET U(85) = O(89) * R5
```

has the meaning it would have with normal variables. Note that R5 is *not* an element of an array. It is a regular variable. $R(5)$, on the other hand, because of the parentheses involved, would be an element of the array called R. The computer keeps R5 and $R(5)$ separate, and you must do so as well if you are to stay on good terms with the machine.

Dimension Statements   Our good friend, the compiler, arranges for memory spaces for the numbers that we store in an array. In return for making the reservations, the compiler demands to know in advance how many numbers you plan to store in the array. The *dimension statement* gives it this information. It consists of the word DIM followed by the letter designating the array name and then the number of elements in parentheses. For example,

```
44 DIM Q(35)
```

tells the compiler that the array called Q is to have 35 elements in it. Depending on your system, these elements of the array may be $Q(0)$ to $Q(34)$, or $Q(1)$ to $Q(35)$, or perhaps even $Q(0)$ to $Q(35)$, which actually has 36 elements.

The dimension statement must appear before the array is used in the program. On some systems, dimension statements must appear before ANY statement. (This is why one begins with statement 10. When you forget to dimension your array and get an error message, you can then put the dimension statement in statement 9.)

Some systems assume that an array that you have not dimensioned has some arbitrary size, say 10 or 15. Whether or not your system does this, it is a good idea to dimension every array. Arrays are important enough that an announcement of their presence will be extremely helpful to readers of your program.

If you attempt to use a bigger array than you have dimensioned, you will be assailed with error messages. For example, if you dimension K with 35 elements and subsequently try to store a number in K(78), you can expect trouble. Try to anticipate this possibility by dimensioning your arrays large enough in the first place. An array that is dimensioned too large wastes only a small amount of space; the loss of space is important only if you are straining the capacities of your computer.

Use of Arrays   Armed with arrays, let us rewrite the program that keeps track of the list of 25 numbers. We will store the numbers in an array called Q. In the program shown below, note the way that FOR-NEXT loops and arrays go together:

```
10    DIM Q(25)
20    FOR I = 1 TO 25
30      INPUT Q(I)
40    NEXT I
50    REM *** LOOP ***
55      PRINT "WHAT NUMBER SHOULD BE CHECKED";
56      INPUT M
60      LET S = 0
70      FOR I = 1 TO 25
80        IF M <> Q(I) THEN 100
90          LET S = 1
100     NEXT I
110     IF S = 1 THEN 140
120       PRINT M;" IS NOT A MEMBER OF THE SET. "
130       GOTO 160
140     REM
150       PRINT M;" IS A MEMBER OF THE SET. "
160 GOTO 50
170 END
```

The loop from statement 10 to statement 40 is repeated 25 times, and the computer inputs a number each time. The first number goes into Q(1), since I equals 1 the first time through the loop. On the second time through, I equals 2, and thus the next number goes into Q(2). In this way, all 25 numbers are inputted and stored in Q(1) to Q(25). The variable S keeps track of whether or not our number M is on the list. Initially, S is 0, as we have not found a matching number on our list. We set S to 1 if we find a number on the list matching M. When we come out of the FOR-NEXT loop, we use S to find out which of the two messages is appropriate.

Note that in statements 70 to 100, we again use an array inside a FOR-NEXT loop to do all the work for us. This is a basic principle of arrays. A FOR-NEXT loop similar to the one below is common:

```
100 FOR I = 1 TO 40
...     .......
...     ......        Do something of interest with Q(I).
...     .......
200 NEXT I
```

This loop performs the same operation on 40 elements of the array Q. It is this technique that makes arrays worthwhile.

Improvements in the Search Program   The program just discussed could be more efficient. Once it found an element of the array which matches the number M, it could quit searching. Such a time saving is obviously unimportant with a list of only twenty-five numbers, but with longer lists, it could be a matter of some concern. The problem with the program as it stands is that the FOR-NEXT loop searches from one end of the array to the other even if it finds the desired element early on. It would be far better to write our own program loop which stops (1) because it has run out of array elements to check, or (2) because it has found the element. The FOR-NEXT loop stops only for the first condition. The program that follows allows for the second as well. Although this program could have been written with a FOR-NEXT loop, it might prove confusing to the reader. Since it is the iteration variable that makes FOR-NEXT loops meld well with arrays, we have simply created our own iteration variable for the more efficient program shown at the top of the next page.

Exercises

1. Write a program which reads a sequence of numbers. When the number 0 is typed in, the computer should type back the numbers typed in in the reverse order. (Hint: Remember negative STEP?)
2. Write a program which inputs an array of ten elements. Subsequently, when you type in a number, it should either type back

```
NO ELEMENT OF THE ARRAY IS LARGER THAN YOUR NUMBER.
```

or it should type out a table:

```
ELEMENTS OF THE ARRAY LARGER THAN 26:

ELEMENT NO    VALUE

    1         29
    3         332
    8         40

THERE ARE  3  ELEMENTS OF THE ARRAY LARGER THAN 26.
```

```
3    REM *****************************************************
4    REM *** THIS PROGRAM KEEPS A LIST OF 25 NUMBERS AND      ***
5    REM *** DECIDES IF A GIVEN NUMBER IS ON THE LIST.        ***
6    REM *****************************************************
7    REM
8    REM *** INPUT THE 25 NUMBERS ***
9    REM
10   DIM Q(25)
20   FOR I = 1 TO 25
30     INPUT Q(I)
40   NEXT I
43   REM
44   REM *************************************************
45   REM
46   REM
47   REM *** MAIN LOOP ***
50   REM
55     PRINT "TYPE NUMBER TO COMPARE WITH NUMBERS ON LIST. ";
60     INPUT M
70     LET I = 1
80     LET S = 0
90     REM *** LOOP TO COMPARE M WITH EACH Q(I) ***
100      IF Q(I) <> M THEN 130
110        LET S = 1
120        GOTO 160
130      IF I = 25 THEN 160
140      LET I = I + 1
150    GOTO 90
160    IF S = 1 THEN 190
170      PRINT M;" IS NOT A MEMBER OF THE LIST. "
180      GOTO 210
190    REM
200      PRINT M;" IS A MEMBER OF THE LIST. "
210    REM
220    PRINT "TYPE 0 TO END THE PROGRAM"
225    PRINT "TYPE ANY OTHER NUMBER TO CONTINUE"
230    INPUT X
240    IF X = 0 THEN 260
250  GOTO  50
260  END
```

3. Write a program which inputs an array of ten elements and then either types the message

```
                NO TWO ELEMENTS OF THE ARRAY ARE EQUAL.
```

or types a table:

```
        ELEMENT   1   IS EQUAL TO ELEMENT(S)   7
        ELEMENT   2   IS EQUAL TO ELEMENT(S)   5   6
        ELEMENT   5   IS EQUAL TO ELEMENT(S)   2   6
        ELEMENT   6   IS EQUAL TO ELEMENT(S)   2   5
        ELEMENT   7   IS EQUAL TO ELEMENT(S)   1
```

4. Write a program which deals a five-card poker hand. To deal each card, use the random number function to give you a number from 1 to 52. There are two difficulties: The first is to get a decent looking output. (Try for QUEEN OF HEARTS or 6 OF DIAMONDS rather than CARD #23, CARD #47.) The second is to prevent the computer from dealing the same card more than once. To solve this problem, create a 52-space array corresponding to the 52 cards in a deck. Set all elements to 0. When a card is dealt, change the corresponding element to a 1. When you are about to deal a card, check the corresponding element to see if you have dealt it before. If you have, get another random number and try again.

    A second method is to keep a five-space array whose elements contain the numbers of the cards you have dealt and to compare new cards to all the elements of that array. Which method do you like better?

5. Write a program which keeps a list of numbers for the user in the following manner. If the user types in a number that is not already on the list, the computer adds the new number to the end of the list. If the user types a number that is on the list, the computer deletes that number from the list. When the user types a −1, the program should type out the list. When he types a −2, the program should end. Here is a sample of the interaction between this program and its user:

```
?1
?7
?12
?7
?9
?-1
YOUR LIST IS  1   12  9
?8
?7
?12
?-1
YOUR LIST IS  1   9   8   7
?-2
*READY
```

Hint: You must somehow keep track of where the user's list ends, since its length varies. Also, when the user deletes a number from the list, you must either move all subsequent elements of the list up one space or you must somehow indicate that there is a hole in the list where the number was deleted.

6. The Caves of Computeraria consist of fifteen rooms, each of which has a one-way tunnel into it from another room and a one-way tunnel out. The tunnel leading out of a room may, however, lead you right back to the same room and therefore also be the tunnel into that room (in which case, of course, there is no escape from that room). Have the computer (1) create such a set of caves, and (2) find all the loops in the caves it has created. The output might be like that on the next page.

ROOM	TUNNEL FROM ROOM	TUNNEL TO ROOM
1	3	7
2	4	8
3	7	1
4	15	2
5	5	5
6	8	11
7	1	3
8	2	6
9	14	10
10	9	14
11	6	15
12	13	13
13	12	12
14	10	9
15	11	4

LOOPS IN THE CAVES:

1 TO 7 TO 3 BACK TO 1

2 TO 8 TO 6 TO 11 TO 15 TO 4 BACK TO 2

5 BACK TO 5

9 TO 10 TO 14 BACK TO 9

12 TO 13 BACK TO 12

Hint: To generate the caves, put the numbers 1 to 15 in order in array spaces R(1) to R(15). Then exchange random pairs of elements by picking two random numbers, A and B, from 1 to 15 and exchanging R(A) and R(B). Do fifty exchanges. The number in each element of array R represents the room to which the tunnel from that room leads. If R(6) equals 12, for example, then the tunnel from room 6 leads to room 12. It is left to you to figure out an algorithm to find from whence the tunnel into a room comes and to figure out the loops in the caves.

4.5 Collections of Letters (Strings)

It is by now an established phenomenon that people prefer being names to being numbers. Some people carry this to a mania. It is also an established phenomenon that banks are reluctant to cash checks that are made out to numbers instead of to people. A computer engaged in letter-writing or in printing paychecks, therefore, is stuck with writing out names. So is the computer that makes up the telephone book. Where would we be if it printed only numbers and not names?

As we shall see, the reason that people are often assigned numbers when they are put in the computer's den is that whereas computers cope handily with numbers, they are hard put to deal with the series of letters that make up a name.

A series of characters is called a *string*. A string may include characters besides letters: digits, punctuation marks, blanks, and so on. For example, QW#$ 56;; is a perfectly good string, even if unlikely looking. The computer does not differentiate among the types of characters in a string.

As with numbers, the principal thing that the computer can do with strings is to remember them, and as with numbers, a string can be stored in a variable. Unlike number variables, the name of a variable containing a string consists of a single letter followed by a dollar sign. Examples are B$, D$, and S$.

Stop and think about how strings are stored in a computer's memory. Remember that everything in the computer consists of circuits that are on or off, representing 1's and 0's. Strings are no exception, and each character in a string must first be converted into a series of 1's and 0's to be stored. These 1's and 0's are called the *ASCII code* of the character. The letter X, for example, has the code 1011000. Often there is space for four characters in each memory space in the computer, and a string variable consists of a series of memory spaces, each with four characters in it. Thus, in the computer, a string looks rather like an array—a series of memory locations with data in them.

Again it is the compiler's or interpreter's task to reserve the memory spaces for the string variable, and in some systems the computer wants to know how many memory spaces it should reserve. You must tell it how many characters you will have in the string. (The computer itself will figure out how many memory spaces it needs, based on the number of characters.) The dimension statement (as before) looks like the following:

```
10 DIM S$(73)
```

This example indicates that the variable S$ may have as many as 73 characters in it. As with arrays, if you try to stick a seventy-fourth character in the string, you can expect trouble; therefore, it pays to dimension your strings a little larger than you think that you will need. Some systems assume that a string with no corresponding dimension statement is some arbitrary length, often 16 or 32 characters. Some systems, in fact, do not allow dimensioning of string variables, and all string variables are assumed to have the same length. Read your system manual, or do some experimenting to find out.

Behavior of String Variables   A string variable acts in many ways like a numeric variable. You can, for example, PRINT K$ or INPUT E$. You can LET F$ = G$. There are situations in which you must be a little careful, though, because BASIC requires quotes around strings to tell the computer when the strings begin and end. Therefore, you must write

```
10 LET D$ = "DINGDONG"
```

if you want D$ to be DINGDONG. Since strings may well contain spaces, the quotation marks are the computer's only way of knowing that the string has ended.

It is possible to "add" strings. The second string added is simply appended to the tail end of the earlier string. Thus

```
10 LET D$ = "FIRST AND"
20 LET E$ = D$ + " LAST"
```

puts the value FIRST AND LAST in E$. Sticking strings together in this way is often called *concatenation*.

Comparing Strings Strings may be compared in an IF statement. For example,

```
10 IF D$ = E$ THEN 70
```

skips to 70 only when D$ and E$ are the same length and contain the same characters in the same order. The statement

```
20 IF F$ <> G$ THEN 90
```

skips of course, if F$ and G$ differ either in length or in one or more characters.

The question remains as to when you should consider one string to be greater than another. One possible way would be that longer strings should be considered larger. But what is the most common way of sorting words? Alphabetically, of course, and this is how the computer orders strings. Smaller strings are ones that come earlier alphabetically. Hence,

```
APE < BEG < BOG < CAST < CASTE < CAT < DOG
```

The above rule works for strings that are words, but what about strings containing digits and other characters? How does the computer decide which of two such strings is the larger? The method is as follows. The computer looks at the first character of each. If they are different, then the string whose first character has the smaller ASCII code is the smaller. (A quick look at the table of ASCII codes in the Appendix will convince you that this sorts letters alphabetically.) If the first characters are the same, then the second characters are similarly compared. If these too are the same, then the third characters are compared, and so on. If one of the strings runs out of characters before a difference is detected, then the longer string is the larger. Therefore, 34#$% is larger than 34#$.

Using Strings for User Input Often when you are writing programs for someone else, you can make his life far simpler by using strings. For example, suppose you have a program which inputs a series of numbers and then asks the user which computations it should perform. It might tell the user to type 0 if he wants the sum of his numbers, 1 if he wants the largest, 2 if he wants the smallest, 3 if he wants the mean, 4 if he wants the mode, 5 if he wants the median, and so on. The user could learn BASIC and write his own program before he figured out how to use yours.

Instead, allow the user to type BIG or MEAN or SUM or whatever. After he has typed in his numbers, have the program accept a string as input. Then compare what the user types with a list of things your program does, as shown below:

```
190 INPUT X$
200 IF X$ = "BIG" THEN 1000
210 IF X$ = "MEAN" THEN 1100
220 IF X$ = "SUM" THEN 1200
. . . . . . . . .
. . . . . . . . .
```

If the user types "BIG," your program skips to the routine to type the largest number. If he types "MEAN," jump to wherever in your program the computer calculates the mean. This program is just as easy for you to write as the one which forces the user to type numbers, but it is far easier to use.

Breaking Strings into Pieces   Note first of all that many BASIC systems do not permit strings to be broken into pieces. Find out if yours does before spending time on this section.

We have already seen some slight similarities between strings and arrays. Here is another: A string can store several pieces of data. One string, for example, might include a first name, a last name, a middle initial, an age, a social security number, and a phone number. The computer user might want to have the computer sort people alphabetically by last name, or he may want a list of people whose ages are 55 and over, or he may want people sorted by social security number. All these things require that the computer look at one piece of data in a stringful and therefore that it be able to look at a *substring*, that is, a piece of the string. Consider also the compiler or the interpreter. It gets input that looks like "10   FOR B1 = 5+4 TO 893 STEP 6" and has to distinguish among line numbers, variable names, numbers, arithmetic operations, statement words, and so on.

There are irritating disparities among BASIC systems that allow substrings. This section first describes various ways that computer systems allow them and then concentrates on one particular method to demonstrate the usefulness of the capacity.

To find substrings, all systems number the characters of a string by one of two methods. In the first method, the first character at the left end of the string is called character number one; the second, character number two; the third, character number three; and so on. In the second method, the first character is called character number zero; the second, character number one; the third, character number two; and so on. This latter method undoubtedly appears horridly confusing, and it is, at least for a while, but eventually you become accustomed to counting from zero when using strings. In what follows, however, we will use the first method.

The first way of breaking off a substring from a string is the subscript method. In this method, the string variable is followed by two subscripts in parentheses, such as

$$R\$(4,9)$$

Depending on the system, this may mean either (1) the fourth character through the ninth character of R$, or (2) nine characters of R$ starting at the fourth. Thus, for example, if R$ = "ABCDEFGHIJKLMNO", then R$(4,9) is equal either to "DEFGHI" or to "DEFGHIJKL". If your computer uses the subscript method, you'll have to look this up.

The second method is the function method. For this method, there are three functions: LEFT, RIGHT, and MID. LEFT(R$,5) means the first (left-most) five characters of R$. RIGHT(R$,8) means the last eight. MID(R$,2,7) means either (1) the second through the seventh character of R$, or (2) seven characters of R$ starting at character 2. MID(R$,2,7) is the same as is R$(2,7) in the subscript method.

It is unfortunate that there are so many ways of extracting substrings from strings, because programmers must be familiar with all the different ways to be able to read one another's programs, and because programs that work on one computer must be rewritten for another that uses a different method. In what follows, we will use the subscript method, and we will assume that R$(4,9) means the fourth through the ninth character of R$. You must determine what method your computer uses; the mannual will say.

Using the subscript method and a numbering system that calls the first character character number one (the method used in all following examples), we have the following examples of substrings:

> *If*   S$ = "LOOK IN THE OTHER ONE"
> *Then*   S$(1,4) = "LOOK"
> S$(9,11) = "THE"
> S$(14,16) = "THE"
> S$(3,7) = "OK IN"
> S$(4,4) = "K"

To give an example, let us suppose that A$ through E$ contain the names of five people, first name first, last name last, and suppose that we want to print the names of those whose first name is John. Of course, none of the strings exactly equal "JOHN" since all the strings also contain a last name, but if a person's first name is JOHN, the first four letters of his name equal "JOHN", which gives rise to the following program:

```
10 IF A$(1,4) = "JOHN" THEN PRINT A$
20 IF B$(1,4) = "JOHN" THEN PRINT B$
30 IF C$(1,4) = "JOHN" THEN PRINT C$
```

and so on. (At this point we might wish seriously that there were such a thing as string arrays—that is, collections of strings. Some BASIC systems fortunately have these.)

As another example, suppose we have a 40-character sentence stored in A$, and suppose we wish to know if the letters "THE" appear in that order anywhere in the sentence. In the program below, the variable N will be 0 if we have not found "THE"; 1, if we have:

```
10   LET N = 0
20   LET I = 1
25   REM
26   REM
27   REM *** LOOP TO SEARCH STRING A$ FOR THE LETTERS 'THE' ***
30   REM
40     IF A$( I, I+2 ) <> "THE" THEN 70
50       LET N = 1
60       GOTO 90
70     IF I = 38 THEN 90
80   GOTO 30
90   REM
100  REM
105  REM *** PRINT WHETHER 'THE' IS IN A$ ***
106  REM
110  IF N = 1 THEN 140
120    PRINT "NO"
130    END
140  REM
150    PRINT "YES"
160    END
```

On the first time through the FOR loop, since I is 1, we check A$(1,3) to see if it is "THE". The second time through, I is 2, and we compare A$(2,4) to "THE". And so on through the string. Note that this does not check if the word *the* is in the sentence, for if the word *other* were in the sentence, the program would find "THE" in the middle of "OTHER" and give an affirmative answer. If you want to check for the word THE, check to see if the five characters " THE " are in the sentence. (Note the spaces in " THE ".)

The length function tells you the number of characters in a string. LEN(B$), for example, returns the number of characters in B$. This feature is useful in the following situation, among others: If you input B$ from the teletype with, say, fifteen characters, and your program refers to the sixteenth character of B$, it will not exist, and you will get an error message.

Suppose that you want to check if the letter A is in the input string. You want to write a loop as in the previous example, but you dare not let the iteration variable go beyond the length of the inputted string. To avoid this, let the LEN function set the limit of your loop, as shown at the top of the next page.

Note that the variable I jumps you out of the loop at the last character of A$ and thus saves you the embarrassment of referring to a nonexistent character.

```
5    INPUT A$
10   LET N = 0
20   LET I = 1
25   REM
26   REM
27   REM *** LOOP TO SEARCH STRING A$ FOR THE LETTER 'A' ***
30   REM
40     IF A$(I,I) = "A" THEN 70
50       LET N = 1
60       GOTO 90
70     IF I = LEN(A$) THEN 90
80   GOTO 30
90   REM
100  REM
105  REM *** PRINT WHETHER THE LETTER 'A' IS IN A$ ***
106  REM
110  IF N = 1 THEN 140
120    PRINT "NO"
130    END
140  REM
150    PRINT "YES"
160    END
```

Four Functions   Four library functions useful in string processing are commonly found in BASIC systems:

1. STR—This function turns a numeric variable into an equivalent string. For example, if you want N$ to contain someone's name and age, and N$ already contains his name and A his age, you can't simply write

```
50 LET N$ = N$ + A
```

since A is not a string and hence cannot be "added" to string N$. But you can write

```
50 LET N$ = N$ + STR(A)
```

This concatenates the age to the name in N$.

2. NUM—This does the opposite of STR by turning a string variable back into the number it represents. This operation might be useful, for example, if you input a date in the form "12/27/61" and want to have the computer figure out how many months ago that was. You could use the statements,

```
20 LET Y = NUM(P$(7,2))
30 LET M = NUM(P$(1,2))
```

to put the month number in M and the year in Y. If you try NUM on some string that is not the string representation of a number, such as "AX932Y", for example, then you will get an error message.

3. ASC—This returns the ASCII code of the first character of a string. ASC("DDFGTR") is 68, the ASCII code for D.

4. CHR—This returns a one-character string whose ASCII code is the argument of the function. CHR(70) is the string "F". The statement,

```
90 LET P$ = CHR(89) + CHR(69) + CHR(83)
```

puts "YES" in P$.

For each of these functions, you must remember whether it takes a string for an argument and returns a number, or vice versa. The computer objects if you put one kind of data where it was expecting another kind.

Exercises

All exercises except the first require the capability of breaking strings into pieces.

1. Write a program which inputs eight numbers and stores them in an array. The user should then be able to type any of the following words and get an appropriate computer response: LARGEST, SMALLEST, MEAN, LIST, BACKWARDS LIST.
2. Palindromes (symmetric strings):
   (a) Write a program which inputs a string and then types it back backwards.
   (b) Write a program which inputs a string and decides if it is symmetric. (*Symmetric* means that it reads backwards the same as it reads forwards. "AXE B EXA" is symmetric, for example.)
   (c) Write a program which inputs a string, removes all the spaces from it, and then decides if the result is symmetric. This program should say that MADAM IM ADAM is symmetric, since with the spaces removed, it is MADAMIMADAM.
3. Write a program that inputs a name in any of these four formats:

   JOHN DOE
   JOHN ALFRED DOE
   DOE, JOHN
   DOE, JOHN ALFRED

No matter which of these inputs the computer gets, it types back the name in the format:

   DOE, JOHN

4. Write a program to check if the word THERE is somewhere in an inputted sentence. (Note that the suggestion in the text is a little too simple, for the word THERE may be either the first five letters or the last five, or it may be followed immediately by a punctuation mark. These possibilities will require some improvements in the program.) If you feel fancy, you might have the computer count the number of times that the word THERE appears in the string. You might even create this output:

```
INPUT STRING:
?THERE IS A POINT THERE, THERE IS!
THERE IS A POINT THERE, THERE IS!
*****              *****  *****
```

4.6 Putting Things in Order

As was remarked upon in the very first section, one of the great uses of the computer is doing filing work. Any well-kept file is always in order, and computer-kept files are no exception. As we have observed, the computer can search rapidly through large quantities of information, but even a computer can bog down if the amount of information gets large enough. In such circumstances, keeping some order among the data can speed up search routines tremendously. A computer keeping track of a million credit accounts, for example, cannot do its work efficiently if the accounts are not stored in some kind of order.* Although a large computer system may be able to search through a million unsorted names in a matter of seconds, it might very well get twenty user requests for information at once. The twentieth user could be waiting quite a while for the first nineteen people to be served.

Sorting is even more useful when the computer is printing out large quantities of data. Names in the phone book *have* to be sorted if the phone book is to be of any use to anyone. Then they must be re-sorted for the yellow pages. The utility company wants the computer to sort its bills by zip code so that the bills can be speeded to the proper post office.

The method of sorting described in this section is the *bubble sort*. If you have a million pieces of information to sort, it is not the fastest known way, but significantly faster programs are significantly more complicated. For small amounts of data, the speed of the bubble sort is competitive.

The routine is called the *bubble sort* because the smaller numbers (if you are sorting numbers) appear to "bubble" to the top of the list. (The larger numbers also appear to "sink" to the bottom, but *sediment sort* is a less appealing name.)

To illustrate the bubble-sort algorithm, let's take a list of five numbers: 7 10 6 9 8 (which would, of course, be in an array were they in a computer). To sort the list so that smaller numbers precede larger ones, we choose certain pairs of numbers. If the larger is on the right, we make no change; if the larger is on the left, we exchange the two. We look first at the first and second numbers, then the second and third, then the third and fourth, and finally the fourth and fifth. The first pair to be considered is 7 10. Since they are in the right order, we make no change. Then we look at 10 6, and since they are in the wrong order, we exchange them and end up with 7 6 10 9 8. Now we look at the pair 10 9, exchange the two, and get 7 6 9 10 8. Last we look at 10 8, exchange them, and

---

*Typically, though, a computer does not keep files in any order that would be useful to a human. Instead, it puts the ASCII codes of the letters of the name of the file item into an algebraic formula and uses the resulting number to figure out where to look for the item. This procedure is called *hashing* into the file.

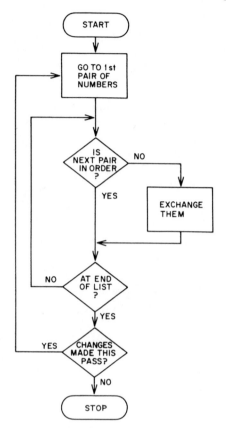

Fig. 4.2 Flowchart of bubble sort process

get 7 6 9 8 10. (Note that the largest number, 10, is now at the bottom.) It is now time to repeat the process. The underlined numbers are the ones compared:

7 6 9 8 10	Exchange 7 and 6
6 7 9 8 10	Make no change
6 7 9 8 10	Exchange 9 and 8
6 7 8 9 10	Make no change

We note that the sequence is now in order. What happens if we continue the process?

6 7 8 9 10	Make no change
6 7 8 9 10	Make no change
6 7 8 9 10	Make no change
6 7 8 9 10	Make no change

No exchanges are made when the list is in order. The computer keeps track of whether it made any exchanges on each pass through the list. If it did not make any, it has finished its job. A flowchart of the process is shown in Fig. 4.2.

Before writing the program for sorting, consider how to exchange A(I) and A(I+1). If you write just the following,

```
10 LET A(I) = A(I+1)
20 LET A(I+1) = A(I)
```

the value of A(I) is erased by statement 10 and can never be recovered. Since A(I) and A(I+1) now contain the same value, statement 20 has no effect. You must save the value of A(I) in some other variable first, as follows:

```
10 LET X = A(I)
20 LET A(I) = A(I+1)
30 LET A(I+1) = X
```

Now let us turn the flow chart into BASIC. Assume that five numbers are stored in A(0) to A(4) and that N is 0 if we have made no changes on the list and 1 if we have. The program follows:

```
5    REM *** PROGRAM FRAGMENT TO SORT ARRAY A ***
10   REM
15     LET N = 0
20     FOR I = 0 TO 3
30       IF A(I) <= A(I+1) THEN 80
40         LET X = A(I)
50         LET A(I) = A(I+1)
60         LET A(I+1) = X
70         LET N = 1
80     NEXT I
90     IF N = 0 THEN 110
100 GOTO 10
110 END
```

One Slight Improvement   There is one thing to note about the bubble sort. After the first time through, the largest number is inevitably the last. In the previous example, the 10 sinks to the bottom of the list the first time through. It is, therefore, unnecessary to worry about the last position thereafter. Similarly, on the second time through, the second largest number ends up second from the last. Therefore, after the second time, we can ignore the bottom two positions. After P times through, we can skip the bottom P places.

Let us rewrite the previous program to incorporate this improvement, assuming now that the array to be sorted is stored in A(0) to A(Q) and that the computer knows the value of Q. Note that statement 20 is the biggest difference between the original program and its improved version, as shown at the top of the next page.

Statement 90 subtracts 1 from Q. If we continue sorting, the iteration variable in the FOR-NEXT loop stops one value earlier than before; the last pair of numbers is not checked. Each time through, statement 90 deletes one more array space from consideration. If Q gets to 0, we have deleted from considera-

```
4    REM ***********************************************
5    REM *** THIS PROGRAM FRAGMENT SORTS THE ARRAY A ***
6    REM ***********************************************
7    REM
8    REM
9    REM *** MAIN LOOP ***
10   REM
15     LET N = 0
20     FOR I = 0 TO (Q - 1)
30       IF A(I) <= A(I+1) THEN 80
40         LET X = A(I)
50         LET A(I) = A(I+1)
60         LET A(I+1) = X
70         LET N = 1
80     NEXT I
90     LET Q = Q - 1
100    IF Q = 0 THEN 130
110    IF N = 0 THEN 130
120  GOTO 10
130  END
```

tion all the spaces but the first. In this case, the list must be in order whether or not any changes were made on the last pass through. Play computer on this program with the sequence 6 5 4 3 2 1 to see that this is the case.

Exercises

Note: When you get tired of typing "typical" array values into the computer, use the following program segment to load an array with numbers:

```
3 DIM A(15)
4 FOR I = 1 TO 15
5   LET A(I) = INT(100*RND(0)) + 1
6 NEXT I
```

This yields an array with fifteen numbers from 1 to 100 and should give you plenty of fodder with which to check out your programs.

1. Write a program that finds the median of a set of input numbers. (The *median* is the number in the middle. Half the numbers are larger; half are smaller. If the number of elements in the list is even, the median is the average of the two most central numbers.) The user should be able to type in a list of numbers in any order, and when he types a −1, the computer should print the median.
2. Write a program that finds the mode of a set of input numbers. (The *mode* is the number that occurs most frequently in a list in which numbers are repeated. You must decide what your program should do if no such number exists.) Rewrite the array-filling program fragment above to fill a 25-element array with numbers from 1 to 7. Possible output from the mode program might be:

```
THE LIST IS

2  6  1  3  2  6  2  1  2  6
2  1  3  2  7  4  5  2  5  6
1  7  1  5  4


THE SORTED LIST IS

1  1  1  1  1
2  2  2  2  2  2  2
3  3
4  4
5  5  5
6  6  6  6
7  7


THE MODE IS   2
```

3. Write a program that keeps an array sorted. It starts with an empty array, and whenever the user types in a number, it either (a) inserts that number in the array if it is not already there, (b) deletes that number from the array if it is already there, or (c) prints the array if the number is −1. Here is an example of the interaction between the user and this program:

```
NUMBER?6
NUMBER?22
NUMBER?14
NUMBER?15
NUMBER?-1
YOUR LIST IS ---  6   14   15   22
NUMBER?15
NUMBER?-1
YOUR LIST IS ---  6   14   22
NUMBER?8
NUMBER?-1
YOUR LIST IS ---  6   8   14   22
```

4. Write a program that allows the user to input two already-sorted five-element arrays and types back all ten numbers in one sorted list. An example of this program in action might be:

```
FIRST ARRAY
    ELEMENT 1    ?5
    ELEMENT 2    ?8
    ELEMENT 3    ?22
    ELEMENT 4    ?35
    ELEMENT 5    ?60
SECOND ARRAY
    ELEMENT 1    ?9
    ELEMENT 2    ?23
    ELEMENT 3    ?24
    ELEMENT 4    ?25
    ELEMENT 5    ?55

YOUR NUMBERS ARE   5   8   9   22   23   24   25   35   55   60
```

(Simply adding the second array at the end of the first in one big array and sorting the big array is ridiculously slow. Devise a better algorithm using the fact that the two arrays are sorted. You should have the computer make sure that the two arrays which the user types in are sorted.)

5. It is possible to sort a list by looking through the list for the smallest element and putting that element first in a new array, then looking for the smallest of the remaining elements and putting that second, and so on. Write this program. In some circumstances, this program is as fast as the bubble sort, but in many cases a well-written bubble sort is faster. Why is this?

6. Improve the program in the text so that it skips the last part of a sequence if it is already in order. For example, if in the process of sorting an array your program gets as an intermediate list 1 7 3 8 6 37 38 39 40 41 45 48, it should subsequently ignore the last seven numbers on the list after checking them at most once more.

7. Write a program that sorts integers by their last digits. The user inputs ten numbers, and the computer then sorts the list. Numbers with the same last digit may be in any order. Interaction between the user and this program might be:

```
INPUT TEN NUMBERS:
?255
?19
?23
?25
?1105
?26
?51
?52
?33
?100

THE LIST SORTED BY LAST DIGITS IS:

100   51   52   23   33   255   25   1105   26   19
```

(Hint: Create a separate array containing only the last digits. Then sort this second array. Whenever you exchange two elements of the second array, exchange the corresponding two elements of the original array, also.)

4.7 More About Packaging (GOSUB and RETURN Statements)

Subroutines A *subroutine* is a program that is a piece of a bigger program; it performs one facet of the main program's work. The following is what happens. A program runs until it needs done what a subroutine does; it then turns control over to the subroutine. When the subroutine has been executed, the main program continues from wherever it left off.

For example, a program that processes purchase orders may have a subroutine to keep track of customer credit accounts. Whenever it wants to cope with credit transactions, the program stops and waits while the subroutine takes care of the matter.

A program is said to *call* a subroutine, which is, in effect, a slave program at the beck of the main program. A program may have several subroutines, and it may call each several times. For example, a program might call a subroutine to sort an array. The subroutine finishes and the main program continues. Later the program might call the same subroutine to sort another array. When the main program continues, it may later call a subroutine that has the computer throw blue fits, and so on. The terms *subprogram*, *routine*, and *procedure* are synonymous with *subroutine*.

GOSUB and RETURN   Subroutines are written just like programs. Write a program starting, say, at statement 1000. If the END statement comes at line number 1090, then to make this into a subroutine, you need only replace the END statement with a RETURN statement:

```
1090 RETURN
```

The purpose of this procedure will be discussed momentarily.

Suppose now that you are writing your main program and you come to statement 60 and want the subroutine to do its work. Of course, you want the program to come back to the next statement after 60 when the subroutine is finished. You can't write GOTO 1000 because the program might never get back. However, if you write

```
60 GOSUB 1000
```

everything happens for you the way you want. The program goes to 1000, where your subroutine begins. When the subroutine is over, the program goes back to whatever statement is immediately after 60. That's why you wrote RETURN at the bottom of your subroutine; it makes the computer return where it should when the subroutine has ended.

If at statement 120 you want the subroutine to perform again, you write

```
120 GOSUB 1000
```

This causes the computer to jump down to 1000, and when it has finished the subroutine, it will return to the statement following 120. Note the magic here: The computer remembers where it came from.

Examples   Our first example will use two programs that we have already discussed. The problem is to decide which of the first 20 terms of the Fibonacci sequence are powers of 2. Let's assume that you have written a program starting on line 1000 which stores 20 terms of the Fibonacci sequence in the array A, in A(0) to A(19). (The computer will *renumber* your steps for you if you have started your program at some line number other than 1000. The REN command with some numbers following it does the trick. Check your manual for details.) Assume that you have put in a RETURN statement at the end of your program.

The program which decides whether or not the number X is a power of two is given in the section on the REM statement. The subroutine at statement

500 below is a slightly rewritten version which prints the number if it is a power of two and does nothing otherwise.

```
4     REM  *************************************************************
5     REM  *** THIS PROGRAM FINDS WHICH ELEMENTS OF THE        ***
6     REM  *** FIBONACCI SERIES ARE POWERS OF TWO.             ***
7     REM  *************************************************************
8     REM
9     REM
10    GOSUB 1000
20    FOR I = 0 TO 19
30      LET X = A( I )
40      GOSUB 500
50    NEXT I
60    END
70    REM  *************************************************************
80    REM
500   REM  *** THIS SUBROUTINE PRINTS A NUMBER IF IT IS A ***
501   REM  *** POWER OF TWO AND NOT OTHERWISE             ***
502   REM
505   LET N = 2
506   REM
510     IF N = X THEN 550
520     IF N > X THEN 560
530     LET N = N * 2
540   GOTO 506
550   PRINT X
560   RETURN
570   REM  *************************************************************
580   REM
1000  REM  *** THIS SUBROUTINE FINDS FIBONACCI SERIES ***
1001  REM
1010  LET A( 0 ) = 1
1020  LET A( 1 ) = 1
1030  FOR I = 2 TO 19
1040    LET A( I ) = A( I-2 ) + A( I-1 )
1050  NEXT I
1060  RETURN
```

Statement 10 calls upon your program (now a subroutine) to figure out those first 20 numbers. When it has finished, the main program continues at line 20. It successively places each of the numbers that your subroutine has found in space X and then calls the subroutine to check if the number is a power of 2. The subroutine prints the number if it is a power of 2 but does nothing otherwise. The steps in the subroutine happen 20 times, once for each of the numbers.

As a second example, let us write a program which reads a series of 20 numbers, checks to make sure that they are positive integers, sorts them, and finally prints those that are multiples of 2, then those that are multiples of 3, and then those that are multiples of 5. This program will be found on the following page.

```
4      REM ************************************************************
5      REM *** THIS PROGRAM INPUTS 20 NUMBERS, SORTS THEM,     ***
6      REM *** AND DECIDES WHICH ARE DIVISIBLE BY 2, 3, AND 5. ***
7      REM ************************************************************
8      REM
9      REM
10     GOSUB 1000
20     GOSUB 1500
30     LET Y = 2
40     FOR I = 1 TO 20
50       LET X = A(I)
60         GOSUB 500
70     NEXT I
75     REM
80     LET Y = 3
90     FOR I = 1 TO 20
100      LET X = A(I)
110        GOSUB 500
120    NEXT I
125    REM
130    LET Y = 5
140    FOR I = 1 TO 20
150      LET X = A(I)
160        GOSUB 500
170    NEXT I
180    END
190    REM
200    REM ************************************************************
210    REM
500    REM *** THIS SUBROUTINE PRINTS X IF IT IS ***
501    REM *** DIVISIBLE BY Y AND NOT OTHERWISE  ***
502    REM
505    LET N = Y
508    REM
510      IF N = X THEN 550
520      IF N > X THEN 560
530      LET N = N + Y
540    GOTO 508
550    PRINT X
560    RETURN
570    REM ************************************************************
580    REM
1000   REM *** THIS SUBROUTINE INPUTS 20 NUMBERS AND   ***
1001   REM *** CHECKS THAT THEY ARE POSITIVE INTEGERS ***
1002   REM
1010   FOR I = 1 TO 20
1020     INPUT A(I)
1030     IF A(I) <> INT(A(I)) THEN 1060
1040     IF A(I) < 0 THEN 1060
1050     GOTO 1100
1060       PRINT "YOU MUST INPUT POSITIVE INTEGERS"
1070       GOTO 1020
1100   NEXT I
1110   RETURN
1120   REM ************************************************************
1130   REM
1500   REM *** THIS SUBROUTINE SORTS ARRAY A ***
1501   REM
1510   REM *** LOOP ***
1515     LET N = 0
1520     FOR I = 1 TO 19
1530       IF A(I) <= A(I+1) THEN 1580
1540         LET X = A(I)
1550         LET A(I) = A(I+1)
1560         LET A(I+1) = X
1570         LET N = 1
1580     NEXT I
1590     IF N = 0 THEN 1610
1600   GOTO 1510
1610   RETURN
```

The program first reads the numbers, checks that they are positive integers, and sorts them. Since the subroutine at statement 500 checks whether or not the numbers are divisible by Y, we have informed it in statement 30, where Y is set to 2, that we are interested in their divisibility by 2. Statements 40 to 70 successively place each of the 20 numbers in space X and then call the subroutine to check divisibility by 2. When this has been done, Y is set to 3. In statements 90 to 120 the subroutine checks divisibility by 3. Finally, statements 140 to 170 check divisibility by 5.

This example exhibits the main program communicating information to the subroutine. The program uses the variable Y to tell its subroutine the number it wants to check divisibility by and the variable X to tell the subroutine what number to check. This method of exchange of information is common: Just before the subroutine call, the program fixes the values of the variables that the subroutine uses, in this case X and Y. This procedure is called *parameter passing*. Variables which are used to communicate to a subroutine just what it is expected to do, like X and Y of this example, are called *parameters*; their values are *passed* from the program to the subroutine.

Another example of a program in which parameter passing is useful is shown at the top of the next page. The subroutine starting at line 1000 sorts a 20-space array X. We want to use our subroutine to sort arrays A, B, and C, each with 20 members. Before calling the subroutine, we must load the contents of the array to be sorted into array X.

The FOR-NEXT loop in statements 10 to 30 puts the array A into X, where it can be sorted. Then the subroutine is called to sort array X. The sorted array X is moved back into A by the statements 50 to 70, and the process is repeated for B and then for C. Note that the two FOR-NEXT loops from 50 to 100 could be replaced by only one loop, as was done in statements 120 to 150. The program may seem long, but it is far shorter than copying the sort routine three times, once for each of the arrays.

Advantages of Subroutines   The advantages of subroutines are numerous. In the first place, they can be used to break a long program into manageable pieces. This is the case even if some subroutines are called only once. It is much easier to figure out how a program works if instead of one big mass of statements, it consists of several short subroutines, each of which does one aspect of the work. Finding mistakes is easier since subroutines can work as programs by themselves. If your big program isn't working, and it is broken into subroutines, you can check each subroutine one by one until you find the culprit among them. Since the subroutine is shorter, it will probably be easier to correct than a long program would be. Subroutines make it simpler both to add to and delete from a large program. If you decide that part of your program is excessive frippery, it is easy to exorcise that particular subroutine. It might be harder to dig statements out from among other more essential things if the program were one massive block.

A second advantage of subroutines is that you can write a long program

```
4       REM *******************************************************
5       REM *** THIS PROGRAM FRAGMENT SORTS ARRAYS A, B, AND C ***
6       REM *******************************************************
7       REM
8       REM *** SORT ARRAY A ***
10      FOR I = 1 TO 20
20        LET X(I) = A(I)
30      NEXT I
40      GOSUB 1000
50      FOR I = 1 TO 20
60        LET A(I) = X(I)
70      NEXT I
75      REM *** SORT ARRAY B ***
80      FOR I = 1 TO 20
90        LET X(I) = B(I)
100     NEXT I
110     GOSUB 1000
120     FOR I = 1 TO 20
130       LET B(I) = X(I)
140       LET X(I) = C(I)
150     NEXT I
155     REM *** SORT ARRAY C ***
160     GOSUB 1000
170     FOR I = 1 TO 20
180       LET C(I) = X(I)
190     NEXT I
200     END
210     REM *******************************************************
220     REM
1000    REM *** THIS SUBROUTINE SORTS ARRAY X ***
1001    REM
1010    REM *** LOOP ***
1020      LET N = 0
1030      FOR I = 1 TO 20
1040        IF X(I) <= X(I+1) THEN 1090
1050          LET T = X(I)
1060          LET X(I) = X(I+1)
1070          LET X(I+1) = T
1080          LET N = 1
1090      NEXT I
1100      IF N = 0 THEN 1120
1110    GOTO 1010
1120    RETURN
```

in sections and check each section before trying to paste them together, after which things may become unbearably complicated. In practice, large programs are always written this way. Often, several different programmers will write various subroutines of the same big program before any attempt is made to fit all the pieces together. (This method, of course, also makes it easy to assign blame if things don't work, but that isn't the idea.)

The third advantage of subroutines is that they can save you writing out the same series of statements more than once. For example, to write a program to sort arrays A, B, C, and D, you could write out a bubble sort four times, once for each array, or you could write the bubble sort as a subroutine and have your program call it four times, once for each array. The second method saves you from copying the bubble sort three times. It would also save you from copying the bubble sort a thousand times, if that were the number of arrays you needed sorted.

A fourth advantage is that, once written, a subroutine can be used as a tool in more than one program. We have already seen the sort subroutine used repeatedly in various programs. Another subroutine that might be useful is one which inputs a number, checks to see if it is a positive integer, and if it is not, warns the user to input a positive integer and gives him another try. You should take time to make this subroutine convenient both for yourself and the user since once it has been written, you can tack it onto any program that needs it. Furthermore, when such a subroutine is improved, every program using it is improved. If, for example, you have a subroutine that checks if a given date is a reasonable birth date for someone alive today, and you write a new, better subroutine, every program containing the old subroutine is automatically bettered when you replace the old version of the subroutine with the new one.

Two Good Ideas   To make your own life a little simpler, you can do two things when writing subroutines. The first is simply to start your subroutines at numbers that are easy to remember. You must know where your subroutines start when you write GOSUB statements, and if you start your subroutines at places like 3596, you will probably have to look up their starting points every time that you write a GOSUB statement. It is better to start subroutines at places like 4000 or 6500, which you have an outside chance of remembering.

A second technique is to start your subroutines with a REMARK statement. Aside from the obvious advantage of having your subroutines labeled, there is the additional advantage that you can easily add statements at the beginning of your subroutine if you wish. For example, if you have a subroutine starting at 7000 with the statement,

```
7000 FOR I = 23 TO 79
```

and you decide that G6 should be set to 0 before the FOR-NEXT loop, you must add the statement,

```
6999 LET G6 = 0
```

Then you must go back and change all the GOSUB's in your program from GOSUB 7000 to GOSUB 6999. Contrast this annoyance with the relative ease of alteration had you originally written

```
7000 REM *** THIS IS A VERY FOOLISH SUBROUTINE ***
7010 FOR I = 23 TO 79
```

Now you can write the following new statement in the space beween 7000 and 7010:

```
7005 LET G6 = 0
```

Your GOSUB 7000's need not be altered.

Binomial Coefficients   The expression 9! means 1*2*3*...*8*9, which is a very large number. Similarly, 22! means 1*2*3*4*...*21*22, which is even larger. (It is about 1,000,000,000,000,000,000,000.) These products, called *factorials*, pop up frequently in calculations involving probability (among other places), and calculating them by computer is, of course, far easier than calculating them by hand. Let us write a subroutine which calculates F!. We will give it the number F, and it will put F! in the variable F1. The subroutine is as follows:

```
1000 REM *** THIS SUBROUTINE FINDS F! AND STORES ***
1001 REM *** IT IN F1.                           ***
1002 REM
1010 LET F1 = 1
1020 FOR I = 2 TO F
1030    LET F1 = F1 * I
1040 NEXT I
1050 RETURN
```

Note that, as recommended, the subroutine starts with a REMARK statement at a nice, easy number, 1000.

You could play computer on this subroutine to see if it works. You might also type it into the computer and check it by changing 1050 to an END statement and adding these two statements:

```
1005 INPUT F                    1045 PRINT F1
```

You could then run the program, type in the value of F, and see if the printed value of F1 agrees with what it should be. For example, if you type in 3, the computer should type back 6 (1*2*3). When you are convinced that this subroutine really works, take out the statements 1005 and 1045 and change 1050 to a RETURN.

Let us now turn to the problem of calculating the *binomial coefficient*. If p and q are two integers, and if p is greater than q, then the *binomial coefficient*, written $\binom{p}{q}$, is defined as

$$\frac{p!}{q!*(p-q)!}$$

Thus, for example, $\binom{9}{4}$ equals 9!/4!*(9−4)!, which equals 9!/4!5!, which equals 362,880/24*120, which equals 362,880/2880, which equals 126. Needless to say, calculating this accurately by hand would be tedious, but having written a subroutine to do factorials, we can easily get the computer to figure binomial coefficients.

Let's assume that the user will type in P and Q, and that the computer should print the value of $\binom{P}{Q}$. The outline of our program is this: We input P and Q, and store the difference between the two in D. Then we call our subroutine first to find P!, which we put into P1, then to find Q!, which we put in Q1, and finally to find D!, which we put in D1. The binomial coefficient equals P1/(Q1*D1). Since our subroutine finds the factorial of the number stored in F, we must do some parameter passing. Our program is shown below:

```
4      REM  *********************************************************
5      REM  *** THIS PROGRAM FINDS THE BINOMIAL COEFFICIENT ***
6      REM  *** GIVEN P AND Q.                              ***
7      REM  *********************************************************
8      REM
9      REM
10     INPUT P, Q
20     LET D = P - Q
25     REM
26     REM *** FIND P! ***
30     LET F = P
40     GOSUB 1000
50     LET P1 = F1
55     REM
56     REM *** FIND Q! ***
60     LET F = Q
70     GOSUB 1000
80     LET Q1 = F1
85     REM
86     REM *** FIND D! ***
90     LET F = D
100    GOSUB 1000
110    LET D1 = F1
120    PRINT P1/(Q1*D1)
130    END
140    REM  *********************************************************
150    REM
1000   REM *** THIS SUBROUTINE FINDS F! AND STORES ***
1001   REM *** IT IN F1.                           ***
1002   REM
1010   LET F1 = 1
1020   FOR I = 2 TO F
1030      LET F1 = F1 * I
1040   NEXT I
1050   RETURN
```

In statement 30, we put the value of P into F so that the subroutine will know that it is to find the factorial of P. The subroutine stores the factorial in F1, and this value is transferred to P1 by statement 50. In statements 60 to 110, Q and D get the same treatment. Having found all three factorials, we calculate the coefficient and print the result.*

This example illustrates the technique of writing the subroutine first and checking it out before writing the rest of the program. If this final program contains errors, they must be in statements 10 to 130, because we know that the subroutine works. This knowledge gives us a great advantage in finding whatever

---

*Those familiar with the binomial coefficient will realize that there are better methods of calculating it. Writing a more efficient program would be an interesting exercise, although not one related to subroutines.

mistakes there may be, since there are fewer places in our program where they could lurk.

Exercises

1. Do the following:
   (a) Write a subroutine to which you pass the number X and which prints X if it is positive, prints a blank if X is zero, and prints the absolute value of X enclosed in parentheses if X is negative. For example, if X = −5.66, then the routine should print (5.66)
   (b) Use exercise 1(a) as a subroutine to help write a program which inputs six numbers and outputs them in the format below. If the numbers input are 453.66, −551.02, 0, 0, 0,223.11, then the output should be:

```
          BUSINESS INCOME                     453. 66
          CAPITAL GAINS OR LOSSES            ( 551. 02 )
          NET GAINS FROM FORM 4797
          PENSIONS, RENTS, ETC.
    ·     FARM INCOME
          ALIMONY                             223. 11
```

2. Do the following:
   (a) Write a subroutine into which the user can type a date in the form MM/DD, where MM represents the month (01, 02, ... 11, 12) and DD represents the day (01, 02, 03, ... 30, 31). The program decides if the user typed in a valid date. (For example, it makes sure that the month is not bigger than 12 and that the day is not bigger than the number of days in the given month. Assume that the year is not a leap year.) The program sets the variable X equal either to the number of days since the beginning of the year that the input date represents or to −1 if the date is invalid.
   (b) After checking that the routine in exercise 2(a) works, use it for a program that inputs two dates and prints back the number of days between the two dates. If the user types an invalid date on either try, the computer should politely inform him of this and let him try again.
   (c) Use exercise 2(a) as a subroutine for a program into which the user types three dates and which decides which date is between the other two. Note: Here is yet another advantage of subroutines. Once you have written a subroutine such as the one in exercise 2(a), you can use it to make other problems easier. The subroutine in exercise 2(a) can be used as a tool to make this problem very easy.

3. Do the following:
   (a) Write a routine which allows the user to input a string consisting of two numbers divided by a comma (for example, "334.5,12.006")

and sets x equal to the first number and y to the second (in the above case, sets x to 334.5 and y to 12.006).

(b) Use the subroutine in exercise 3(a) for a program that finds the area of a rectangle when the user types in its base and height with a comma between the numbers.

(c) Use the routine in exercise 3(a) in a program that inputs the coordinates first of one point and then of another and figures the distance between the points. The distance between the points (x_1, y_1) and (x_2, y_2) is $\sqrt{(x_1-y_2)^2+(y_1-y_2)^2}$.

(d) Use exercise 3(a) above again as a subroutine in a program which inputs the coordinates of two points and finds the equation of the line running through the points. (Hint: The easiest way is to use the slope intercept form, $y = mx + b$, where m and b must be calculated. Formulas for m and b in terms of the coordinates of the points are as follows:

$$m = \frac{y_2 - y_1}{x_2 - x_1} \qquad b = y_2 - mx_2$$

4. Do the following:

(a) Write a subroutine that draws a single card from a deck (using the random number function), checks to see that it hasn't already drawn this card, and then prints what the card is. (See exercise 4 in section 4.4.)

(b) Use the subroutine in exercise 4(a) above to reprogram exercise 4 in section 4.4.

(c) Use the routine in exercise 4(a) above to program the computer to deal blackjack.

5. Write a subroutine to throw a pair of dice using the RND function, and teach the computer to play craps, print out the results of each throw, and analyze whether it has won or lost or whether the game is continuing.

5
GARGOYLES, GINGERBREAD, AND GILT

5.1   Making the Big Decision (ON-GOTO Statement)

Suppose that you were writing a guessing game in which the computer picks a random number between 1 and 25, and the user tries repeatedly to guess it. After each guess, the computer tells the player whether his guess was higher or lower than the computer's number, and whether his guess is close. Suppose that you want the computer to print one of the following responses based on the absolute value of the difference between the number and the guess:

```
YOU GOT IT!!!

YOU'RE GETTING REALLY CLOSE, BUT

THE NUMBER IS NEAR THIS ONE, BUT

YOU'RE WARM, BUT
```

After the messages in the last three cases and whenever the guess differs from the number by more than 6, one of the statements,

```
YOUR GUESS IS TOO SMALL.   or   YOUR GUESS IS TOO LARGE.
```

will be printed. Here again we see the technique of printing different phrases of the sentence to accord with different PRINT statements. A sample of the interaction between the user and the computer is shown below:

```
TRY TO GUESS THE NUMBER BETWEEN 1 AND 25.
WHAT IS YOUR GUESS?5
YOUR GUESS IS TOO SMALL.
WHAT IS YOUR GUESS?20
YOU'RE WARM, BUT YOUR GUESS IS TOO LARGE.
WHAT IS YOUR GUESS?15
YOU'RE GETTING REALLY CLOSE, BUT YOUR GUESS IS TOO SMALL
WHAT IS YOUR GUESS?16
YOU GOT IT!!!
```

The program for this exchange might be as follows:

```
4    REM ************************************************
5    REM *** THIS PROGRAM PLAYS A NUMBER GUESSING GAME ***
6    REM ************************************************
7    REM
8    REM
9    REM
53   PRINT "TRY TO GUESS THE NUMBER BETWEEN 1 AND 25"
55   LET N = 25 * INT(RND(0)) + 1
58   REM
59   REM
60   REM *** LOOP TO GET A NUMBER OF GUESSES ***
62   REM·
65     PRINT "WHAT IS YOUR GUESS";
70     INPUT G
80     PRINT
90     LET D = ABS(G - N)
100    REM
110    IF D = 0 THEN 200
120    IF D = 1 THEN 300
130    IF D = 2 THEN 300
140    IF D = 3 THEN 400
150    IF D = 4 THEN 500
160    IF D = 5 THEN 500
170    IF D > 5 THEN 600
200    REM
210      PRINT "YOU GOT IT !!!"
220      GOTO 700
300    REM
310      PRINT "YOU'RE GETTING REALLY CLOSE, BUT ";
320      GOTO 600
400    REM
410      PRINT "THE NUMBER IS NEAR THIS ONE, BUT ";
420      GOTO 600
500    REM
510      PRINT "YOU'RE WARM, BUT ";
520      GOTO 600
600    REM
610    REM
620    IF G > N THEN 650
630      PRINT "YOUR GUESS IS TOO SMALL. "
640      GOTO 670
650    REM
660      PRINT "YOUR GUESS IS TOO LARGE. "
670 GOTO 60
700 END
```

N is the computer's number, G is the user's guess, and D is the difference between the two. In statements 100 to 160 the program decides on the basis of D which, if any, of the four preliminary messages the computer should print. This program does the job, but it is possible, and more convenient, to compress all seven IF-THEN statements into one statement, an ON-GOTO statement.

The ON-GOTO statement consists of a line number, the word ON, a numerical expression (which includes variables), the word GOTO, and then a list of line numbers. The computer evaluates the numerical expression, truncates it to an integer (applies the INT function), and then counts through the list of line numbers and goes to whichever line number in the list its count ends on. For example,

```
25 ON J GOTO 400,500,600,700,800
```

goes to 400, if J is 1; to 500, if J is 2; to 600, if J is 3; to 700, if J is 4; and to 800, if J is 5. If J is 4.2, the computer truncates this to 4 and goes to 700. And so on. The statement numbers in the list of places to go may be in any order. What the computer does if J is none of the numbers from one to five varies from system to system. Some stop promptly with the customary type of salutation to the programmer. Some just skip the statement. Some skip the statement if the truncated value of J is bigger than 5 but go to 100, the first listed place to go, if J is less than 1. Check your manual.

To finish the program above, we can use D in an ON-GOTO statement. We add 1 to D (so that it won't ever equal zero), and then if D is 7 or bigger, set D to 7 (to avoid the error just mentioned). Statements 90 to 170 of the above program are replaced by the following:

```
90  LET D = ABS(G - N) + 1
100 IF D < 7 THEN 120
110 LET D = 7
120 ON D GOTO 200,300,300,400,500,500,600
```

If the user guesses the number, then D equals 1, and at statement 200 the computer prints the messages informing the user that he has guessed the number. If the user is off by 6 or more, statement 110 insures that D equals 7; then statement 120 sends the program to statement 600 (the seventh line number on the list). If the guess is off by some intermediate amount, D equals something between 2 and 6, and the program goes to 300, 400, or 500. The entire program is shown on the page opposite.

Note that this program is liberally interspersed with instructions and help for the user. A flowchart for the "Guess the Number" program is shown in Fig. 5.1.

An Alternative Form   On some systems, instead of

```
120 ON D GOTO 200,300,300,400,500,500,600
```

you use

```
120 GOTO D OF 200,300,300,400,500,500,600
```

The execution of this statement is exactly the same as the other.

Note also that whereas some systems allow you to write statements like

```
400 ON 5*W - P GOTO . . .
```

```
4      REM ***************************************************
5      REM *** THIS PROGRAM PLAYS A NUMBER GUESSING GAME ***
6      REM ***************************************************
7      REM
8      REM
9      REM
50     REM *** LOOP TO PLAY THE GAME SEVERAL TIMES ***
52       REM
53       PRINT "TRY TO GUESS THE NUMBER BETWEEN 1 AND 25. "
55       LET N = 25 * INT(RND(0)) + 1
58       REM
59       REM
60       REM *** LOOP TO GET A NUMBER OF GUESSES ***
62         REM
65         PRINT "WHAT IS YOUR GUESS";
70         INPUT G
80         PRINT
90         LET D = ABS(G - N) + 1
100        IF D < 7 THEN 120
110          LET D = 7
120        REM
130        REM
140        ON D GOTO 200,300,300,400,500,500,600
150        REM
200        REM
210          PRINT "YOU GOT IT!!!"
220          GOTO 700
300        REM
310          PRINT "YOU'RE GETTING REALLY CLOSE, BUT ";
320          GOTO 600
400        REM
410          PRINT "THE NUMBER IS NEAR THIS ONE, BUT ";
420          GOTO 600
500        REM
510          PRINT "YOU'RE WARM, BUT ";
520          GOTO 600
600        REM
610        REM
620        IF G < N THEN 650
630          PRINT "YOUR GUESS IS TOO SMALL. "
640          GOTO 670
650        REM
660          PRINT "YOUR GUESS IS TOO LARGE. "
670      GOTO 60
700      REM
710      REM
720      PRINT
730      PRINT
740      PRINT "DO YOU WISH TO PLAY AGAIN (YES/NO)";
750      INPUT A$
760      IF A$ = "NO" THEN 780
770    GOTO 50
780    END
```

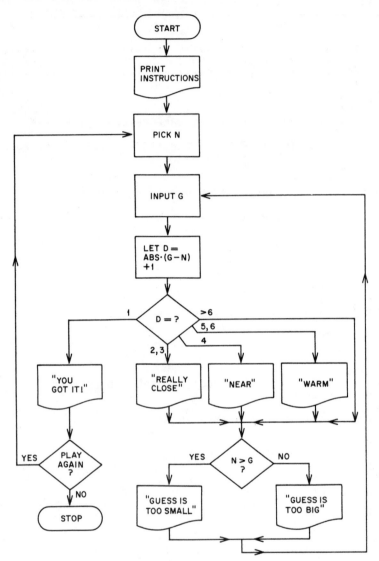

Fig. 5.1   Flowchart of "Guess the Number" example

others allow only a single variable in the ON-GOTO statement itself, and you have to write

```
399 LET S9 = 5*W - P
400 ON S9 GOTO . . .
```

Exercise

1. Use an ON-GOTO statement to write a program which inputs numbers from the terminal. Any number greater than zero is stored in an array. If the user types a 0, the computer types back the number of numbers that he has stored so far. If he types a −1, he gets the largest number stored. If he types a −2, he gets the smallest. If he types a −3, the computer prints back all the numbers in the order that he typed them in.

5.2   More Ways of Moving Numbers Around (READ and DATA Statements)

Consider this irregular collection of numbers:

$$2\ 3\ 5\ 7\ 11\ 13\ 17\ldots$$

These are the first of the prime numbers, and without too much difficulty, you could probably contribute many more primes to the sequence. Suppose that you wanted to write a program that factored numbers into their prime factors. (The number 12 so factored, for example, would equal $2*2*3$.) A reasonable algorithm would be to divide the number by 2 as many times as possible, then to divide the result by 3 as many times as possible, then by 5, then by 7, and so on. For example, the number 140 factors in this way: $140/2 = 70$ and $70/2 = 35$. Obviously, we can no longer divide by 2. Moreover, $35/3$ will not work, but $35/5 = 7$. Neither will $7/5$ work, but 7 goes into 7 once. Fully factored, therefore, 140 equals $2*2*5*7$. We divided by 2 twice, by 5 once, and by 7 once.

To use this algorithm, the computer must have a list of prime numbers. Three rather distasteful ways to implement such a list spring to mind. The first way would be to write a little section of program that divides by 2 as many times as possible, followed by an identical section that divides by 3 as many times as possible, followed by another identical section that divides by 5, and so forth. The second way would be to write a subroutine to find prime numbers as the computer went along. The third way would be to write the program to stop for the user to type in the prime numbers one at a time as they are needed. Let us concentrate on this last lousy little program and subsequently show how to improve it.

Suppose that the number to be factored is input into N. The computer inputs each prime into F in turn, divides F into N as many times as possible, and then prints the prime F every time it goes into N. The program is shown at the top of the next page.

Let us see how this program works with the number 84. Initially, N and F are 84 and 2, respectively. When the program finds that $84/2 = 42$, it prints a 2, sets N equal to 42, and goes to statement 30, where D is set to $42/2$, or 21. Since 21 is an integer, the program prints another 2. Since 2 does not go into 21, the program goes to statement 20 to ask for another prime. You type in 3, and the computer tries $21/3$, which is 7. The computer types a 3, sets N to 7, and

```
5    REM *** THIS PROGRAM FRAGMENT FACTORS A NUMBER ***
6    REM
10   INPUT N
15   REM
20   REM *** LOOP TO DIVIDE BY DIFFERENT PRIMES ***
23     REM
25     INPUT F
28     REM
30     REM *** LOOP TO DIVIDE BY SAME PRIME REPEATEDLY ***
33       REM
35       LET D = N/F
40       IF D <> INT(D) THEN 80
50       PRINT F;
60       LET N = D
70     GOTO 30
80     IF N = 1 THEN 100
90   GOTO 20
100  END
```

continues. Since 3 doesn't go into 7, the computer asks for a new prime. Since 5 doesn't go into 7, either, it asks for yet another prime. Since 7 goes into 7 once, N equals 1, and the computer stops. Your output will be something like that below.

```
?84
?2
2   2
?3
3
?5
?7
7
*READY
```

Since the computer typed two 2's, one 3, and one 7, you can correctly divine that 84 = 2*2*3*7.

What a disaster! To the rescue come two new statements.

READ and DATA Statements   A DATA statement looks like this:

```
100  DATA   45.7, 89, 17, 22, -900, 24E+19
```

The 100 is the statement number. Then comes the word DATA and then a series of numbers separated by commas. When the computer comes to the DATA statement, it does *absolutely nothing*. That is not too interesting. What *is* interesting is that DATA statements in your program allow you to use READ statements such as the following:

```
107  READ X
```

The READ statement is just like an INPUT statement except that instead of stopping the computer to wait for a number from the teletype, the READ statement takes the initiative. If this is the first READ statement in the program, it will get the first number from the lowest numbered DATA statement in the program. If statement 100 above is the lowest numbered DATA statement, then the number 45.7 lands in X. If the next statement is

```
108 READ Y
```

then the next number, 89, lands in Y. Whenever it comes to a READ statement, the computer uses the next item from the DATA statement. If there are so many READ statements that the computer runs out of numbers in this one particular DATA statement, it looks for the next lowest numbered DATA statement and continues with the first item in that. If there are so many READ statements that the computer runs out of all DATA statements, the computer assumes that it is your fault, of course, and sends its usual insulting error messages.

The relative locations of READ and DATA statements in the program have no effect on the program's execution. Whenever the computer encounters a READ statement, it looks for the lowest-numbered unused DATA statement. It doesn't matter whether the READ statement has a higher or lower number than the DATA statement. The computer doesn't even check.

Factoring a Number   With this in mind, let us rewrite that factoring program by listing the primes in DATA statements and including a READ statement at the appropriate place, as shown below:

```
5    REM *** THIS PROGRAM FRAGMENT FACTORS A NUMBER ***
6    REM
10   INPUT N
15   REM
20   REM *** LOOP TO DIVIDE BY DIFFERENT PRIMES ***
23     REM
25     READ F
28     REM
30     REM *** LOOP TO DIVIDE BY SAME PRIME REPEATEDLY ***
33       REM
35       LET D = N/F
40       IF D <> INT(D) THEN 80
50       PRINT F;
60       LET N = D
70       GOTO 30
80     IF N = 1 THEN 100
90   GOTO 20
100  END
110  REM
120  REM
130  REM
140  DATA  2, 3, 5, 7, 11
150  DATA  13, 17, 19, 23, 29, 31
160  DATA  37, 41, 43, 47, 53
```

This program works just like the previous one did, except that at statement 25, instead of hassling the user, the computer looks up the primes in the DATA statements. The output has also improved, as shown below:

```
?84
2   2   3   7
*READY
```

Getting rid of the INPUT statement also got rid of all those annoying question marks the computer typed when it needed a new prime number. Of course, if your number has a prime factor that is greater than 53, this program isn't going to work, but then again, neither would the other unless the user had the patience of a saint and would be willing to type in all those primes one after the other.

Using RESTORE   Suppose that you had several numbers that you wanted to factor with this program. You might think that changing statement 100 to

```
100 GOTO 10
```

would do the trick, but there is a problem with this procedure that has to be ironed out. Suppose that the computer has just factored 35 (5*7), and the program goes back to statement 10 and is asked to factor the number 18. This is what will happen: The computer comes to statement 20 and, having just read the 7 in order to factor the 35, it reads the 11 and puts it in F. The smallest prime that the computer ever tries in factoring 18 is 11. "No! No! No!" you might berate the computer, "You're supposed to start over with the prime 2 when I give you a new number to factor!" But yelling at the machine is a hopeless way to get the program to work (although it can relieve your frustrations). The way to tell the computer to start over with the prime 2 is to insert the statement,

```
95 RESTORE
```

After the computer executes this statement, it starts over at the first item in the lowest numbered DATA statement the next time it encounters a READ statement. A RESTORE statement makes the computer act as if there have been no previous READ statements in the program. The addition of the RESTORE statement will make our modified factoring program work.

RESTORE to a Specific Statement   Suppose that while we are factoring numbers, we have several numbers to factor which for some reason we know ahead of time have no prime factors less than 13. In that case, the computer could start at DATA statement 150 and skip statement 140. When executed, the statement,

```
1010 RESTORE 150
```

makes the computer start reading DATA at the beginning of DATA statement 150. We could have the program ask whether or not the number had primes less than 13 in it and then use an IF-THEN statement based on the response to decide whether to RESTORE 150.

Strings and Parsing Through Data   A DATA statement can have strings in it. Strings can be mixed among the numbers, or a DATA statement might consist entirely of strings. In the next program, the following DATA statements come in handy:

```
200 DATA "JANUARY", "FEBRUARY", "MARCH", "APRIL"
201 DATA "MAY", "JUNE", "JULY", "AUGUST"
202 DATA "SEPTEMBER", "OCTOBER", "NOVEMBER", "DECEMBER"
```

Our program inputs D (the day of the month), M (a number from 1 to 12 representing the month), and Y (the year). It prints the date in this readable form:

```
JULY 23, 1945
```

To type out the name of the month, the computer must find the correct entry in the DATA statements. If M equals 7, then the month we want to type is July (the seventh month). Since the computer always starts reading data at the first item in the first DATA statement, it must read the first six items and throw them away. That is, the computer reads them and then does nothing with them. The program is shown below:

```
4    REM *** THIS PROGRAM FRAGMENT CONVERTS A DATE ***
5    REM *** FROM NUMBERS TO LETTERS.              ***
6    REM
7    REM *** LOOP ***
8       REM
10      INPUT D, M, Y
20      DIM M$(10)
30      RESTORE
40      FOR I = 1 TO M
50         READ M$
60      NEXT I
70      PRINT M$; " "; D; ", "; Y
80   GOTO 10
200 DATA "JANUARY", "FEBRUARY", "MARCH", "APRIL"
201 DATA "MAY", "JUNE", "JULY", "AUGUST"
202 DATA "SEPTEMBER", "OCTOBER", "NOVEMBER", "DECEMBER"
```

If M is 7, the computer will READ M$ seven times in the FOR-NEXT loop. The first six values, the names of the first six months of the year, are each in turn erased the next time through the FOR-NEXT loop. M$ comes out of the loop with the value "JULY", which is duly printed. The other month names are simply lost. When the program starts in on a new date, statement 30 makes sure that the computer starts over with JANUARY again when it starts looking for the month.

This program seems rather wasteful until one tries out the alternatives. One possibility would be

```
40 IF M = 1 THEN PRINT "JANUARY";
50 IF M = 2 THEN PRINT "FEBRUARY";
60 IF M = 3 THEN PRINT "MARCH";
```

and so forth. In comparison, the program with the DATA statements is rather neat.

Exercises

1. Write a program that inputs an amount of money, such as $4.57, and figures out how that amount of money can be given in bills, quarters, dimes, nickels, and pennies. Assume that the amount of money will be less than $20.00. (Hint: This problem is similar to the factoring problem discussed in the text except that here, whenever you give out, say, a dollar bill, you subtract a dollar from the amount of change that you have yet to give. Your DATA statement will have in it the values of the bills and coins, arranged from highest to lowest.)

2. High school administrators delight in organizing class schedules so that no class ever begins or ends at a sensible time. A typical schedule might have each period lasting 42 minutes with a five minute break between each pair. Suppose that there are nine periods in a day:

1	8:15– 8:57
2	9:02– 9:44
3	9:49–10:31
4	10:36–11:18
5	11:23–12:05
6	12:10–12:52
7	12:57– 1:39
8	1:44– 2:26
9	2:31– 3:13

Write a computer program so that when we type RUN, the computer looks up the time of day (there is always such a function on a large computer, often called TIM), then compares it to the daily schedule, which it has stored in DATA statements, and then decides where in the school day we are. It might print, for example:

```
WE ARE IN PERIOD #4
```

or

```
WE ARE BETWEEN PERIODS 7 AND 8
```

Your DATA statements must use the same format for the time as does the TIM function on your machine.

3. Write a program to construct and print a random sentence. You can do this by writing a DATA statement with six possible subjects of the sentence, another DATA statement with six verbs, another with six objects, and perhaps one with six adverbs. Have the computer pick a random number from 1 to 6 and print the subject, then randomly pick the verb, the object, and the adverb. Remember to restore to the appropriate DATA statement before choosing the next part of the sentence.

4. Do the following:

 (a) Write a program in which the user types in a number from 1 to 99 and the computer spells it out in letters; for example,

```
ONE
TWELVE
TWENTY-EIGHT
SEVENTY-SIX
```

(Hint: You need DATA statements which have the numbers 1 through 19 written out, and then other DATA statements with the numbers 20, 30, 40, and so on through 90 in them. If the number typed in is less than 20, the program can simply find it in a DATA statement and type it. If a number is greater than 20, have the program find the first digit with the INT function and then print 20 or 30 or 60 or whatever is appropriate. Then use the second digit to find and type 1 or 2 or 3 or whatever at the end.

 (b) Improve exercise 4(a) to take numbers up to ten thousand. You can make this less difficult by noting that you need few, if any, new DATA statements. The number 503 is spelled out by finding the FIVE you already have, printing HUNDRED, and then working on the 03 part. A subroutine might be useful here.

5.3 Yet More Collections (Matrices)

The arrays we have already discussed are usually known as *one-dimensional arrays*. You can visualize one of these arrays as a row of variables, as seen below:

A(0)   A(1)   A(2)   A(3)   . . .

Each member of the array is designated by the letter name of the array and the value of the one subscript in parentheses. The members of array A are numbered from 1 (or 0, on some systems) to whatever the dimension of A happens to be. You tell the computer how big the array is going to be with a dimension statement, such as:

```
23 DIM A(18)
```

which warns the computer that array A will have eighteen spaces in it.

A *matrix* (the plural is *matrices*) is a two-dimensional array. The display below illustrates the most intuitive way for humans to think about matrices, although they are organized differently in the computer:

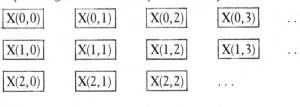

Each box in the display represents one variable in computer memory, and each such variable is called an *element* of the matrix. The collection of variables is referred to as the *matrix X*. Each element of matrix X is designated by the letter X, followed by two subscripts in parentheses separated by a comma. For example,

$$X(3,6)$$

The first subscript, 3 in this case, tells the horizontal row of the desired element, and the second subscript, 6, tells the vertical column. With these two pieces of information, the computer can pick the designated element from matrix X.

As with one-dimensional arrays, you must warn the computer about the size of your matrices; you do this with a dimension statement. Since there are two measurements to a matrix—the number of rows and the number of columns—a dimension statement must include two numbers:

$$12 \text{ DIM } X(3,5)$$

This tells the computer that the matrix X is to have three rows and five columns. In the absence of a dimension statement, some computers assume that the matrix is of a certain size, seven by seven, or something like that, but as with one-dimensional arrays, it is a good idea to dimension all matrices anyhow. BASIC systems almost universally include on every matrix a row numbered zero, called the *zero row*, and a column numbered zero, called the *zero column*. The dimension statement above therefore creates a matrix with four rows, numbered 0, 1, 2, and 3, and six columns, numbered 0, 1, 2, 3, 4, and 5, for a total of 24 elements. You can refer to $X(0,0)$ or $X(0,2)$ or $X(1,0)$, and the computer will have saved a space for these elements. See the matrix created by DIM $X(3,5)$ below:

$X(0,0)$	$X(0,1)$	$X(0,2)$	$X(0,3)$	$X(0,4)$	$X(0,5)$
$X(1,0)$	$X(1,1)$	$X(1,2)$	$X(1,3)$	$X(1,4)$	$X(1,5)$
$X(2,0)$	$X(2,1)$	$X(2,2)$	$X(2,3)$	$X(2,4)$	$X(2,5)$
$X(3,0)$	$X(3,1)$	$X(3,2)$	$X(3,3)$	$X(3,4)$	$X(3,5)$

Example   Data that a matrix stores in a computer would best be organized on paper as a table. Suppose, for example, that we are keeping track of an inventory of men's slacks in the computer. The size of a pair of finished slacks depends on the waist measurement and the length of the inseam (crotch to cuff), both of which we will assume to be between 30 and 40 inches, inclusive. On paper, you might well organize the inventory in a table such as the one shown below, in which the number in each box represents the number of pairs of pants of that size in stock (the circled 13 means that there are 13 pairs of pants with waist 37 and inseam 33):

WAIST SIZE				INSEAM LENGTH							
	30	31	32	33	34	35	36	37	38	39	40
30	12	19	20	17	11	4	3	3	1	0	0
31	12	13	15	16	15	7	3	0	0	0	0
32	14	13	18	21	24	22	8	2	0	0	1
33	8	5	12	26	21	20	14	6	3	2	0
34	9	11	19	23	20	22	18	14	6	0	0
35	5	4	9	14	20	20	19	18	12	9	4
36	5	6	11	22	24	21	14	19	12	3	3
37	2	4	3	(13)	15	24	25	22	22	11	10
38	0	0	0	0	12	17	20	19	23	15	9
39	0	2	1	6	13	15	18	14	14	11	8
40	0	0	0	5	6	4	11	12	15	3	6

To store this data in the computer, dimension the matrix P as follows:

```
44 DIM P(10,10)
```

This gives us the variables $P(0,0)$, $P(0,1)$, $P(0,2)$, ... $P(0,10)$, $P(1,0)$, $P(1,1)$, ... $P(10,10)$. In each of these variables we store the number of pairs of pants of one particular size. The first subscript tells the waist size, and the second subscript, the inseam length. We add 30 to each of the subscripts to find the size of the pants that the matrix element represents. If $P(4,7)$ contains the number 14, for example, then we have on hand 14 pairs of pants with waist 34 and inseam 37. If $P(10,10)$ is 6, then we have six pairs of pants with waist 40 and inseam 40.

Let us write a few useful subroutines using this matrix. First suppose that the data is already stored and that we are writing a subroutine that subtracts a pair of pants from inventory when it is sold. The salesman types in the size of the pair, and the computer subtracts 1 from the appropriate matrix element. Our routine is as shown below:

```
1000 REM *** THIS SUBROUTINE SUBTRACTS PANTS ***
1001 REM *** FROM INVENTORY                  ***
1010 INPUT W, I
1020 LET W1 = W - 30
1030 LET I1 = I - 30
1040 LET P(W1, I1) = P(W1, I1) - 1
1050 RETURN
```

The salesman inputs the waist size W and the inseam length I. If they are 35 and 36, respectively, then W1 and I1 will be 5 and 6, respectively, and the computer subtracts 1 from $P(5,6)$ in statement 1040. This represents in the computer that there is now one fewer pair of 35 × 36 pants in stock.

Note that we could have written:

```
1000 REM *** THIS SUBROUTINE SUBTRACTS PANTS ***
1001 REM *** FROM INVENTORY                   ***
1010 INPUT W, I
1020 LET P(W - 30, I - 30) = P(W - 30, I - 30) - 1
1030 RETURN
```

which has the same effect. There are three problems with this approach: First, it is hard to type; second, it is hard to read; third, it does not run as fast in the computer as the former routine. In that routine, $W - 30$ and $I - 30$ are each calculated once and stored in W1 and I1, whereas in this routine, they are calculated twice, once to look up the old value of $P(W - 30, I - 30)$, and then once again to figure out where to store the new number after it has done the subtraction. Expressions typed twice are evaluated twice.

Perhaps you want to know how many pairs of pants have waist size 34 with any leg length. To find out, you must total the numbers in row four of the matrix:

$$P(4,0) + P(4,1) + P(4,2) + \ldots + P(4,10)$$

A subroutine to do this is as follows:

```
2000 REM *** THIS SUBROUTINE FINDS THE PAIRS ***
2001 REM *** OF PANTS WITH 34 WAISTS          ***
2010 LET T = 0
2020 FOR K = 0 TO 10
2030   LET T = T + P(4,K)
2040 NEXT K
2050 PRINT T
2060 RETURN
```

As K goes from 0 to 10, $P(4,0)$, $P(4,1)$, $P(4,2)$, and on up to $P(4,10)$ are added to T. At the end, T contains the number of all pairs of pants with waist size 34.

Matrices and FOR-NEXT   In the last example, the elements of a row of a matrix were added up using a FOR-NEXT loop. Just as FOR-NEXT loops make one-dimensional arrays useful, they also enhance the utility of matrices. One FOR-NEXT loop can investigate a single row or column of a matrix. Two nested FOR-NEXT loops are able to check all of the entries in an entire matrix.

Suppose that at the end of the day you wish to know if you have fewer than four of any size in stock. You intend to order new inventory and want the computer to list the sizes that you are short of. The computer must look at each matrix element in turn, decide whether it is less than four, and if it is, print out the size of pants that this matrix element represents. The subprogram is as follows:

```
3000 REM *** RE-ORDER SUBROUTINE ***
3010 PRINT "INVENTORY IS SHORT OF THE FOLLOWING SIZES:"
3011 PRINT "(WAIST X LENGTH)"
3020 PRINT
3030 FOR I = 0 TO 10
3040   FOR J = 0 TO 10
3050     IF P(I,J) >= 4 THEN 3070
3060       PRINT I+30;" X ";J+30
3070   NEXT J
3080 NEXT I
3090 RETURN
```

Review nested FOR-NEXT loops to see that this routine does indeed check every element of the matrix P.

MAT-ZER Statement   On most systems a statement which looks similar to

```
493 MAT P = ZER
```

has the effect of setting each of the elements of the matrix P to zero. It saves you the effort of having to write out the nested FOR-NEXT loops that would otherwise be necessary. Of course, what happens in the computer is similar to what would happen if you did write out the FOR-NEXT loops, but the statement above is far easier to write, and since the interpreter or compiler knows exactly what you are up to when you write MAT P = ZER (which it doesn't when you start into a FOR-NEXT loop), it may know a more efficient way. Take warning that if your computer's matrices have zero rows and zero columns, they may be unaffected by the MAT-ZER statement. If you want these elements set to zero, you may have to do it yourself. Note that on some considerate systems, the MAT-ZER statement can also be used on one-dimensional arrays. That means that you can set all the elements of an array to zero using a MAT-ZER statement instead of a FOR-NEXT loop.

If your pants store burns down, you now know how to tell the computer that your inventory is zero.

MAT-INPUT, MAT-READ, and MAT-PRINT Statements   The statement,

```
44 MAT INPUT C
```

causes the computer to print a question mark and then wait for all the elements of the matrix C to be typed in from the teletype, row by row. If C is dimensioned as follows,

```
11 DIM C(2,3)
```

the computer expects numbers to be typed in to fill the spaces C(1,1), C(1,2), C(1,3), C(2,1), C(2,2), and C(2,3), in that order.

On encountering the statement,

25 MAT READ K

the computer looks in DATA statements for the elements of the matrix K. The computer starts off from wherever the last READ statement ended and will READ the elements of K, one at a time, in the same order as in an INPUT statement.

The statement,

27 MAT PRINT Q

has the computer print out the elements of the matrix Q (except for the zero row and the zero column) in some tabular format that the system programmer thought would be most useful for most programmers. Since the format is usually uselessly illegible, most programmers end up printing out matrices using nested FOR-NEXT loops and a generous smattering of the TAB function. For matrices with five or fewer columns, though, the MAT PRINT statement often does a creditable job. Experiment with MAT PRINT (the manual, although informative, never quite does justice to a statement as complicated as MAT PRINT) to find out how useful you think it is in various situations.

You can, of course, INPUT or READ or PRINT a single element of a matrix as though it were a simple variable. For example,

27 INPUT Q(5,8)

prints a question mark and stores the single inputted number in $Q(5,8)$. The statement,

29 INPUT Q(M*2, M-6)

looks up the value of M and finds $M*2$ and $M-6$ to decide in which element of Q to store the inputted number. The statement,

44 READ .Q(7,4)

looks up a value for $Q(7,4)$ in a DATA statement. The statement,

76 PRINT Q(0,8);Q(3,4)

prints the values of elements $Q(0,8)$ and $Q(3,4)$.

Mathematical Matrices   BASIC offers a number of matrix manipulations. If you know about the mathematical uses of matrices, read on. Otherwise, skip this section, since this text will not attempt to explain the mathematics involved. BASIC will do matrix arithmetic for you. In what follows, we assume that A, B, and C are matrices, that M is a variable, and that the computer knows the values of M and of all the elements of B and C. You can write any of the following statements:

```
10 MAT A = B + C
15 MAT A = B - C
20 MAT A = B * C
30 MAT A = ( M ) * B
```

In statement 10, matrices A, B, and C must be dimensioned to the same size. The computer performs the usual element by element matrix addition of B and C and stores the result in A. Statement 15 is similar. In statement 20, the dimensions of A, B, and C must be such that normal matrix multiplication is possible. Statement 30 multiplies the matrix B by the scalar M and stores the result in A. The parentheses around M are usually mandatory. As usual, since some systems use slightly different formats for these statements, it is advisable to check your manual. If you care about what happens to the zero row and column in these statements, you had better check that, too. Also, on some systems, you are not allowed to have the same matrix on both sides of the equal sign in a multiply statement; for example,

```
24 MAT D = D * Y
```

would not be allowed.

In addition to the zero matrix, you can access two other literal matrices. You can fill a matrix with ones (except that the zero row and column remain unchanged) by writing

```
67 MAT Y = CON
```

and you can get the identity matrix (except for the zero row and column) by writing

```
107 MAT Z = IDN
```

The computer will invert and transpose matrices if they are correctly dimensioned and if the matrix to be inverted is invertible:

```
45 MAT F = INV( G )
46 MAT H = TRN( G )
```

Here again, having the same matrix on both sides of the equal sign is often prohibited.

Representing the Plane   In addition to using the matrix as a large storage space, the matrix is useful for representing things that happen on a plane. For example, a matrix can be used to represent a checkerboard, a game of battleship, or the game of life explained in a later section of this book. Mazes and floor tile patterns can be represented in the computer using matrices (see the Exercises).

Exercises

Note: Exercise 4 requires knowledge of matrix multiplication. Exercises 5(a) and 5(b) are quite difficult.

1. Since sizes are always approximate (cuts differ and so on), and since customers' ideas of their sizes are sometimes clouded by ignorance or vanity, when a customer tells you that he has a waist size 35 and a leg length 34, his waist size may be 34, 35, or 36 and his leg length 33, 34, or 35. Assume that the size he gives is no more than 1 inch off. Write a program in which you can input a waist and inseam size, and the computer will tell you how many pairs of pants you have on hand whose sizes are within 1 inch one way or the other of both measurements. (Suggestion: First write this program assuming that the numbers 30 or 40 will never appear. Then deal with the pathological cases 30 and 40; they must be treated differently since no matrix elements correspond to size 29 or size 41, and if you try to discuss such elements with the computer, you will get an error message.)

2. Using the TAB function and FOR-NEXT loops, write a subroutine that prints an 11-by-11 matrix neatly like a table. (The author bets that your system won't do this with MAT-PRINT.) Then use the subroutine to write a program that prints a multiplication table of the numbers 1 through 11. Put the number I*J in matrix element M(I,J). Then use your subroutine to print it out neatly. (Also try MAT PRINT and watch it make a mess.)

3. Write a program that "designs" floor tiles. You can do this by filling a five-by-five matrix with random numbers. Then wherever the matrix has a random number greater than .5, print a block of six X's, as follows,

```
                    XXX
                    XXX
```

and wherever the random number is less than .5, leave a block of six blanks. If you are feeling fancy, put a line of I's around the whole block.

The matrix might turn out to be the following,

```
        .97  .80  .70  .52  .69
        .84  .12  .94  .18  .97
        .70  .13  .97  .36  .02
        .74  .34  .75  .55  .65
        .20  .79  .07  .62  .58
```

in which case the output would be

```
        IIIIIIIIIIIIIIIII
        IXXXXXXXXXXXXXXXXI
        IXXXXXXXXXXXXXXXXI
        IXXX    XXX    XXXI
        IXXX    XXX    XXXI
        IXXX    XXX       I
        IXXX    XXX       I
        IXXX    XXXXXXXXXI
        IXXX    XXXXXXXXXI
        I    XXX    XXXXXXI
        I    XXX    XXXXXXI
        IIIIIIIIIIIIIIIIII
```

4. Write your own matrix multiply routine. Afterwards, see if you understand why

23 MAT B = B * C

is often not permissible on BASIC systems. (Assume that BASIC systems multiply matrices in a manner similar to your program. Will your program multiply matrices B and C and leave the result in B without blowing a fuse?)

5. Map tracing:

(a) Write a program that traces a road map in the following way: There are eight cities, numbered 1 to 8. The user indicates locations of roads by inputting pairs of numbers. Inputting 2,5, for example, indicates that a road connects cities 2 and 5. When the user inputs 0,0, he has input all the roads. Then he inputs a final pair of cities, and the computer is to determine if it is possible to get from one to the other. (If the user inputs 2,6, there may not be a road from 2 to 6, but there may be roads from 2 to 3, from 3 to 8, and from 8 to 6, in which case you can get from 2 to 6.)

(b) Improve the program in exercise 5(a) by initially inputting triples of numbers so that 2,5,67, for example, indicates that the road from 2 to 5 is 67 miles long. When the user inputs the pair of cities he wishes to travel between, the computer should find the length of the shortest route, if any route exists.

(c) Improve exercise 5(b) so that the computer outputs not only the length of the shortest route, but also the cities through which the route passes in the order in which they are visited.

5.4 Long Term Memory (Files)

It is not hard to imagine situations in which data stored in a computer might be used at different times for different purposes. Dingaling Phone Company may have a computer list the phone calls made by each subscriber. At the end of the month, it uses these figures to calculate each bill. At the end of the year, it may want to know the total number of calls from Nowheresville to Exchange City. Later, Dingaling, considering new rates, may want to know how much money the company might have made last year had the new rates been in effect. In every case, the same phone-call data is used.

An organization that has just taken an extensive political poll may have printed out the number of Republicans, Democrats, and Independents interviewed, the number of people for and against the bond issue to build a new city hall next to the monkey island at the zoo, and the number of people who want to exile the mayor. Two weeks later, it may become clear that an important statistic is the number of Democrats favoring the bond issue or the number of Independents against His Honor's exile. If the data is still in the computer, a program can be written to determine these figures.

A payroll program may store the weekly paycheck of each worker. At the end of the year, this data can be used to print tax forms, figure the total labor costs of the company, or add up the incomes of only those workers involved in making ersatz octopus hides. This data might be saved in the computer for comparison with next year's statistics just in case the new manager at the hide plant, for example, wants to know if the plant has improved productivity.

These situations illustrate instances in which a large amount of data in the computer might be subjected to various analyses by different programs at different times. In each of them, the amount of data is large enough that saving it in the computer is far easier than typing it in each time it is wanted. One of the strengths of the computer is that it can arrange for the storage of vast amounts of data for long periods of time. This section will explain how BASIC gives you access to this ability.

Most data stored for long periods of time in a computer is stored either on disc or on magnetic tape so that the central memory may be saved for things that the computer is currently working on. Since a disc that stores eighty million 1's and 0's is not uncommon, a computer with several discs can store a good sized chunk of data. Magnetic tape, as previously discussed, is somewhat slower than disc, but it is very cheap and durable.

BASIC Files   The methods of handling data storage files in BASIC differ drastically from system to system. Every system has its own quirks, partly because every programmer writing a program to manage computer files thinks (possibly correctly) that he can make a faster or more convenient program than the next man, and partly because every programmer writing a BASIC compiler thinks (possibly correctly) that he knows a better way to merge BASIC into existing file management software. The exposition that follows, therefore, discusses the principles behind one type of filing system, *serial files*; describes the statements that some systems use for handling files; and suggests that you read your manual. Only one example is presented since solutions to file problems require the use of specific BASIC statements pertaining to files, and these are not standard. It is hoped, nevertheless, that this discussion will give you enough background to be able to read your manual intelligently.

Creating and Opening Serial Data Files   To have a data file, you must first create one and put data in it. Some systems insist that before a file is mentioned in any statement in any BASIC program, a command must be given to the monitor telling it about the new file. The monitor will demand certain information about the file, such as its name (all computer systems allow you to name your files), its size, its location on the disc, and so forth. Your manual has the details on how to input this information. Typical restrictions on file names, for example, are that they can be no longer than six characters, that blanks are not allowed in the first three characters, that the first character may not be a number, and that quotation marks are not allowed. Some easy-going computer systems automatically create files for you the first time you use them in a BASIC program.

Although computer systems always require that their data files be named, you must often refer to a file during a BASIC program by a number rather than by its name, and at the beginning of the program (or at least before you refer to the file), you must have a statement connecting the file names and numbers. For example,

```
10 FILE #1, "APPLE"
```

tells the computer that file number 1 is the file called "APPLE", and

```
11 FILE #2, "ORANGE"
```

means that file number 2 and a file called "ORANGE" are the same file. Some systems use a statement such as

```
11 OPEN #2, "ORANGE"
```

instead of the FILE statement. If files called ORANGE and APPLE already exist, they are used when you refer to file number 1 or file number 2. If no such files exist, then either they are created by these statements, or you get an error message. On some systems, you use one statement to announce all the files you are going to use; for example,

```
10 FILES "APPLE", "ORANGE", "PEAR", "PEACH"
```

makes "APPLE" file number 1; "ORANGE", file number 2; "PEAR", file number 3; and "PEACH", file number 4. The process of telling the computer that you are going to use a file is called *opening* the file.

Once you have opened a file, the computer can write on it for you as though it were a long strip of paper. The first data item is written at the left end of the strip; subsequent items are written in adjacent spaces to the right. The statement that tells the computer to put an item in a file is similar to one of the following:

```
25 WRITE #1, Q
```

or

```
25 PUT #1, Q
```

Whichever of these is allowable writes the value of Q in the first space in file number 1—"APPLE", in this case. Subsequent WRITE or PUT statements write values in the following spaces in the file.

If the computer, for example, were presented with the statements,

```
20 WRITE #1, 29, "WHO?", 18
30 WRITE #1, "XYZ", "ME!"
```

it would write out

| 29 | WHO? | 18 | XYZ | ME! | . . . |

Most filing systems allow you to mix strings, numeric variables, and literals indiscriminately. For example, the following sort of statement is permissible:

```
25 PUT #1,1,R$,3.1415,"THE CAT IN THE HAT"
```

This puts the four items of data in order in the file. Some systems permit a statement such as

```
35 MAT PUT #2,M
```

which writes matrix M into file number 2 in the same order that numbers are typed into a matrix for a MAT INPUT statement, that is, left to right across the rows. As usual, the zero row and zero column probably won't go into the file automatically.

Getting Data Out of a File   Data files are useful only if you know how to get the data out of one. In many systems, the first problem to deal with is that at any one time, you can write data on a file or read data from it, but not both. There is, though, always a way to get around this difficulty. Often, when you first open a file, the computer doesn't decide whether it is a read file or a write file until the first time you use it. In such systems, you can *close* the file that you want to change from a WRITE file to a READ file and then reopen it. The statements that would make this change for "APPLE" (file number 1) might be as follows:

```
345 CLOSE #1
346 FILE #1, "APPLE"
```

At statement 345, the computer forgets about the connection between file number 1 and the file called APPLE. Statement 346 re-establishes the connection, but now the computer doesn't know whether this is a file to write on or to read from. As a result, it is now possible for you to do either. Other systems might use

```
345 RESTORE #1
```

or

```
345 RESET #1
```

or

```
345 REWIND #1
```

for the same purpose. These statements have the effect of rewinding the strip of paper to its beginning.

Files to be read from usually behave like DATA statements. The statement,

```
18 READ #1, A, B
```

puts the first two items from file number 1 in variables A and B. Subsequently,

```
19 READ #1, C, D
```

puts the next two in C and D. Some systems use

```
19 GET #1, C, D
```

instead of READ. If an item in a file is a string, you must be careful to provide the computer with a string variable to put it into:

```
20 READ #1, K$
```

Otherwise, you will get an error. The computer usually lacks the capacity to warn you ahead of time if the next item is a string, so it is your responsibility to know in what order data is stored in your file and when a string can be expected. The statement,

```
349 RESTORE #1
```

usually sends you back to the beginning of the file. Some systems use a statement like

```
349 RESET #1
```

or

```
349 REWIND #1
```

instead. These are equivalent to a RESTORE statement for DATA statements. On many systems, there is a statement of this kind:

```
670 MAT READ #2, M
```

You ought to be able to figure out what this does by yourself.

Usually, an *end-of-file marker* hides at the end of a data file. This marker tells the computer that the file is over. If you read from a file so many times that the computer runs into this end-of-file marker, the computer will bang out an error message on the terminal. When you write on a data file, the end-of-file marker is simply moved down the strip of paper to the end of whatever you have written.

Example   The following program stores data from a political poll (the poll previously discussed) in a file. The user types in the precinct name, P$, and then the number of Democrats, Republicans, and Independents; the number of people favoring the bond issue; and the number of people favoring exile for the mayor. These are written in the file called "POLL". Remember that differences in computer systems might make this program look rather different on your computer.

```
10 DIM P$(20)
20 FILE #1, "POLL"
30 REM *** LOOP ***
35    INPUT P$,D,R,I,B,E
40    WRITE #1,P$,D,R,I,B,E
50    PRINT "MORE PRECINCTS (Y/N)";
60    INPUT A$
70    IF A$ = "N" THEN 90
80 GOTO 30
90 END
```

A file that this program might create is shown below:

DOWNTOWN	28	197	3	117	1	UPTOWN	104

117	24	156	14	SUBURB	87	104	111	283	26

WRONGSIDEOFTRACKS	0	0	106	0	106	EOF	...

The following program will print a table of the number of Democrats in each precinct:

```
10 DIM P$(20)
20 FILE #1, "POLL"
30 REWIND #1
35 PRINT "PRECINCT","# OF DEMOCRATS"
40 REM *** LOOP ***
45    READ #1,P$,D
50    PRINT P$,D
60    READ #1,W,X,Y,Z
70 GOTO 40
80 END
```

Statement 30 may or may not be necessary, depending on the system. However, statement 60 is necessary—unless your files are divided into records (see below)—because after we read the precinct name and the number of Democrats, four more file items precede the next precinct name, and the only way of getting rid of them is to read them and forget them, the same technique we used with DATA statements. This program will probably end with an error message when it gets to the end-of-file marker.

A Variety of Filing System Features   BASIC files store data in various ways. In some systems, every element in the file is stored as a string. A number like 4.56E+09 is turned into a string—"4.56E+09"—and then stored in the file that way.

Often you can get a listing of such a file on your terminal with the LIST command. When you read a numeric variable from such a file, the computer attempts to convert the string back to a number. This conversion is always possible if the data entry was a number to begin with. In other types of files, numbers are stored in base two, the same way that they are stored in the central memory.

Files can be classified as *serial* files or *random access* files. A serial file is one in which you can only access file elements by starting at the beginning of the file and stepping through it element by element. Often, you can only write onto the end of such a file. If you wish to make corrections to the file, you must copy the entire file over again, making the corrections on the way through central memory. An inadvisable way to correct a serial file is shown below:

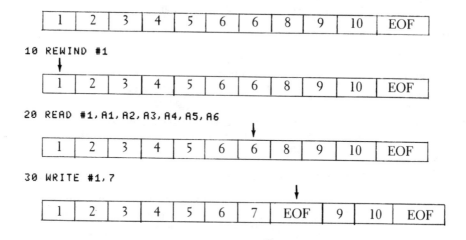

The write statement puts an end-of-file marker after the item it has written. Now your file ends with the number 7.

You can restart your reading at the beginning of the file, but if you want just one data entry out of the middle, you must read all the elements in the file ahead of it.

The so-called random access file allows you to read or write over any piece of data without affecting the rest of the file. The statement

347 RESTORE #1: 90

or a similar one allows you to pick any element of the file. After statement 347, a READ or a WRITE on file number 1 will start at the ninetieth data entry of the file (the ninety-first on some systems). It is like a RESTORE 90 statement for DATA statements.

Some filing systems divide their files into *records*. At the end of each file WRITE statement, an *end-of-record marker* is put in the file. When you read from the file, each READ statement starts at the beginning of the next record. If a record has five data items in it and you read two of them, the next READ statement will skip the next three, find the end-of-record marker, and resume reading at the item following the marker. This system can be very convenient. It would, for example, allow us to skip statement 60 in the program for printing a table of the number of Democrats in each precinct. It can also be very frustrating, for if you want all the various items in a record, but want them at different times in your program, you nonetheless must read them all in one READ statement.

Some filing systems allow you to name each of the records in a file and subsequently access them by name. The name of a record is often called its *key*. For example, if you have a file containing the classes for which each student at your school is enrolled, records could be keyed by students' names. By asking the computer to look in this file in the record labeled JONES, for instance, you could retrieve the data concerning Jones' class schedule.

Exercises

1. Write a program that prints out the contents of a file on your terminal. Then use this program to check whether other programs are writing correct data into files.
2. Do the following:
    (a) Write a program that creates a file which contains a list of student names and test scores. There are five scores for each student. For example, the file might read

    JONES,31,45,67,37,99,SMITH,35,45,66,96,88,SMALL, etc.

    The computer should input names and scores until you type in "END" as the name of a student (perhaps with all test scores equal to zero). The computer should store "END" on the file as a student's name along with the "scores" (your own end-of-file marker).
    (b) Write a program that uses the data file of exercise 2(a) to type out a table with each student's name and his average score for the five tests. (When the computer gets to the name "END", it knows that it is finished.)
    (c) Write a program that uses the data file of exercise 2(a) to type out the name of the student who got the highest score on each test and the name of the student who got the lowest. (The name "END" tells the computer to stop looking.)
3. Do the following:
    (a) Write a program that copies the contents of a file into another file. (The method is to read out of the first file and write into the other.)
    (b) After you have done exercise 2, write a program that allows you to make corrections to the file. You type in a student's name and his correct test scores, and the computer corrects the file. (Hint: Copy the file, student by student, making the correction when you get to that student in the file.) If the student whose test scores are being corrected is not on the file, the computer should offer to add him to the file. A student whose corrected test scores are five zeros should be removed from the file.

4. Do the following:

    (a) Write a program which inputs a set of numbers in order from lowest to highest and stores them in a file. The computer checks that the numbers are in order and refuses to accept numbers if they are not. When you type − 1, the computer should put this − 1 in the file as an end-of-file marker, and the program should end. Use the program in order to create a file called ALEPH and a file called BETH.

    (b) Write a program which combines the contents of ALEPH and BETH into one large file, GIMEL, also sorted. Use the program from exercise 1 to check this program.

5.5 Prettier Output (PRINT USING Statement)

Suppose that you want your answers to be printed out only to the nearest tenth, despite the fact that the computer is figuring them to umpteen decimal places of accuracy, or that you are printing dollar amounts and you want them to come out looking like dollar amounts. As you may have noticed, the computer has a nasty habit of printing

$$\$4.5$$

to mean $4.50, or

$$\$6?.98776$$

to mean $67.99. Suppose that your output will be a column of numbers like the following:

```
34.965
2.77431
2458.1
```

and you wish that they would come out with the decimal points aligned:

```
34.96500
2.77431
2458.10000
```

The PRINT USING statement and the IMAGE statement will assign the number of decimal places to be printed, align decimal points, organize text, and save you from statements like

```
44 PRINT TAB(15); "$"; K; TAB(22); M; "C"; TAB(40); "@"; J; "PER OUNCE"
```

and the grief caused when you have to retype this because it should be "TAB(41)" instead of "TAB(40)".

As an example of the use of the PRINT USING statement, here is the "widgets" program, the object of which is to input the necessary data and then to print it in the format shown below:

```
AMT       DESCRIPTION AND PRICE       COST

  15 WIDGETS AT $ 8.74           $ 131.10
   4 WIDGET WRENCHES AT $14.25   $   57.00
     TOTAL                       $ 188.10

     TAX ( 6%)                   $   11.29

     GRAND TOTAL                 $ 199.39
```

After reading the section on the INPUT statement, you may have tried this problem, and with a combination of commas, semicolons, quotation marks, PRINT statements, and frustration, you probably created output somewhat less attractive than the above. The program that prints the output above is shown below:

```
4    REM *** PROGRAM TO SOLVE THE WIDGETS PROBLEM ***
5    REM
10   PRINT "INPUT NUMBER OF WIDGETS FOLLOWED BY PRICE PER WIDGET"
20   INPUT W, P
30   PRINT "TYPE IN NUMBER OF WRENCHES AND PRICE PER WRENCH"
40   INPUT R, Q
50   PRINT "INPUT TAX RATE"
60   INPUT T
70   LET T1 = W*P
80   LET T2 = R*Q
90   LET T3 = T1 + T2
100  LET T4 = T3*T*.01
110  LET T5 = T4 + T3
115  PRINT
116  PRINT
120  PRINT "AMT.    DESCRIPTIONS AND PRICE        COST"
125  PRINT
130  PRINT
140  PRINT USING 300 W, P, T1
150  PRINT USING 310 R, Q, T2
160  PRINT USING 320 T3
170  PRINT
180  PRINT USING 330 T, T4
190  PRINT
200  PRINT USING 340 T5
210  END
295  REM
296  REM
297  REM
298  REM
300  :   ## WIDGETS AT $##.##           $####.##
310  :   ## WIDGET WRENCHES AT $##.##    $####.##
320  :      TOTAL                        $####.##
330  :      TAX  (##%)                   $####.##
340  :      GRAND TOTAL                  $####.##
```

The variables in this program are defined as follows:

W = number of widgets bought
P = price per widget

R = number of widget wrenches bought

Q = price per wrench

T = tax rate as a percent (if T = 6, the tax rate is 6%)

T1 = cost of widgets

T2 = cost of widget wrenches

T3 = subtotal

T4 = tax

T5 = grand total

When the computer comes to statement 140, the PRINT USING statement tells it to make the output look like statement 300. At statement 150, the computer is told to look at statement 310 to find the output format. The IMAGE statements 300 through 340 provide templates into which the computer puts its output.

The IMAGE Statement When the computer comes to a statement like

140 PRINT USING 300 W, P, T1

it prints out the values of the variables W, P, and T1 in accordance with the IMAGE statement located at statement 300. An IMAGE statement is not executed if the program comes to it; it is used only to help out PRINT USING statements. An IMAGE statement begins with a colon (:), and the rest of it is constructed according to the following rules:

1. A contiguous group of number signs (#), possibly with a decimal point among them, designate a *field* into which a number is to be printed. In statement 300:

300 :   ## WIDGETS AT $##.## $####.##
         1   2   3

there are three fields. At statement 140,

140 PRINT USING 300 W, P, T1

the computer prints W in field number 1, P in field number 2, and T1 in field number 3. The locations of these numbers on the printed line are determined by the positions of the fields in the IMAGE statement. Since field number one above occupies columns 4 and 5 of the IMAGE statement, the value of W is printed in columns 4 and 5. Since field number 2 occupies columns 19 through 23, the value of P is printed in those columns.

2. If there is no decimal point in the field, such as in field number 1 above, then the computer rounds the number to be printed—W in this case—to an integer. (Some systems round and some systems truncate. Check your manual.) Then it prints the integer in the field as far to the right as it can. If W equals 2, then a 2 is printed in column 5, and column 4 is left blank. If W equals 16, then a 1 is printed in column 4

and a 6 in column 5. If W is 3 or more digits, the computer prints asterisks (*) in both columns and does not print the value of W at all. It plays this asterisk trick whenever a number proves too large for the field.

3. If there is a decimal point in the field, then the computer prints the decimal point exactly where it appears on the line in the IMAGE statement and organizes the number around the decimal point. The computer prints as many digits to the left of the decimal point as it needs, filling unused columns in the field with blanks. To the right of the decimal point, it prints exactly as many digits as are shown, rounding the number if necessary and filling in trailing zeros if necessary. Suppose that the computer has to print 131.1 in the field

####.##

It puts the decimal point exactly where it belongs, types 131 to the left of the decimal point preceded by a blank, puts the 1 to the right of the decimal point, and puts a zero in the other space to the right of the decimal point. It prints

__131.10

where the underline (__) indicates that a blank is left. If the computer has the same field in which to print 11.286, it rounds it to 11.29 to make it fit into two decimal places, and prints

__11.29

If the field is not large enough to hold the number, the computer fills it with asterisks. For example, since 12465.8 could not be squeezed into the field ####.##, the computer would print asterisks in the field.

4. A group of four exclamation points (!) immediately following a field tells the computer to use scientific notation. The four exclamation points may be replaced by E+34 or E−09, or whatever. On encountering ###.##!!!!, the computer prints a number with up to three places to the left of the decimal point, exactly two to the right of the point, and an exponent.

5. A + sign at the beginning of a field indicates that the computer is to print a plus sign or a minus sign, as appropriate. Thus +###.## produces + 34.79 from the number 34.793.

6. A minus sign at the beginning of a field indicates that the computer is to print a minus sign if the number is negative, but to leave a blank in this column if the number is positive. If no sign precedes a field, some systems print negative numbers with no sign in front of them, making them appear positive. This practice is extremely unsettling.

7. Any other character in an IMAGE statement is printed exactly as it is. This includes periods (.) not embedded in number fields, any exclamation point not in a group of four following a field, and any letters, numbers, or symbols.

String Fields   The IMAGE statement can also specify how string variables are to be printed. In the program,

```
5    DIM L$(20)
6    DIM F$(20)
7    DIM M$(20)
10   INPUT L$,F$,M$
30   PRINT USING 100 L$,F$,M$
40   END
100  :##########, ##### #.
```

the computer inputs a last name, a first name, and a middle name. Then, using IMAGE statement 100, it prints up to ten letters of the last name. (Ten spaces is the length of the first field.) If the last name is longer than ten letters, the computer prints the first ten. If it is shorter than ten letters, the computer prints it at the left end of the field. The comma and space are then printed and then the first five letters of the first name. (There are five spaces in the second field.) Then the computer prints the middle initial. Note that whatever the user types for a middle name, the computer only types the first letter of it. See the input and output below:

INPUT	OUTPUT
SMITH, JAMES, ALLEN	SMITH JAMES A.
VANDERWAERDEN, HANS, Q	VANDERWAER, HANS Q.
WELLS, H. , GEOFFREY	WELLS , H. G.
WELLS, H, G	WELLS , H G.
HUMPERDINK, ENGLEBERT, R	HUMPERDINK, ENGLE R.

An IMAGE statement can contain both numeric and string fields. When the computer comes to a field, it prints the next variable on the list of variables to be printed. If that variable is a string, then the field is assumed to be a string field. If the variable is a number, then the field is assumed to be numeric.

The program at the top of the next page is a slight improvement on the widget program.

The variables of this improved widget program are defined as follows:

A$, B$, C$ = names of first, second, and third items bought
A1, B1, C1 = prices of the items
A2, B2, C2 = number of each item bought
A3, B3, C3 = cost of each item bought
T1 = subtotal
T = tax rate
T2 = tax
T3 = grand total

```
4    REM *** THIS IS AN IMPROVED WIDGETS PROGRAM ***
5    REM
10   PRINT "FOR EACH OF THREE ITEMS, TYPE THE NAME OF THE ITEM,"
20   PRINT "ITS UNIT COST, AND THE NUMBER OF SUCH ITEMS BOUGHT."
30   INPUT A$,A1,A2
40   INPUT B$,B1,B2
50   INPUT C$,C1,C2
60   LET A3 = A1 * A2
70   LET B3 = B1 * B2
80   LET C3 = C1 * C2
90   LET T1 = A3 + B3 + C3
100  PRINT "INPUT THE TAX RATE"
110  INPUT T
120  LET T2 = T1 * T * .01
130  LET T3 = T1 + T2
140  PRINT
141  PRINT
145  PRINT "AMT.    DESCRIPTION AND PRICE                        COST"
150  PRINT
160  PRINT USING 300 A2,A$,A1,A3
170  PRINT USING 300 B2,B$,B1,B3
180  PRINT USING 300 C2,C$,C1,C3
190  PRINT USING 310 T1
200  PRINT
210  PRINT USING 320 T,T2
220  PRINT
230  PRINT USING 330 T3
240  END
250  REM
260  REM
270  REM
300  :    ## ############### AT $##.##        $#####.##
310  :       TOTAL                            $#####.##
320  :       TAX (##%)                        $ ###.##
330  :       GRAND TOTAL                      $#####.##
```

At statement 160, the computer is to print A2, A$, A1, and A3. Since A2 is a number, the first field of statement 300 is a number. The next field is used to print string A$, and the last two fields are numbers. The output might possibly be as follows:

```
AMT.    DESCRIPTION AND PRICE                        COST

   12 DYNAMITE STICKS AT $ 6.22              $   74.64
    6 LOCK PICKS       AT $ 1.98             $   11.88
    1 GETAWAY CAR      AT $24.33             $   24.33
      TOTAL                                  $  110.85

      TAX ( 4%)                              $    4.43

      GRAND TOTAL                            $  115.28
```

Alternate Formatting on Some Systems   Some systems do not provide a PRINT USING statement but allow the programmer to specify how each variable is to appear on the page as each appears within a PRINT statement. An example of a PRINT statement on such a system is

```
140 PRINT "   ";W:"##";" WIDGETS AT ";P:"##.##";TAB(40);
          "$";T1:"####.##"
```

The user specifies the field for each variable by typing a colon followed by the field specification. Often, the field specification must be enclosed in quotes, which is a nuisance, but on the other hand, it is usually possible to use a string variable as a field specification, which can be a blessing:

```
10 LET Z5$ = "#####.###!!!!"
      .
      .
      .
      .
1025 PRINT A:Z5$;B:Z5$;C:Z5$
```

Here, you are saved from typing that mammoth field format three separate times. The colon tells the computer not to print the value of variable Z5$ but to use it to format the values of A, B, and C.

Systems that use this kind of formatting also often allow options such as specifying that commas should be inserted every three digits, that a dollar sign should immediately precede the first digit, that negative numbers should be enclosed in parentheses, that leading zeros should be printed, that worthless trailing zeros should be suppressed, that asterisks should be placed in all unused spaces to the left of the number (a fantastic provision for printing checks, for example), that numbers should be printed at the left end of the field, or that strings should be printed as far to the right as possible instead of as far to the left. Thus this system allows you considerably more freedom in formatting although it is perhaps more tedious to use.

Exercises

1. Improve the widgets problem yet further with the following technique. The user is allowed to type the purchase data for any number of items, and the data is put onto a file as he types it in. Then the computer pulls all the items off the file one at a time and prints out the bill of sale in the format shown.
2. Print a table of square roots of the numbers from 50 to 70, but round the square roots to the nearest one hundredth. You can use a FOR-NEXT loop and one IMAGE statement.
3. Write a program into which a user can type his name, and it types back his initials, such as

M. J. B.

4. Write a program which inputs first a number of transactions to be entered, T, and an initial balance, B, followed by a series of T positive or negative dollar amounts representing deposits or withdrawals. The computer should then print the following:

```
INITIAL BALANCE          $  479.83

DEPOSIT                  $  629.14
BALANCE                  $1108.97

DEPOSIT                  $    .98
BALANCE                  $1109.95

WITHDRAWL                ($ 576.12)
BALANCE                  $ 533.83
```

Hint: You need four IMAGE statements.

6
ADMIRING THE EDIFICE: PROBLEMS FOR COMPUTER SOLUTIONS

6.1 Calculating with Very Large Integers

You have no doubt noticed that the computer gives you only six digits of accuracy, or maybe a very few more. For example, 3.14159265 is rounded to 3.14159. Numbers larger than some arbitrary size, maybe one million, are changed into scientific notation to fit into those six decimal places. Thus, 93,000,000 is changed to 9.3E+07, for example. Since six digits of accuracy is often all that you need or want, this is a sensible arrangement. But suppose that you happened to want more digits than that? In that case, BASIC does you a definite disservice.

Some languages allow you to determine the accuracy of the computer's computations. At the expense of some computer speed, you can specify *long precision* for numbers that you want stored and calculated to more decimal places. Although seldom offered in BASIC, long precision is common in FOR-TRAN, since the scientific work done in FORTRAN occasionally demands more digits of accuracy. This section introduces you to programming the computer to calculate with outrageously large numbers in spite of the BASIC compiler. It is not very effective to write programs using these methods if the programs demand repeated computations in long precision; they would run too slowly. These are, nevertheless, useful techniques.

The first problem that crops up is that the BASIC compiler keeps only six digits for the very good reason that six digits is often as much precision as can be squeezed into one memory space in the computer. As previously discussed, there is a largest number that can be stored in a word of memory. Storing a larger number is rather akin to writing a seven digit number when you may write only three digits on a line. The solution is to use more than one line, and the solution to the computer problem is to use more than one memory space to store one number. To store the number 1234567, we might put a 1 in one of the memory spaces, 234 in the next, and 567 in the next. Each of the three numbers, 1, 234, and 567, fits easily into a word of memory, and from the three of them, we can reconstruct the original number 1234567.

We will find the number 2^{275}, which is equal to 275 factors of 2. If you ask your computer to find this number, you will probably exceed the largest number that it can handle. (The answer is 83 digits long!) You may get the answer $6.07E+82$, but you will more likely get an error message, and under no circumstances will you get all 83 digits.

Let us write a program to find all 83 digits. (This is not quite the same as providing extra digits of accuracy; we have merely simplified the problem by dealing only in integers.) To find this gargantuan number 2^{275}, the computer must obviously handle some rather large numbers. It must, in fact, store numbers up to 83 digits long and multiply these numbers by two. An array is used to provide the many memory words needed to store a number of this size. Call the array A and dimension it with 35 spaces, numbered 0 through 34. In each of the array spaces, the computer stores three digits of the number, for a total capacity of 3 times 35, or 105 digits. This will suffice with a few extra digits left over. For example, when the computer has calculated 2^{25}, it has the number 33554432, which is stored in array A as follows:

$$\ldots A(4) = 0 \quad A(3) = 0 \quad A(2) = 33 \quad A(1) = 554 \quad A(0) = 432$$

All the elements from A(3) on up are equal to 0. The reason for putting no more than three digits in any element is that three-digit numbers are far enough away from the one-million mark, where the computer may convert to scientific notation, that there is no danger of conversion. On the other hand, putting fewer digits in an element means a larger array and a slower program.

To find 2^{275}, put the number 2 in array A [A(0) = 2; all other elements equal 0], and multiply it 274 times by 2. When multiplying by 2, the computer must always check that none of the array spaces contain more than three digits. Watch the process when the computer multiplies 2^{25} by 2 to find 2^{26}:

$$2^{25} = 33554432$$
$$2^{26} = 2^{25} * 2 = 67108864$$

Now 2^{25} is stored in the array A as shown above. We want 2^{26} to be stored as

$$\ldots\ldots A(4) = 0 \quad A(3) = 0 \quad A(2) = 67 \quad A(1) = 108 \quad A(0) = 864$$

but if we multiply each of the elements of A (2^{25}) by 2, we get

$$\ldots A(4) = 0 \quad A(3) = 0 \quad A(2) = 66 \quad A(1) = 1108 \quad A(0) = 864$$

We see that A(0) is correct, but that A(1) has four digits in it instead of three and that A(2) is too small. We need to carry! Since every time the number in A(2) gets bigger by 1 it has the same effect on the total number as A(1) getting 1000 bigger, that 1000 in A(1) is the same as a 1 would be in A(2). Therefore subtract 1000 from A(1) and add 1 to A(2). We get just what we wanted:

$$\ldots A(4) = 0 \quad A(3) = 0 \quad A(2) = 67 \quad A(1) = 108 \quad A(0) = 864$$

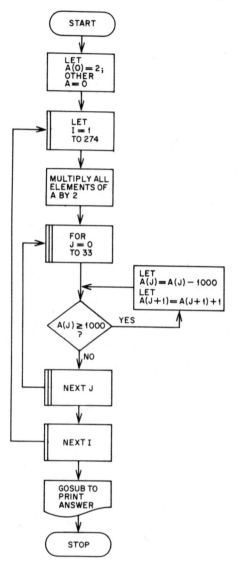

Fig. 6.1 Flowchart to find 2^{275}

The computer must multiply each array space by two, then carry. The process is shown below, and the flowchart is shown in Fig. 6.1.

	A(4)	A(3)	A(2)	A(1)	A(0)
2^{25}	0	0	33	554	432

First multiply each array element by two, getting

	0	0	66	1108	864

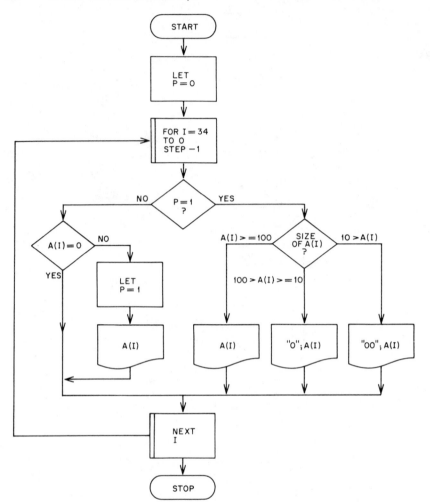

Fig. 6.2 Flowchart to print 2^{275}

Then carry, getting

	2^{26}	0	0	67	108	864

Multiply by 2

		0	0	134	216	1728

Carry

	2^{27}	0	0	134	217	728

Multiply by 2

		0	0	268	434	1456

Carry

$$2^2— \qquad 0 \qquad 0 \qquad 268 \qquad 435 \qquad 456$$

and so on.

When the computer gets the answer, it must print it out by printing out each of the array elements one at a time (see the flowchart in Fig. 6.2.) There are two little problems, however. Although the array A is storing 105 digits, 2^{275} has only 83. If you just ask the computer to print the elements of array A, it will start off with a string of zeros, and you want the computer to start printing only when it first comes to some element that is not zero. The second problem is that if the number turns out to be

$$60\ 708\ 400\ 096\ 001\ldots$$

the computer will print

$$60\ 708\ 400\ 96\ 1\ldots$$

leaving out those important zeros. Each time that you print out one of the array spaces after the first one, you must be sure that place-holder zeros are put in.

The complete program for finding and printing 2^{275} is shown on the following page.

You may end up with peculiar spaces in your output, since BASIC systems often shovel in extraneous spaces when they print numbers. You can usually suppress these if you look on the right page of your manual or ask the right person the right question. The STR function is often useful in this context.

Exercises

1. Improve on the program in the text by having it input a number X less than 1000 and a number Y, and then find X raised to the Yth power. You had better check that X is less than 1000 and that the numbers that you generate do not overflow the array. If A(34) gets bigger than 1000, then the number is too big, even for your program. Your program should stop if overflow occurs.
2. Write a program that finds the factorial of any number that the user types in up to, say, 69. (Since 69! has ninety-nine digits, it is large enough for interest.)
3. Improve the efficiency of the programs in exercises 1 and 2 by improving the carry routine. To see the use of this, suppose that your program is finding 998^{11}. At the beginning, A(0) is 998. To find 998^2, this is multiplied by 998 for a result of 996004 in A(0). You want to carry the 996 to A(1), leaving the 4 in A(0), but carrying by subtracting 1000 from A(0) and adding 1 to A(1) 996 times (the method suggested in Fig. 2.1 is outrageously slow). Instead, divide A(0) by 1000 (996.004), and apply the INT function to the result (996), thereby finding out how much to carry. Then add this 996 to A(1) and subtract 996,000 from A(0).
4. Write a program that allows the user to type in two enormous numbers, puts each in an array as above, adds the two numbers together, and prints the sum. The adding part of this program is fairly easy, but getting the computer to input a

```
4      REM **********************************************
5      REM *** THIS PROGRAM FINDS 2 TO THE 275TH POWER ***
6      REM **********************************************
100    REM
110    REM
120    REM *** INITIALIZE VARIABLES ***
130    REM
140    FOR I = 1 TO 34
150      LET A(I) = 0
160    NEXT I
170    LET A(0) = 2
180    REM
190    REM
200    REM *** MULTIPLY BY 2- -274 TIMES ***
210    REM
220    FOR I = 1 TO 274
230      FOR J = 0 TO 34
240        LET A(J) = A(J) * 2
250      NEXT J
280      REM
290      REM *** CARRY ROUTINE ***
300      REM
310      FOR J = 0 TO 33
320        REM *** LOOP ***
330          IF A(J) < 1000 THEN 370
340          LET A(J) = A(J) - 1000
350          LET A(J+1) = A(J+1) + 1
360        GOTO 320
370      NEXT J
380    NEXT I
390    REM
410    REM **********************************************
1000   REM
1010   REM *** PRINT ANSWER ***
1020   REM
1030   LET P = 0
1040   FOR I = 34 TO 0 STEP -1
1050     IF P = 1 THEN 1100
1060       IF A(I) = 0 THEN 1200
1070         LET P = 1
1080         PRINT A(I);
1090         GOTO 1200
1100     REM
1110       IF A(I) < 100 THEN 1140
1120         PRINT A(I);
1130         GOTO 1200
1140       IF A(I) < 10 THEN 1170
1150         PRINT "0";A(I);
1160         GOTO 1200
1170       REM
1180         PRINT "00";A(I);
1190         GOTO 1200
1200   NEXT I
1500   REM
1510   REM
1520   END
```

large number and to store it in an array can be troublesome. Clearly, if you just input

$$969795827384116253224$$

the computer will not be nice enough to store it in an array without a lot of help. You might input the number into a string variable and then peel off three digits at a time. The NUM function is often useful for this.

5. Do the following:
>   (a) Once you conquer the input hassles of exercise 4, try the more challenging problem of writing a program that multiplies the two numbers together.
>   (b) Write the relatively easy program to figure out which of the two input numbers is larger and then to subtract the smaller from the larger.
>   (c) Division is extremely difficult, but the ambitious might want to try. Simply subtracting repeatedly is out because the computer time necessary to do one division by this method is probably several trillion centuries.

6. Make one of your programs more efficient by keeping a record of how big the numbers are. For example, when the program to find 2^{275} first starts, it need look only at A(0), because the rest are all zero for quite some time. If the variable A(1) stored the length of the number in A, the program could look at array spaces A(0) to A(1) and skip the rest.

6.2   Printing Graphs of Functions

You can get a computer to give you a table of the x and y values for a function by having it check all the x values from -3 to 3 at intervals of .1, and you can then use this table to plot points and find the general shape of the graph of the function. It is, however, more fun and less work (once you write the program) to have the computer itself draw the graph. This section gives some suggestions for having it do this. Examine the computer-produced graph of the function $y = 3e^{-(x+1.5)^2} + e^{x-2} - 2$ (e symbolizes a number equal to about 2.718281828) and also the conventional graph of the same function in Fig. 6.3.

Note first that the computer graph is "sideways." Although all you need do to get it "right side up" is to give the paper a quarter turn counterclockwise, this turn is easier done by hand than by computer. Second, note that although the graphs are roughly the same shape, the computer version looks "stretched" from left to right (from top to bottom of the teletype page). The reader is left to solve this problem in his own way, although hints are given later in this chapter.

When you graph a function, you probably plot just a very few points (calculating the y-values is a nuisance) and then draw smooth curves or lines connecting your points. For the computer, however, finding y-values is easy whereas extrapolating curves between plotted points is a tough problem in the

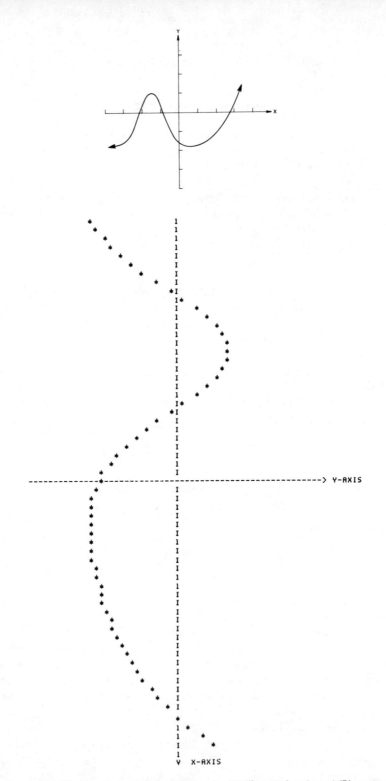

Fig. 6.3 (A) Conventional graph of the function $3e^{-(x+1.5)^2} + e^{x-2} - 2$, and (B) computer-produced graph of the same function

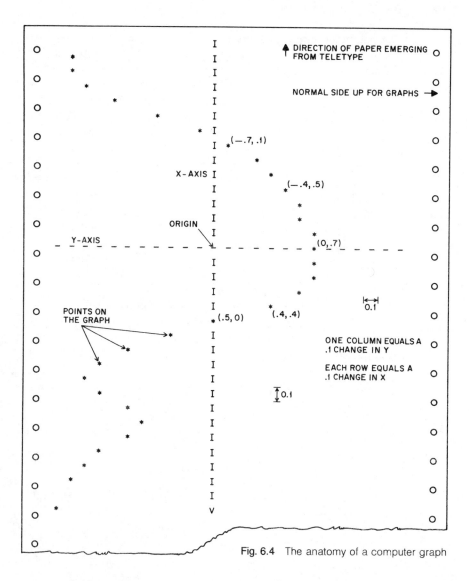

Fig. 6.4 The anatomy of a computer graph

field of artificial intelligence. The computer's method, therefore, is to pick every x-value between certain limits, find the y-value with the function formula, and plot each of the points. Such is the typical, plodding computer's way of doing things. In the discussion that follows, assume that the graphs depict a domain for x from −3 to 3 in increments of .1. The first teletype line is the collection of points whose x-coordinates are −3; the next line has points with x-coordinate −2.9; the next, −2.8; and so on. At each line, the computer must calculate the corresponding y-value from the function formula, and then put an asterisk in the appropriate column. Each column on the teletype is assumed to represent a change of .1 and the x-axis (the row of "I"s) is in column 30. Points for which y equals 0 are in column 30. A positive y-value puts the point further to the right; a negative value, to the left. (See Fig. 6.4.)

The computer comes to the first line, where x equals -3. If the function we are graphing is $y = x^2 - 11$, then y equals -2. The teletype must be instructed where to place the "I" representing the x-axis and the asterisk representing the point of the function. The TAB function can space the teletype to the proper column for each. We are assuming that the "I" goes in column 30, and thus at the appropriate time, the computer will TAB to column 30 and print the "I". But what about the asterisk? In what column should the computer print a point whose y-coordinate is -2? To figure that out, we must find a formula which turns the y-value of a point into a column number for the TAB function.

If y equals 0, then the asterisk should fall in column 30, right on the x-axis. But every time that the y-coordinate gets .1 bigger, the point should move one column to the right. In other words (assuming for the moment that y is positive), we want to know the number of times that .1 goes into y and then space that number of columns to the right of column 30.

$$\text{column} = 30 + y/.1$$

If $y = .1$, the point is in column 31; if $y = .4$, in column 34. If y is negative, then for every .1 that y is less than zero, this formula puts the point that many columns to the left of the axis. If $y = -2$, for example, then $y/.1 = -20$. So $30 + y/.1$ is 10. The asterisk lands in column 10, 20 columns to the left of the x-axis in column 30, which is where it belongs. The column formula therefore

x	y	Teletype column for y-value
-3.0	-1.67706	13
-2.9	-1.56998	14
-2.8	-1.43821	16
-2.7	-1.28012	17
-2.6	-1.09536	19
-2.5	-.885253	21
-2.4	-.653148	23
-2.3	-.404554	26
-2.2	-.147125	29
-2.1	.109602	31
-2.0	.354718	34
.	.	.
.	.	.
-1.5	1.03020	40
.	.	.
.	.	.
-1.0	.386189	34
0.0	-1.54847	15
1.0	-1.62633	14
2.0	-.999980	20
3.0	.718282	37

Fig. 6.5   Partial Table of Values for the Function $3e^{-(x + 1.5)^2} + e^{x - 2} - 2$

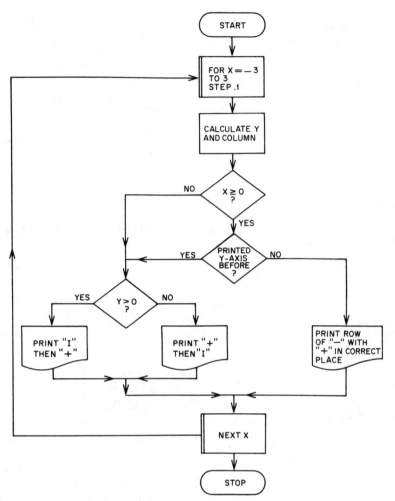

Fig. 6.6 Flowchart of program to graph functions

works whether y is positive or negative (see Fig. 6.5). You will have to cope with the situation that arises if the column turns out to be either greater than 70 or less than 0.

To print the x-axis, the computer must first decide which of the symbols "I" and "*" is on the left and print that one first. Since a teletype cannot backspace, this step is essential. To type the y-axis, the computer checks before typing each row whether the x-coordinate has passed zero (*not* whether it is equal to zero; remember that the inaccuracy of binary numbers may lurk here.) Then it checks if it has typed the axis before. If it hasn't, then this is the time to do it. Some variable must change when the y-axis is printed to remind the computer that it has typed the y-axis (see Fig. 6.6).

Improvements   After this much of the program is working, there are several features that you may want to add. Two of the nicest are the following:

1. Define the function to be graphed as a user-defined function. When your program starts, it should instruct the user about how to type in the statement that defines the function he wants graphed and then stop for him to type it in. Then the user types RUN a second time, and the computer jumps into the graphing routine. An example of the interaction with this routine follows:

```
RUN
WAIT FOR ### AND READY.   THEN TYPE

100 FNA(X) =

FOLLOWED BY THE FORMULA FOR THE FUNCTION YOU WANT GRAPHED
AND A CARRIAGE RETURN.   THEN TYPE

RUN


###

*READY
100 DEF FNA(X) = X↑2 - 2*X + 34
RUN
```

The computer then graphs the function. The user has added the function definition statement to your program. Your program must set some variable so that when the user types RUN the second time, it skips into the graphing routine.

2. Allow the user to set some of the parameters. You might ask him to input the minimum and maximum x-values he wants to see on his graph (easy change in the major FOR-NEXT loop). You might ask him how much change in x each teletype line should represent. (You figure out this simple improvement.) You might ask him which column to put the y-axis in and how much change in y each column represents. (This problem is more troublesome since you have to change the column formula using the data that the user puts in. You also have to change where the "I"s are printed, but that is easy.) By making these changes, the user can affect the scale of the graph, stretching it along the x- and y-axes. What change in x and y should each row and column represent in order to create a "normal" graph?

Exercises

1. Write the programs outlined in the text.
2. Write a program to which a user can add a function definition of FNA at statement 10 and which automatically picks the following parameters and creates the "best possible" graph of the function FNA:

(a) The least and greatest values of x
(b) The change in x that each line represents
(c) The change in y that each column represents
(d) The column in which to place the x-axis

The best possible graph is one which is the size of one page, 8 1/2″ × 11″ or 11″ × 17″, shows all the zeros of the function and all of the places at which it changes from increasing and decreasing and vice versa, and never runs off the side of the page.

3. After doing exercise 2, you may decide that the definition given for the "best possible" graph can be improved. Improve the definition and rewrite the program.

4. Write a program that graphs functions right side up, that is, with the x-axis horizontal and the y-axis vertical. Since you must print first those points with the highest y-coordinates, you must first find all of the x- and y-coordinates of the points you are going to print and then sort them with highest y-coordinates first. Among those points that have y-coordinates close enough to one another to be printed on the same line, you must first print those with the lowest x-coordinates. You must therefore re-sort this subcollection of points.

6.3 Playing the Game of Life

The "Game of Life" was described in the mathematical games section of the October, 1970 issue of *Scientific American,* and when that description first appeared, programmers across the country rushed to their terminals to bang out programs. The game cries out for computer analysis, since it is relatively easy to program but tedious to play by hand. The original article raised several unanswered questions about the game, and readers scrambled to find the answers. The fascination of the game was so great that part of a subsequent column was devoted to a discussion of the answers to the earlier questions. Some of the most startling contributions to the discussions came from people who had programmed their computers to assist them in playing the game.

Rules of "Life"   The so-called "Game of Life" is not a game but rather a process which the player starts but in which he subsequently plays no part. The player specifies a pattern which acts as the original "population" or "first generation," and then the rules of the game specify a single process for finding the second generation from the first, the third from the second, and so on. Each generation is found from the previous one by applying the rules. The process of finding the next generation is called a "move."

Each generation consists of a number of "individuals," all of whom are represented by an X in a square on a sheet of graph paper. The graph paper is assumed to extend indefinitely in all directions. An individual never changes his position, but in passing from one generation to the next, an individual may survive or die, and new individuals may be born in previously empty squares. The sole criterion which determines birth, survival, and death is the number of individuals of the population who are adjacent horizontally, vertically, or diagonally to the square in question. If an individual in a population is adjacent to two or three other individuals, he survives to the next generation. If he is adjacent to one or none, he is "isolated" and dies. If he is adjacent to four or more, he is "overcrowded" and dies. After an individual dies, there is an empty square where he used to live. A birth occurs in a square which is unoccupied and is adjacent to precisely three individuals. A birth can occur in a square left vacant by a death in an earlier move. These rules are applied to each generation to find the next generation. In passing from one generation to the next, births and deaths happen simultaneously. An individual who dies in this "move" may thus contribute to a birth in the next.

In Fig. 6.7, the player specified three individuals in a vertical row as the original population. (The outlined square is just a reference position which remains unmoved.) Let us calculate subsequent generations. First consider which of the three individuals in the first generation are to survive and which to die. The individual at the top of the row has only one neighbor; hence he is isolated and will die. The same is true for the bottom individual. The center individual, however, has two neighbors and will survive. Now consider where births will occur. The numbers in the empty spaces in the second picture of the first generation indicate the numbers of individuals adjacent to each of those spaces (check them). Births can occur only in those squares adjacent to three individuals; as you can see, there will be two births (in the squares with the number three in them). Now erase the top and bottom individuals who died, draw new individuals where the births occurred, and get the second generation as shown. Notice how the individuals who died helped create the ones who were born.

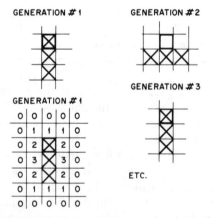

Fig. 6.7   First example of generational growth

To continue the game, apply the rules to this second generation. The left-hand and right-hand individuals are isolated and die; the center individual survives; two new individuals are born top and bottom. We now have the third

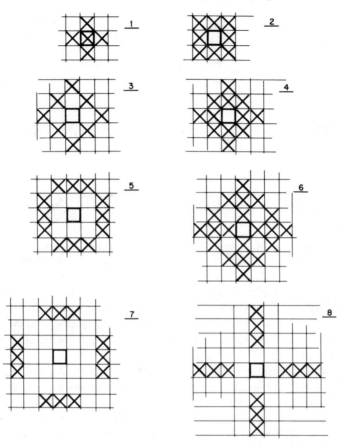

Fig. 6.8   Second example of generational growth

generation. This process can continue ad nauseum, for this particular population obviously oscillates between the two patterns indefinitely.

In the first generation of Fig. 6.8, the central individual is overcrowded and dies, whereas the other four live. Four new individuals are born. Going from the second generation to the third, the individuals at the corners of the square survive (two neighbors each) whereas the sides of the square are overcrowded (four neighbors each) and die. Four new individuals are born around the perimeter. All the individuals of the third generation have two neighbors and hence survive. Four new members are born. After the fourth generation, overcrowding sets in, and all the individuals adjacent to the reference square die. New births occur at the periphery. It is left to you to verify that this population eventually oscillates between the patterns of the seventh and eighth generations.

Figure 6.9 is included to display the unpredictable effect of the addition of an extra individual to the initial population of Fig. 6.8. Work through this example to see that although this population is very similar to that of Fig. 6.8, it

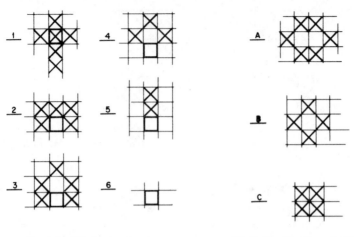

Fig. 6.9 Third example of generational growth

Fig. 6.10 Fourth example of generational growth

shortly dies out completely! Figures 6.10(A), (B), and (C) show populations which are stable. In each of these populations no births occur and no deaths. Every subsequent generation is identical to the original population. Notice how similar are the initial populations of Fig. 6.8 and Fig. 6.10(B) and how divergent the results.

One can imagine five possibilities in the long run. We have seen populations that oscillate, populations that die out, and populations that are stable. It is conceivable that a population might grow indefinitely or that a population might travel, not growing in size, but moving itself, say, from left to right across the page. It is not clear whether there are any such populations, however, and it was to either discover them or prove their nonexistence that *Scientific American* readers so eagerly sprang. The mysteries were eventually solved, and you may check the solution in the subsequent article in *Scientific American*.

The Computer's Role   Before programming a computer to work out this problem, and before looking up the answers to the questions posed in the previous paragraph, try several initial population patterns and see what happens. You will probably discover that the results are seldom what you expect and that calculating new generations accurately is tedious. As an example, you might try an initial straight row of four individuals. This pattern becomes stable. An initial row of five eventually oscillates. A row of six attains a population of 16 at two generations in its career, but after about a dozen generations, it dies out! What happens to a row of seven? Of eight? What happens to other familiar patterns?

The computer can do the drudgery of calculating the generations given a first generation, leaving for you the enjoyment of seeing what happens to your initial population. One possible technique is to represent the graph paper as a matrix in the computer. A 20-by-20 matrix is large enough for satisfying experimentation and small enough not to crowd the data space in the computer.

P(0, 0)	P(1, 0)	P(2, 0)	P(3, 0)	P(4, 0)	P(5, 0)
P(0, 1)	P(1, 1)	P(2, 1)	P(3, 1)	P(4, 1)	P(5, 1)
P(0, 2)	P(1, 2)	P(2, 2)	P(3, 2)	P(4, 2)	P(5, 2)
P(0, 3)	P(1, 3)	P(2, 3)	P(3, 3)	P(4, 3)	P(5, 3)
P(0, 4)	P(1, 4)	P(2, 4)	P(3, 4)	P(4, 4)	P(5, 4)

Fig. 6.11   Numbering of graph paper squares

Each square of graph paper is represented by one space in the matrix, a 1 representing an individual in that space and a 0 representing an empty space. Call the matrix P; then $P(0,0)$ is the upper left-hand corner of the graph paper; $P(10,10)$ is at the center; $P(20,20)$ is the lower right corner (see Fig. 6.11). Although the graph paper is supposed to be infinite, have the computer give up if the population extends off the edge of this size "paper." Assume further that the population does not extend into row zero, column zero, row twenty, or column twenty, for reasons to be explained in a moment.

Three subroutines are needed for this program. The first one allows the player to input the initial population, the second calculates a new population from the old one, and the third prints the new population. The reader is left to write the input routine. Having the user input the subscripts of the locations of the initial individuals is one possible way. To calculate a new population from an old one, assume that the present population is stored in matrix P. We construct the new population in matrix Q, and then copy Q back into P, erasing the old population. Using two nested FOR-NEXT loops, the computer looks at each square of the matrix P to decide whether there is birth, survival, or death:

```
FOR X = 1 TO 19
FOR Y = 1 TO 19
```

We go only from 1 to 19 (and assume that there is no population in row or column zero or twenty) because the computer checks all squares adjacent to the square under consideration. Were we to work with rows zero and twenty, the computer would try to check nonexistent matrix elements such as those in row twenty-one. The empty rows and columns around the outside of our matrix solve this problem. We can check the row below row nineteen or the column to the left of column one with impunity.

At the square $P(X,Y)$ there are two facts we need to know: (1) Is there an individual there now? (2) How many individuals are in adjacent squares? The adjacent squares are the following:

$$P(X - 1, Y - 1)$$
$$P(X - 1, Y)$$
$$P(X - 1, Y + 1)$$
$$P(X, Y - 1)$$
$$P(X, Y + 1)$$
$$P(X + 1, Y - 1)$$
$$P(X + 1, Y)$$
$$P(X + 1, Y + 1)$$

We can count the number of these matrix elements that equal 1 just by adding them all. Now we can put a 1 in $Q(X,Y)$ if birth or survival occurs and otherwise put a 0 there. After this process is performed for the entire matrix, Q contains the new population. Copy Q back into P.

The print subroutine must display the matrix P by printing an X where a 1 occurs in the matrix and a blank where a 0 occurs. It would be useful for the computer to print out some sort of reference square to serve the same purpose as the outlined boxes of the previous figures. For example, the computer might type a plus sign at space $P(10,10)$ if it is occupied, or a dot (.) if it is not. The output of the successive generations of Fig. 6.7 would then be as follows:

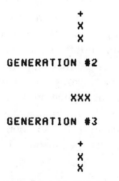

```
        GENERATION #1

              +
              X
              X

        GENERATION #2



             XXX

        GENERATION #3

              +
              X
              X
```

and so on.

A flowchart for the "Game of Life" is shown in Fig. 6.12.

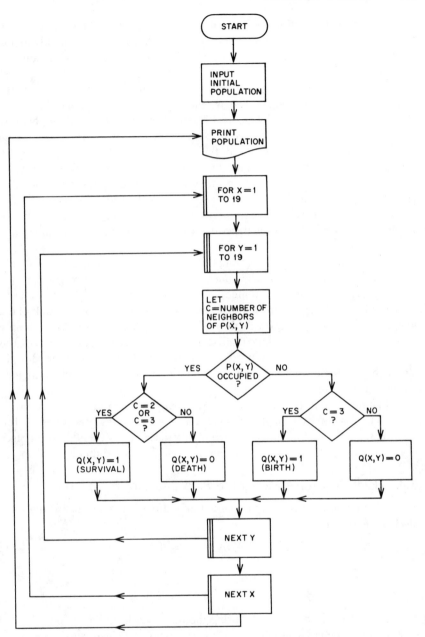

Fig. 6.12 Flowchart to play the Game of Life

Exercises

1. Write the program described in the text. You should be allowed to input the initial population by inputting pairs of numbers representing the subscripts of the members of that population. When you input 0,0, the computer should assume that

you have finished inputting the initial population and ask you how many generations you want it to calculate. It should then calculate and print subsequent generations until (a) it has printed as many as you asked for, (b) the population runs "off the edge" of the matrix, or (c) the population dies out.

2. Improve the new generation subroutine to use only one matrix. When the computer finds an individual who is going to die, it can change the matrix element in P from a 1 to 1.1. The machine must *not* change it to a zero, because the individual may still contribute to births, survivals, and deaths in adjacent squares that we haven't yet checked; the computer must be able to distinguish between an individual who is about to die and an empty square. Similarly, an empty square where a birth is to occur can be changed from 0 to 0.1. After checking all the squares, all 0.1's can be changed to 1's and 1.1's to 0's. Clearly, 0.1 and 1.1 is a better choice of numbers than some because you can still count neighbors to a square by adding the contents of the adjacent matrix elements and taking the integer part of the answer.

3. Improve program efficiency by noting that the computer need not check squares that are near no individual in the population, because nothing happens in such locations. The computer can remember the first subscript of the leftmost individual in L and of the rightmost individual in R, and the second subscripts of the topmost and bottommost individuals in T and B respectively. It then needs only check a rectangular subset of the matrix, from $L - 1$ to $R + 1$ and from $B + 1$ to $T - 1$. The print subroutine need print only from L to R and from B to T, although you might want to increase the boundaries of the rectangle to include the reference point at 10,10.

4. Note that matrix P is used inefficiently. Since each number in the matrix has six digits, why not use each digit to represent a square on the graph paper? In this way, six squares could be stored in each matrix space, and we could store a piece of graph paper six times as large in the matrix. (This is a difficult problem.)

6.4   Using Newton's Method to Find Zeros of Functions *

Suppose that you were interested in writing a program that would solve algebraic equations such as

$$x^2 - 8x + 14 = 0 \qquad\qquad (A)$$

or

$$x^3 - 2.5x^2 - 58.06x + 112.48 = 0 \qquad\qquad (B)$$

The first one could be solved by using the quadratic formula. A formula also exists for cubic equations such as equation (B), but it is a gigantic mess. Suppose that you also want your program to solve equations like

$$x^4 - 24x^3 - 17 = 0 \qquad\qquad (C)$$
$$x^5 + 22x^3 - 112 = 0 \qquad\qquad (D)$$
$$x^4 - \sin(x) - 15 = 0 \qquad\qquad (E)$$

*No calculus is required for this section.

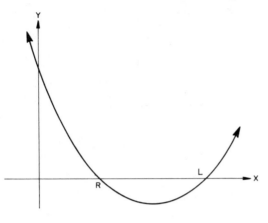

Fig. 6.13   Graph of y = x² − 8x + 14

You could look up the quartic formula to solve equation (C), but it is even messier than the cubic formula. There is no formula for solving the quintic equation (D), nor are there formulas for equations with miscellaneous functions in them such as equation (E). Therefore, instead of depending on formulas, let us write a program which finds approximate solutions for all of these cases.

To use Newton's method, a method which gets approximate solutions to any algebraic equation handily, there are several concepts to note. The first is that to solve the equation

$$x^2 - 8x + 14 = 0$$

is the same as looking at the graph of

$$y = x^2 - 8x + 14$$

and asking for what values of x is y equal to zero, or, what is the same, asking for x-coordinates of the points where the graph crosses the X-axis. A graph of this function is shown in Fig. 6.13. The objects of our search are the x-coordinates of the points R and L. These are the solutions to our equation. We will concentrate on finding point R.

Iterative Methods   Newton's method works by taking a guess at the answer and then using that guess and other data to calculate a second, improved guess. Then this second guess is used in the same way to calculate a third guess. Fourth, fifth, and following guesses are generated, each guess a better approximation of the answer than the previous one, until at a certain point the most recent guess is close enough to serve your purposes. This method of approximating an answer is called the *iterative method* or *iterative process*. A flowchart for iterative processes is shown in Fig. 6.14.

As a straightforward example of an iterative method, here is an algorithm to find the square root of a number N by successive guesses. (This is

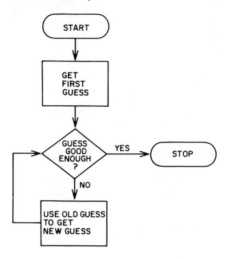

Fig. 6.14   Flowchart for an iterative method

often called Newton's method for finding square roots.) Take a guess, g, as the square root. Then calculate

$$(g + N/g)/2$$

This number will be closer to the true square root; it is your next guess. Repeat the process as long as necessary to get an answer good enough for your purposes. As an example, if you want to find the square root of 67 by this method, the first guess might be 8. This should be close, because $8^2 = 64$ and 64 is close to 67. Then,

g = 8   N/g = 8.375   N/g + g = 16.375   (N/g + g)/2 = 8.1875

Since $(8.1875)^2 = 67.03516$, 8.1875 is closer to the square root than was the original guess. Now use 8.1875 as a guess and repeat the process:

g = 8.1875   N/g = 8.18320   N/g + g = 16.37070   (N/g + g)/2 = 8.185353

If 8.185353 isn't close enough (the correct answer is 8.18535277...), we can repeat the process again and get

g = 8.185353   N/g = 8.185352   N/g + g = 16.37070   (N/g + g)/2 = 8.18535277...

Our guesses close in on the square root of 67, and quite soon our answer is as close as the computer is accurate.

A Curve Is Almost a Line   Newton's method for finding the zeros of a function is an iterative process, but it generates new guesses from old in a more complicated manner than the square root algorithm does. Examine the exploded

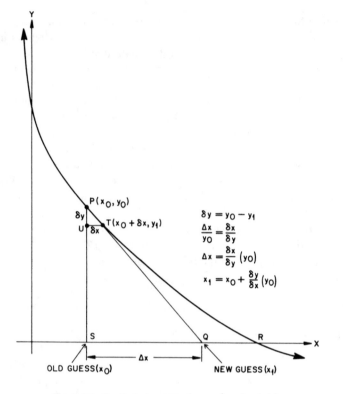

Within the figure:

$P(x_0, y_0)$

δy

$U \, | \, \delta x$ $T(x_0 + \delta x, y_1)$

$\delta y = y_0 - y_1$

$\dfrac{\Delta x}{y_0} = \dfrac{\delta x}{\delta y}$

$\Delta x = \dfrac{\delta x}{\delta y}(y_0)$

$x_1 = x_0 + \dfrac{\delta y}{\delta x}(y_0)$

S   Q   R   X

Δx

OLD GUESS(x_0) NEW GUESS(x_1)

Fig. 6.15   Exploded graph of $y = x^2 - 8x + 14$

picture of our function $y = x^2 - 8x + 14$ in Fig. 6.15, and suppose that our first guess for the point where the graph crosses the x-axis is at S. This guess is way off, but the idea is to use this poor guess to get a better one. If x_0 is the x-coordinate of S, the computer can plug x_0 into the function formula

$$y = x^2 - 8x + 14$$

to find the y-coordinate of P, the point above S on the curve. Call this coordinate y_0. Since y_0 is not zero, the computer knows that x_0 is not the x-coordinate of the point R that it is trying to find. To find a better guess, the computer assumes that the graph of the function is a straight line through P and through T, another point close to P on the curve. The computer finds where this line crosses the X-axis and assumes that this spot is somewhere close to where the curve crosses the X-axis. On the face of it, this seems like a ridiculous idea, but in practice, it works well because short sections of curves don't have a chance to bend much away from a straight line.

The computer takes this step because finding where this line crosses the X-axis is relatively easy, as will be discussed below. First the computer finds the point on the curve close to P. Call it T. (Readers who know calculus may recognize what follows as a way to have the computer calculate an approximate tangent line to the curve.) To get T, the machine adds some arbitrary small number, call it δx, to x_0. For example, δx might be .1, but whatever it may be, we decide what it is ahead of time and it remains constant. The x-coordinate of point T is x_0 + δx, and the computer can use the function formula to find the y coordinate of T, which we will call y_1. The coordinates of the point T are then $(x_0 + δx, y_1)$. If we draw a line through the points P and T, it will go in very much the same direction as the curve for at least a short way.

Since this line is a good approximation of the curve for a short distance, the computer assumes that where the line crosses the x-axis at Q is close to where the curve crosses at R. Since it is certainly a better approximation than was S, the computer calculates the x-coordinate of Q by calculating distance Δx and then adding Δx to the x-coordinate of S. To find Δx, note that the computer knows the length of $\overline{PS}$ (it is the y-coordinate of P) and the length δx (a small number which we picked arbitrarily), and that it can calculate the length δy (it is the difference of the y-coordinates of P and T). Since triangles PUT and PSQ are similar triangles (remember your geometry?), this ratio holds:

$$\frac{\Delta x}{y_0} = \frac{δx}{δy}$$

Solving for Δx by multiplying both sides by y_0, we get

$$\Delta x = \frac{δx * y_0}{δy}$$

Since we know the three quantities on the right hand side of this equation, we can calculate Δx. The x-coordinate of Q is $x_0 + \Delta x$.

We take the x-coordinate of Q as our new guess and repeat the entire process (see Fig. 6.16). We find points A and B as we found P and T, draw a new line, find another Δx, and find another point, M. Using M, we find the point N similarly. We can continue in the same manner indefinitely.

As an example of the process, further consider

$$y = x^2 - 8x + 14$$

and suppose that 1.5 is our first guess. Let us assume that δx is .1. The point S is (1.5,0). We calculate the y-coordinate of P using the formula $y = x^2 - 8x + 14$ and find that point P is (1.5,4.25). We move δx to the right, and the x-coordinate of point T is therefore 1.6. We find that the y-coordinate of point T is 3.76, and therefore T is (1.6,3.76). Now we have

$$y_0 = 4.25$$
$$y_1 = 3.76$$

and

$$δy = y_0 - y_1 = .49$$

Because we picked it to be so,

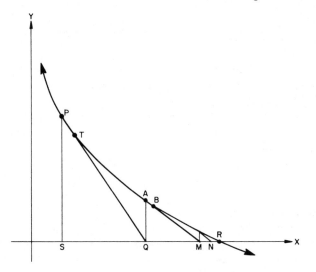

Fig. 6.16   Finding repeated guesses by Newton's method

$$\delta x = .1$$

Therefore,

$$\Delta x = \frac{\delta x * y_0}{\delta y} = \frac{.1 * 4.25}{.49} = .86735$$

This means that the x-coordinate of the point Q, the new guess, is

$$x_0 + \Delta x = 1.5 + .86735 = 2.36735$$

We repeat the process to find point M (Fig. 6.15). The point coordinates and calculations are as follows: Point A is (2.36735,0.66556) and point B is (2.46736,0.34902). Moreover,

$$\delta y = 0.31654$$

$$\Delta x = \frac{.1 * .66556}{.31654} = .21026$$

The x-coordinate of point M is therefore

$$2.36735 + .21026 = 2.57761$$

Continuing the process, the x-coordinate of N turns out to be 2.58541. Our guesses at the answer have been 1.5, 2.3675, 2.57761, and 2.58541, respectively. They are getting closer to one another and closer to the answer itself. The y-coordinates corresponding to the above x-coordinates are 4.25,.66556,.023193, and .009561, which are rapidly approaching zero. The actual answer to this problem is (from the quadratic formula) 2.585786.

Starting and Quitting   Newton's method must be started with an initial guess. One sensible method of getting a first guess is to have the user input one. A method of having the computer take the first guess is the following. Assuming that there are no solutions of the equation less than −100 or greater than 100 (or some other limits that seem reasonable), the computer evaluates the function at each of the integers between these limits. When the resulting y-coordinates change sign between two integers, then the function has crossed the axis some-where in between the last integer and this one. We therefore use the most recent integer as a first guess.

Another method, perhaps better, is to evaluate the function at each of the integers from −100 to 100, and wherever the y-coordinate is close to zero, say is less than 3 and greater than −3, use that integer as a first guess. The reader is encouraged to try both methods and compare.

After the computer gets its first guess for Newton's method, the sub-routine can then calculate an infinite string of subsequent guesses. We must provide some critereon for quitting. Please note first that no matter what else you do, you *must* have the computer stop after some maximum number of calculated guesses, although this number could be large. This precaution is necessary because if the first guess is bad enough, the computer's subsequent guesses may get no better. They may bounce around forever in an area in which the function does not cross the axis. Sensible points at which to stop the computer—in addition to just counting the number of guesses (which is inefficient)—are as follows:

1. If the y values are getting close to zero. ABS(Y) on your most recent guess is less than, say, .0001.
2. If the x values of the guesses are getting close to each other. Δx is getting small, in other words.

A subroutine to handle Newton's method is shown at the right. The variables of this subroutine are defined as follows:

$$D = \delta x$$
$$G0 = \text{old guess}$$
$$G1 = \text{new guess}$$
$$D1 = \Delta x$$
$$C = \text{number of guesses taken (when } C = 25 \text{, we give up)}$$
$$F = 0 \text{ if we gave up without finding a good answer}$$
$$F = 1 \text{ if we did find an answer}$$

The variables X0, X1, Y0, and Y1 are as described in the text and diagrams, and FNA is the function whose zeros are being found.

```
1000 REM ***********************************************
1001 REM *** THIS SUBROUTINE USES NEWTON'S METHOD TO FIND ***
1002 REM *** THE ZERO OF FUNCTION FNA GIVEN A FIRST GUESS ***
1003 REM *** G1.                                          ***
1004 REM ***********************************************
1005 REM
1006 REM
1010 LET C = 0
1020 LET D1 = 1
1030 REM *** LOOP TO FIND GUESSES ***
1035    REM
1036    REM *** DECIDE IF IT IS TIME TO STOP ***
1037    REM
1040    LET Y0 = FNA(G1)
1050    IF C <= 25 THEN 1090
1060       REM *** TOO MANY GUESSES ***
1070       LET F = 0
1080       GOTO 1300
1090    IF ABS(Y0) > .0001 THEN 1130
1100       REM *** ANSWER IS CLOSE ***
1110       LET F = 1
1120       GOTO 1300
1130    IF ABS(D1) > .001 THEN 1170
1140       REM *** ANSWER IS CLOSE ***
1150       LET F = 1
1160       GOTO 1300
1170    REM
1180    REM
1190    REM *** FIND NEW GUESS ***
1120    REM
1210    LET X1 = G1 + D
1220    LET G0 = G1
1230    LET Y1 = FNA(X1)
1240    LET D2 = Y0 - Y1
1250    LET D1 = D * Y0 / D2
1260    LET G1 = G0 + D1
1270    LET C = C + 1
1280 GOTO 1030
1300 RETURN
```

The program shown on the next page illustrates some of these possibilities.

Exercises

1. Write the program to find square roots. Either have the user input a first guess or else always use the number one as a first guess. Compare your results with the SQR function on the computer. How many guesses does it take before the method gives an answer within .001 of the true root?
2. Write a program that uses Newton's method to find the roots of the equations mentioned at the beginning of this section.
3. Do the following:
   (a) There are certain obnoxious functions for which checking whether

```
4     REM *************************************************
5     REM *** PROGRAM TO FIND SOL'NS TO EQUATIONS WITH ***
6     REM *** NEWTON'S METHOD                           ***
7     REM *************************************************
8     REM
10    REM *** THE FUNCTION IS: ***
30    DEF FNA(X) = .. .. .. ..
40    REM
50    REM
60    PRINT "THE ZEROS OF THE FUNCTIONS ARE:"
70    FOR X = - 100 TO 100
80      LET Y = FNA(X)
90      IF ABS(Y) > 3 THEN 140
100       LET G1 = X
110       GOSUB 1000
120       IF F = 0 THEN 140
130         PRINT G1
140    NEXT X
150    END
160    REM
170    REM *************************************************
1000  REM
1001  REM *** NEWTON'S METHOD SUBROUTINE ***
1006  REM
1010  LET C = 0
1020  LET D1 = 1
1030  REM *** LOOP TO FIND GUESSES ***
1035      REM
1036      REM *** DECIDE IF IT IS TIME TO STOP ***
1037      REM
1040      LET Y0 = FNA(G1)
1050      IF C <= 25 THEN 1090
1060        REM *** TOO MANY GUESSES ***
1070        LET F = 0
1080        GOTO 1300
1090      IF ABS(Y0) > .0001 THEN 1130
1100        REM *** ANSWER IS CLOSE ***
1110        LET F = 1
1120        GOTO 1300
1130      IF ABS(D1) > .001 THEN 1170
1140        REM *** ANSWER IS CLOSE ***
1150        LET F = 1
1160        GOTO 1300
1170      REM
1180      REM
1190      REM *** FIND NEW GUESS ***
1120      REM
1210      LET X1 = G1 + D
1220      LET G0 = G1
1230      LET Y1 = FNA(X1)
1240      LET D2 = Y0 - Y1
1250      LET D1 = D * Y0 / D2
1260      LET G1 = G0 + D1
1270      LET C = C + 1
1280  GOTO 1030
1300  RETURN
```

the sign of the y-coordinate has changed will not find guesses close to all of the zeros. Describe these functions.

(b)   A different collection of obnoxious functions will not succumb to the trick of guessing values where the y-coordinates are less than 3. Describe these functions.

(c)   Suppose that you are using both methods of getting first guesses. If there is a change of sign, *or* if the absolute value of y is less than 3, you use that as a first guess. Functions must be really troublesome to evade both of these tests, but they can do it. Draw a picture of one that does.

4. Devise methods of finding the first guesses for the functions in exercise 3.

5. The methods suggested for taking the first guess have overkill in the sense that the computer may often find the same answer from several different initial guesses. Try to reduce this as much as possible to make the program more efficient. Your improvement should come in two phases.

First the computer should never print the same answer more than once, even if it finds it several times.

Second, the computer should avoid calling the subroutine at all when it appears that the proposed first guess will yield a zero that the computer has already found.

6.5   Simulating Probability Problems with the RND Function

Suppose that you want to answer this question: If you flip ten coins, what are the chances that you will flip eight or more heads? You could look up the answer to the question in a table. You could calculate the answer if you know something about binomial distribution probabilities, although you would probably use tables and a calculator to help out. It might, however, be interesting to get an experimental answer to the question by flipping ten coins, seeing if you get eight or more heads, and repeating the procedure a hundred times. On how many of the one hundred trials did you get eight or more heads out of ten coins? This number would be a good approximation of the answer, but it requires flipping a thousand coins, a task which might take you several hours.

To save these hours of coin flipping, spend several hours writing a computer program to flip coins for you instead. Such a program will get you the results while relieving your fingers from flipping duty. Now computers are not noted for the manual dexterity necessary for flipping coins, but they can do this experiment using random numbers. The random number generator returns random numbers between 0 and 1, and these numbers are scattered evenly across the interval.* So, for example, in the long run, half of the random numbers

*Random number generators on computers are in actuality "pseudorandom." Although the numbers are apparently random and can be used for most applications, they are actually calculated by a set formula, often based on the last random number. An example is: Take the previous random number, add 3.14159, take the fifth power of the sum, and take the fractional part of this result to get a new random number.

should turn out to be less than .5, and half greater. A tossed coin behaves in the same manner: In the long run, heads can be expected about half the time, and tails the other half. To simulate a toss of a coin, the computer gets a random number from the random number function. If the random number is less than .5, the computer has tossed a tail, but if it is greater than or equal to .5, the computer has tossed a head.* The following subroutine has the computer "toss ten coins" (one at a time) and count the number of heads it gets:

```
300 REM *** THIS SUBROUTINE TOSSES TEN COINS ***
301 REM *** AND COUNTS HEADS                    ***
302 REM
310 LET H = 0
320 FOR I = 1 TO 10
330     IF RND(0) < .5 THEN 350
340        LET H = H + 1
350 NEXT I
360 RETURN
```

H is initially zero. It is incremented when a head is flipped but left alone when a tail is flipped. At the end of the loop, H contains the number of heads the computer has tossed in ten tries.

To do the experiment at hand, the computer must repeat the above procedure a hundred times, keeping track of the results. We will do a little more than the problem requires and keep track of the number of trials in which each number of heads from zero to ten occurs. To do this, we create a ten-space array X. In X(4), for example, we keep track of the number of times that the computer flipped four heads in ten coins. If the machine goes through the loop above, and H ends up as four, then ten coins turned up four heads. Therefore, the computer adds one to X(4). In all cases, it adds one to X(H) after it comes out of the loop. Adding one to X(H) represents that once again H is the number of heads that came up. The program at the top of the next page tries the ten-coin experiment one hundred times and keeps track of the results. Statements 10 to 40 set the X(I) to zero because the computer has done no coin tossing yet. After the computer flips ten coins, statement 70 stores the fact that it has flipped H heads on this experiment. The ten-coin experiment is tried one hundred times in the loop from 50 to 80.

Printing Results   We must tack statements onto the same program to print out the results of the experiment. One method would be to print a table:

```
90  FOR I = 0 TO 10
100     PRINT I, X(I)
110 NEXT I
120 END
```

A possible output might be the following table, in which the column at the right is the number of occasions on which the number of heads given in the left column came up:

---

*The "extra" number .5 in the range for heads makes no difference.

```
4    REM *********************************************************
5    REM *** PROGRAM TO FIND OUT LIKELIHOOD OF VARIOUS ***
6    REM *** NUMBERS OF HEAD OUT OF TEN COINS           ***
7    REM *********************************************************
8    REM
9    REM
10   DIM X(10)
20   FOR I = 0 TO 10
30      LET X(I) = 0
40   NEXT I
45   REM
46   REM
50   FOR J = 1 TO 100
60      GOSUB 300
70      LET X(H) = X(H) + 1
80   NEXT J
90   END
100  REM
110  REM *********************************************************
120  REM
300  REM *** THIS SUBROUTINE TOSSES TEN COINS ***
301  REM *** AND COUNTS HEADS                  ***
302  REM
310  LET H = 0
320  FOR I = 1 TO 10
330     IF RND(0) < .5 THEN 350
340        LET H = H + 1
350  NEXT I
360  RETURN
```

```
0          0
1          1
2          3
3          17
4          24
5          28
6          13
7          11
8          1
9          2
10         0
```

A more interesting output can be created by having the computer print a *histogram* (bar graph) of the same results such as the one shown below:

```
0
1          X
2          XXX
3          XXXXXXXXXXXXXXXXX
4          XXXXXXXXXXXXXXXXXXXXXXXX
5          XXXXXXXXXXXXXXXXXXXXXXXXXXXX
6          XXXXXXXXXXXXX
7          XXXXXXXXXXX
8          X
9          XX
10
```

A program fragment to produce such a histogram is shown below:

```
90   FOR I = 0 TO 10
100    PRINT I,
110    FOR J = 1 TO X(I)
120      PRINT "X";
130    NEXT J
140    PRINT
150  NEXT I
160  END
```

The loop from 110 to 130 prints an X in row I for each of the times we got I heads out of ten coins. In the histogram, row four has 24 X's in it, indicating that on 24 occasions four heads came up out of ten tries. This more graphic output is easier to comprehend quickly.

Properties of RND   The random number function distributes numbers evenly across the interval from 0 to 1 in the long run. That means, as was previously mentioned, that the probability of getting a random number less than .5 is .5. It also means that the probability of getting a number less than .1 is .1 and that the probability of getting a number less than .3479 is .3479. The length of the interval between .408 and .679 is .271. Therefore, the probability is .271 that a random number will fall in that interval, and you can expect about 271 out of the next thousand random numbers to be in that interval.

In doing random number simulations, the probability of the real world event and the probability of the random number representing that event must be the same. For example, .5 is the probability both of tossing a head and of getting a random number greater than .5. Hence, the event of a random number greater than .5 accurately simulates the event of getting a head on a tossed coin. We could also have said that when the random number is between .3 and .8, the coin is a head, since the chance of a random number falling within this interval is again .5, but such an interval, of course, is far less convenient. The chance of getting a 3 on the roll of one die is 1/6, or, in decimal form, .166666. We could say, therefore, that we have rolled a 3 whenever a random number comes up that is less than .166666.

The formula,

$$INT(N * RND(0)) + 1$$

generates random integers between K and $K + N - 1$, inclusive, with equal frequency. To see why the frequencies are equal, consider the special case,

$$INT(4 * RND(0)) + 1$$

which gives us the integers 1 to 4. The number 1 comes out of the formula when the random number is between 0 and .25. Four times a number between 0 and .25 gives a number between 0 and 1. The integer part of that result is 0, and 1 comes out of the formula. If the random number is between .25 and .50, then multiplied four times it becomes a number between 1 and 2, the integer part of which is 1, and 2 is the result. Similarly, 3 and 4 correspond to the intervals from .50 to .75 and from .75 to 1, respectively. Since each of the numbers 1 to 4 comes from an interval of length .25, each has a 25 percent chance of occurring.

Two warnings: A pair of dice give a number between two and twelve. However, you cannot use the formula

$$INT(11*RND(0))+2$$

because it will give you the numbers 2 to 12 with equal frequency, whereas dice do *not* give you the numbers 2 to 12 with equal frequency. The chances of getting a 7, for example, are better than 16 percent, whereas the chances of getting a 2 are less than 3 percent. To simulate a pair of dice, throw the first one (you can use the formula

$$INT(6*RND(0))+1$$

because the odds of the numbers from 1 to 6 are all equal), then throw the second one, and finally add the two.

Second warning: Adding random numbers does not yield the results your intuition might lead you to expect. The statement,

25 LET X = RND(0) + RND(0)

sets X to a number between 0 and 2, but X does *not* have equal likelihood of being anywhere in the interval. It is much more likely to be towards the center of the interval.* This applies even more strongly to

35 LET Y = RND(0) + RND(0) + RND(0) + RND(0)

which sets Y close to the number two too often. However,

45 LET Z = 4 * RND(0)

distributes Z evenly across the interval 0 to 4. The distinction is that in statement 45, the random number function is called only once, but in statements 25 and 35, it is called more than once.

The Drunkard's Walk   Another problem in probability is the problem of the Drunkard's Walk. The drunkard starts at a lamppost in the center of an open city square and walks randomly (a notion that must be defined). What is the likelihood that the drunkard will be any given distance from the post after a given number of steps? (Being drunk, he is as likely to walk toward the post as away from it.)

To do this problem, we must make assumptions about the meaning of walking randomly, assumptions that you are invited to alter if you try the problem. In what follows, assume that the drunkard walks directly north, south, east, or west, and that he takes some integral number of steps of equal length in one direction before turning. Assume that after each step, the probability of his

---

*Half the length of the interval lies between .5 and 1.5, but X falls in that interval three-fourths of the time.

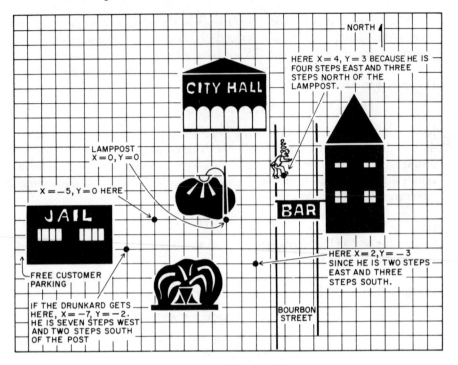

Fig. 6.17   The Drunkard's Walk

turning is .3, and therefore that the probability of his continuing in the same direction is .7. Also assume that when he turns, he turns ninety degrees one way or the other. After 25 steps, we will check to see how far he is from the lamppost. As before, we then repeat the process 100 times for our final result.

The variables X and Y keep track of the drunkard's present position. They are his x and y coordinates if you consider the square he is walking in to be a coordinate plane with the lamppost at the origin. The variable X indicates the drunkard's distance east or west of the lamppost. If X is, say, positive 5, the drunkard is five steps to the east (and an indeterminate number of steps north or south). If X is negative 7, then the drunkard is seven steps to the west of the lamppost. The variable Y similarly contains the drunkard's distance north or south of the lamppost (see Fig. 6.17). To move the drunkard one step to the east, we add 1 to X; to move him one step south, we subtract 1 from Y; and so forth.

The variables D and E indicate the direction in which the drunkard is walking, as defined by the following table:

Direction	D =	E =
North	0	1
South	0	−1
East	1	1
West	1	−1

We set X and Y to 0 (the location of the lamppost, and the initial location of the drunkard), pick an initial direction by picking D and E, and the drunkard starts walking. The variable S counts the number of steps taken. After each step, we decide whether or not the drunkard should turn. If the random number chosen is greater than .3 (a .7 probability), then he continues in the same direction. Otherwise, he changes directions. The subroutine is shown below:

```
1000 REM *** THE DRUNKARD TAKES 25 STEPS ***
1005 REM
1010 LET X = 0
1020 LET Y = 0
1030 LET D = INT(2*RND(0))
1040 LET E = SGN(RND(0) - .5)
1050 FOR S = 1 TO 25
1060    IF D = 1 THEN 1070
1065       LET Y = Y + E
1066       GOTO 1080
1070    REM
1075       LET X = X + E
1080    IF RND(0) > .3 THEN 1110
1090       LET D = ABS(D - 1)
1100       LET E = SGN(RND(0) - .5)
1110 NEXT S
```

In changing the directions, statement 1090 changes D from 0 to 1 or from 1 to 0 to insure that if the drunkard were walking north or south, he will now be walking east or west, or conversely. Statement 1100 sets E randomly to either -1 or $+1$. At the end of 25 steps, the drunkard will be at the location denoted by the variables X and Y. We can calculate his distance to the lamppost using the distance formula:

$$D = \sqrt{X^2 + Y^2}$$

We include this subroutine in a loop and try the walk a hundred times, storing the results in an array. The program is shown on the next page.

Array W serves the same purpose that array X did in the previous example. W(3) is the number of times that the drunkard's final straight-line distance from the lamppost was between 3 and 4 steps. We can arrange to print out the results as before.

A flowchart for the Drunkard's Walk is given in Fig. 6.18.

The Four Suits Pick a card from a standard deck, look at its suit, and return it to the deck. Then pick another card. Repeat this procedure until you have picked at least one card from each suit. How many cards does it take on the average to get a complete collection of the suits? To simulate this problem, the central loop in a program must pick cards repeatedly until it has picked one from each suit. Number the suits as follows:

$$
\begin{array}{ll}
1 = \text{clubs} & 3 = \text{hearts} \\
2 = \text{diamonds} & 4 = \text{spades}
\end{array}
$$

```
4     REM *********************************************
5     REM *** THIS PROGRAM TRIES THE DRUNKARDS WALK ***
6     REM *** 100 TIMES                             ***
7     REM *********************************************
8     REM
9     REM
10    DIM W(25)
20    FOR I = 0 TO 25
30      LET W(I) = 0
40    NEXT I
50    FOR J = 0 TO 100
60      GOSUB 1000
70      LET L = SQR(X*X + Y*Y)
80      LET L = INT(L)
90      LET W(L) = W(L) + 1
100   NEXT J
110   END
120   REM *********************************************
130   REM
1000  REM *** THE DRUNKARD TAKES 25 STEPS ***
1005  REM
1010  LET X = 0
1020  LET Y = 0
1030  LET D = INT(2*RND(0))
1040  LET E = SGN(RND(0) - .5)
1050  FOR S = 1 TO 25
1060    IF D = 1 THEN 1070
1065      LET Y = Y + E
1066      GOTO 1080
1070    REM
1075      LET X = X + E
1080    IF RND(0) > .3 THEN 1110
1090      LET D = ABS(D - 1)
1100      LET E = SGN(RND(0) - .5)
1110  NEXT S
1120  RETURN
```

A four-space array S keeps track of what suits the computer has picked. For example, S(3) is 0 until the computer picks a heart; then it is changed to a 1. The variable T keeps track of the number of different suits so far chosen. When T equals 4, the process is finished. The computer picks a random number from 1 to 4 to simulate choosing a card of one of the suits.* Since we are replacing the chosen cards in the deck, the chances of picking any given suit remain equal, no matter what cards have been picked. The subroutine is shown at the bottom of the opposite page.

It is left to you to write a program to repeat the subroutine a hundred times and keep the results in some array. Note that when you get out of the subroutine, since C in theory may be any size, you may want the statement

```
IF C > 50 THEN C = 50
```

so that the last element of your array will be the number of times that it took fifty *or more* cards to get a complete set of suits. This event is highly unlikely, in any case.

*Note that each of the numbers 1 to 4 is equally likely.

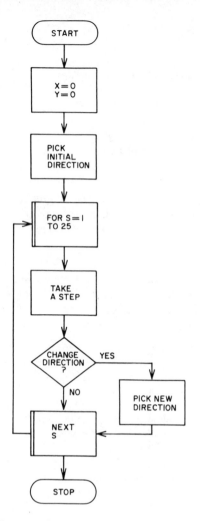

Fig. 6.18 Flowchart for the Drunkard's Walk

```
1000 REM *** PICK CARDS UNTIL ONE OF EACH SUIT ***
1001 REM *** IS DRAWN                           ***
1002 REM
1010 LET C = 0
1020 FOR I = 1 TO 4
1030    LET S(I) = 0
1040 NEXT I
1050 LET T = 0
1060 REM *** LOOP TO PICK CARDS ***
1065    LET C = C + 1
1070    LET R = 4 * INT(RND(0)) + 1
1080    IF S(R) = 1 THEN 1120
1090      LET S(R) = 1
1100      LET T = T + 1
1110      IF T = 4 THEN 1130
1120 GOTO 1060
1130 RETURN
```

Exercises

Answer the questions using a computer simulation.

1. Complete the four suits program.
2. Home-run Harry has a batting average of .325. Find how likely it is that he will get five hits in the next six times at bat.
3. What are the odds of getting 15 or better on a roll of three dice?
4. There are 50 different rugby players on bubblegum cards, and they are distributed randomly in packages of bubblegum. How many packages of bubblegum are you likely to have to buy in order to get a complete set of cards?
5. Suppose that the random walker has one more for the road and consequently has a .4 chance of turning instead of .3 at every step. How does this difference affect the results?
6. Suppose that there is a fountain in the random walker's square which is four steps to the east and extends from four steps north to four steps south of the pole (see illustration). How many steps will it usually take before the walker falls into the fountain? Consider him to have fallen in if he is on the edge.

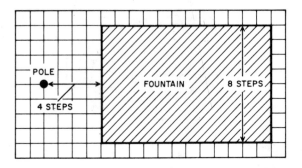

7. The definition of random walking given in the text is not the only possible one. Whether a drunkard takes steps of equal length, for example, is open to discussion. Whether he walks in one of only four directions is not clear either, but you must know some trigonometry to make this alteration. Write a new definition for walking randomly and rewrite the drunkard's walk subroutine to conform to it.
8. Suppose that when you play the suits game, you give up in disgust if you ever pick four of one particular suit before you have completed your collection. How likely is it that you will finish your collection before you give up?
9. Try this old chestnut. What is the chance that two out of 25 random people have the same birthday? Pick 25 random days of the year and see. What about 23 people? Also 40 people?
10. You have two urns filled with 100 balls. The first urn has 100 white balls, and the second has 100 black balls. You take a ball from each urn and exchange them. Then you make 99 more exchanges for a total of 100 exchanges. How many white balls are likely to be in the second urn?

11. Do the following:
   (a) Set Y to RND(0) + RND(0) + ... + RND(0) for a total of ten terms (use a FOR-NEXT loop). Set Z equal to INT(Y). How often does Z take on each of the values from 0 to 9 in the long run? Do the integers occur with equal frequency? Try setting Z to INT(10*RND(0)) instead. Now what?
   (b) Set W to RND(0) * RND(0). How often is W less than .1? Less than .2? Than .5?

6.6   Simulating Physics Problems

An airplane lands at the end of a runway at a speed of 50 meters per second (about a hundred miles per hour), and the pilot slams on the brakes. A wire at the end of the runway can catch and stop the plane if necessary, but the pilot would rather not run into this wire at a speed greater than 10 meters per second. How long need the runway be to give the brakes a chance to slow the airplane to this speed?

To solve this problem, let's first review a few formulas from physics.

Velocity (sometimes called speed or rate) is how fast you are moving. Automobile speedometers in this country measure velocity in miles per hour, but to keep our calculations simple, we will use meters per second (m/s). The distance you travel if your velocity is constant equals your velocity times the amount of time you travel:

$$p = v * t$$

where

p = change in position
v = velocity (assumed to be constant)
t = elapsed time

Thus if your velocity is 8 m/s and you travel for 3 seconds, you go 24 meters.

Acceleration is how fast your velocity is changing. It can be positive (speeding up) or negative (slowing down). The relationship between constant acceleration and velocity is the same as that between velocity and position:

$$v = a * t$$

where

v = change in velocity
a = acceleration (assumed to be constant)

Acceleration is measured in meters per second per second (m/s²). If an object accelerates at 6 m/s², then after every second it is going 6 m/s faster than it was going at the beginning of the second. If it starts from rest (velocity = 0 m/s) and has an acceleration of 6 m/s², then it will be going at 6 m/s after 1 second, 12 m/s after 2 seconds, 18 m/s after 3 seconds, and so on. If its velocity is 18 m/s to begin with and it slows down at a rate of 2 m/s² (acceleration of −2), it will take 9 seconds to stop.

Now about the problem of brakes: You need to know that brakes are in some sense more effective the faster you go. In fact, the deceleration they cause is about proportional to the speed of the object they are slowing. After the airplane decelerates to a speed of 25 m/s, for example, the brakes are only slowing it half as rapidly as when it first touched down at 50 m/s. There is some number k (which depends on the weight of the airplane, the size of the brake pads, etc.) by which you can multiply the speed of the airplane to find its deceleration:

$$a = -k * v$$

(The acceleration is negative because the airplane is slowing down.) The number k must be found experimentally in each situation. If k is large, that means that the brakes are good (or that the airplane is small and slows down easily). If k is small, then the pilot had better not try any landings on aircraft carriers.

In the case of the airplane, the two physics formulas cannot be applied directly. They assume that the velocity or the acceleration remains constant for some period of time, an assumption which ceases to hold since the airplane slows down continuously and since the braking (the acceleration), which depends on the speed, is also changing. When the pilot first applies the brakes, he is thrown against his seat belt, but as the plane slows down, the braking effect dies out, and he is thrown forward less. This process is continuous: The airplane slows down, and the braking effect dies a bit. But since there is still some braking, the plane slows still more, reducing the braking more, and so on.

To get around this problem, let's borrow a trick from the calculus to allow us to apply the formulas mentioned to get an approximate result. Assume that

$$k = .1$$

Consider what happens in the first .01 second after the landing: At the beginning of this time interval, the airplane is going 50 m/s and its acceleration is

$$a = -k * v$$

or

$$a = -.1 * 50$$
$$= -5$$

It is therefore slowing down at the rate of 5 m/s². At the end of the interval, the plane is some short distance down the runway, it has slowed down somewhat, and the braking effect is less. But the change in its speed and its acceleration in .01 second is very slight, so slight, in fact, that we can assume that both the speed and acceleration have stayed the same throughout the interval. Since the speed of the airplane has been 50 m/s for .01 second, the distance it has traveled down the runway is

$$p = v * t$$
$$= 50 * .01$$
$$= .5$$

that is, .5 meter. Since the acceleration is -5 m/s², the velocity change is

$$v = a * t$$
$$= -5 * .01$$
$$= -.05$$

that is, a decrease of .05 m/s. Subtracting this figure from the initial velocity of 50 m/s gives us the new velocity:

$$v = 50 - .05 = 49.95 \text{ m/s}$$

We now repeat this process for the next .01-second interval. Assuming that our calculated velocity of 49.95 m/s stays constant, the change in position is as follows:

$$p = 49.95 * .01 = .4995 \text{ m}$$

Adding this figure to the .5 meter that the plane traveled in the first time interval, it has now traveled a distance of

$$.5 + .4995 = .9995 \text{ m}$$

Since its speed is 49.95 m/s, its acceleration is now

$$a = -k * v$$
$$= -.1 * 49.95$$
$$= -4.995 \text{ m/s}^2$$

The change in velocity is thus

$$v = a * t$$
$$= -4.995 * .01$$
$$= -.04995 \text{ m/s}$$

Adding this change to the old velocity, we get the new velocity:

$$v = 49.95 - .04995$$
$$= 49.90005 \text{ m/s}$$

Repeat this process with a third time interval, a fourth, a fifth, and so on, and thus approximate the planes's speed, position, and acceleration.

Programming the Computer   The program fragment at the top of the next page is the translation of the above process into BASIC:

First, P is set to the initial position of the plane on the runway (at the end of the latter, where the position equals zero), and V is set to its velocity at that point (50 m/s). Then for each interval of .01 second, the computer finds the

```
4     REM *** PROGRAM TO CALCULATE LANDING DISTANCE ***
5     LET K = .1
10    LET P = 0
20    LET V = 50
100 FOR T = 0 TO 1 STEP .01
110     LET P1 = V * .01
120     LET P = P + P1
130     LET A = (-1) * K * V
140     LET V1 = A * .01
150     LET V = V + V1
160 NEXT T
```

change in the position of the plane (P1), the new position, the acceleration, the change in velocity (V1), and the new velocity.

Yet another program will print out the plane's position and velocity at the end of each of the first twenty seconds on the runway:

```
4     REM *** PROGRAM TO CALCULATE LANDING DISTANCE ***
5     LET K = .1
10    LET P = 0
20    LET V = 50
30    PRINT "TIME", "POSITION", "VELOCITY"
50    FOR J = 1 TO 20
100     FOR T = 0 TO 1 STEP .01
110         LET P1 = V * .01
120         LET P = P + P1
130         LET A = (-1) * K * V
140         LET V1 = A * .01
150         LET V = V + V1
160     NEXT T
200     PRINT J, P, V
210 NEXT J
```

It is a simple matter to look through the table created by this program to see how far down the runway the plane has traveled when it has slowed to 10 m/s.

Harmonic Oscillators   The same process will approximate the motion of a weight which is attached to a spring and slides back and forth across a slick surface (one example of a harmonic oscillator). The force that a spring exerts is proportional to the distance that it has been stretched or compressed. The acceleration on the weight is therefore the product of some constant k (depending on the strength of the spring and the mass of the weight) and the position of the weight:

$$a = -k * p$$

We can write the same program that we did for the airplane by using this formula for acceleration in statement 130 instead of the other statement. Try a k that equals .9 and set P initially to 3.

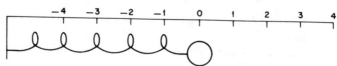

The position of a relaxed spring, in which it neither pushes or pulls (position = 0)

FORCE →

Negative position, in which the velocity is to the left and the spring is pushing to the right (positive acceleration)

← FORCE

Positive position, in which the velocity is to the right and the spring is pulling to the left (negative acceleration)

Fig. 6.19   Keeping signs straight on a harmonic oscillator

The harmonic oscillator can be extremely confusing, since it moves and accelerates in both directions. Correct results can be obtained by following the formulas in the text and by considering motion, acceleration, and position to the right to be positive, and to the left, negative (see Fig. 6.19).

Damped Harmonic Oscillator   The motion of a *damped harmonic oscillator* is calculated in the same way, but with the added assumption that friction is busy slowing everything down. As with airplane brakes, the friction is proportional to the velocity and of course acts in the opposite direction from the velocity. Therefore, the acceleration due to friction is

$$a = -f * v$$

where f is some positive constant. The total acceleration is the sum of the acceleration due to the spring and the acceleration due to friction, as follows:

$$a = -k * p - f * v$$

Use this formula instead of statement 130 in your formula. A good constant to try is f = .3.

Exercises

1. Do the following:
   (a) In the airplane problem, we assumed that there was a constant of braking, k, which was equal to .1. By changing the constant in

statement 5, we can make k anything we want. How much runway length do you need if k is .05? .15? .2? .3?

(b) What is the effect on the runway length if the initial landing velocity is 25? 75? 100?

(c) Suppose that instead of using brakes, the airplane utilizes a drogue parachute attached to the tail to slow it down. The formula for the braking effect of the parachute is

$$a = -.006 * v^2$$

Now how long a runway does the airplane need?

(d) Suppose that the airplane uses both the parachute and the brakes. Then how long a runway does it need? (Add the acceleration of the brakes and of the parachute to get the total acceleration.)

2. A harmonic oscillator is released at a point 3 to the right of center and moves back and forth across its surface. It takes a certain number of seconds, called the *period*, for one cycle back and forth to take place. If k = .9, what is the period? If k = .6? If k = 2? How are the results affected if the oscillator is released at a point only 2 to the right of center instead of 3?

3. Try the damped harmonic oscillator and answer the following: If f is small (very little friction), the oscillator goes back and forth, but its motion dies out eventually. If f is very big (friction great in comparison to the strength of the spring), the oscillator never gets a chance to oscillate but just slides towards the center position and stops. About how big does f have to be for this change to occur?

4. Do the following:

(a) An iron filing flies towards a magnet, and its acceleration is

$$a = -k/p^2$$

where p is the distance from the magnet. Pick a value for k and get a table for the motion of a filing that starts at rest 10 meters from the magnet. What physical measurements does k depend on?

(b) Instead of having the computer print a table of position and velocity values, have it print a diagram of the results which is similar to a histogram. (See the section on probability for an example of a histogram.)

5. When you are landing a rocket on the moon, the acceleration on the rocket is −1.6 m/s² due to the gravity of the moon (where the negative number indicates that you are being accelerated downward). There is also an acceleration due to the engines of the rocket pushing upward. Devise a program which starts the user 1500 meters above the moon heading towards the surface at 150 m/s. The computer should print the altitude and the speed towards the surface at the end of each second and ask the user how much fuel he wants to burn in the next second. The acceleration due to the rocket engines is proportional to the amount of fuel burned. Experiment and select appropriate limits on the speed of impact on the moon that constitutes a "soft" landing, on the total fuel available, and on the rate of fuel consumption.

APPENDIX A
A TABLE OF ASCII CODES

ASCII, the American Standard Code for Information Interchange, is the set of patterns of 1's and 0's used to store characters within a computer and to transmit them from terminal to computer and from computer to terminal. It is used almost universally, although a different code is used for some teletypes.

The table given here shows the bit patterns corresponding to each character and the translations of these patterns from base two into base ten. You will note that there are certain bit patterns for which no characters are supplied. Such patterns correspond to messages interchanged by the terminal and the computer that are of no concern to the user. For example, one bit pattern is used by the computer to turn terminals on and off, and another is used by the terminal to tell the computer that it is on and waiting for data.

Bit pattern	Base ten translation	Corresponding character
0000000	0	Null character; a filler
0000001	1	
0000010	2	
0000011	3	Control C; used to tell the computer to pay attention to you
0000100	4	End of transmission; no more data coming after this character
0000101	5	
0000110	6	
0000111	7	Control G; rings the bell.
0001000	8	Backspace, if the terminal can do it
0001001	9	Advances carriage to next tab stop if terminal has tab stops
0001010	10	Line feed
0001011	11	Advances paper to next vertical tab stop if terminal has vertical tab stops
0001100	12	Advances paper to top of next page; clears screen on video terminals
0001101	13	Carriage return
0001110	14	
0001111	15	

Bit pattern	Base ten translation	Corresponding character
0010000	16	
0010001	17	
0010010	18	
0010011	19	
0010100	20	
0010101	21	
0010110	22	Synchronous idle; makes print head bob up and down once on teletypes
0010111	23	
0011000	24	
0011001	25	
0011010	26	
0011011	27	Escape key
0011100	28	
0011101	29	
0011110	30	
0011111	31	
0100000	32	Space
0100001	33	!
0100010	34	"
0100011	35	#
0100100	36	$
0100101	37	%
0100110	38	&
0100111	39	'
0101000	40	(
0101001	41	)
0101010	42	*
0101011	43	+
0101100	44	,
0101101	45	−
0101110	46	.
0101111	47	/
0110000	48	0
0110001	49	1
0110010	50	2
0110011	51	3
0110100	52	4
0110101	53	5

Bit pattern	Base ten translation	Corresponding character
0110110	54	6
0110111	55	7
0111000	56	8
0111001	57	9
0111010	58	:
0111011	59	;
0111100	60	<
0111101	61	=
0111110	62	>
0111111	63	?
1000000	64	@
1000001	65	A
1000010	66	B
1000011	67	C
1000100	68	D
1000101	69	E
1000110	70	F
1000111	71	G
1001000	72	H
1001001	73	I
1001010	74	J
1001011	75	K
1001100	76	L
1001101	77	M
1001110	78	N
1001111	79	O
1010000	80	P
1010001	81	Q
1010010	82	R
1010011	83	S
1010100	84	T
1010101	85	U
1010110	86	V
1010111	87	W
1011000	88	X
1011001	89	Y
1011010	90	Z
1011011	91	[
1011100	92	\

Bit pattern	Base ten translation	Corresponding character
1011101	93	]
1011110	94	†
1011111	95	— (Underline)
1100000	96	à
1100001	97	a (The first of the small letters printed on terminals that print small letters)
1100010	98	b
1100011	99	c
1100100	100	d
1100101	101	e
1100110	102	f
1100111	103	g
1101000	104	h
1101001	105	i
1101010	106	j
1101011	107	k
1101100	108	l
1101101	109	m
1101110	110	n
1101111	111	o
1110000	112	p
1110001	113	q
1110010	114	r
1110011	115	s
1110100	116	t
1110101	117	u
1110110	118	v
1110111	119	w
1111000	120	x
1111001	121	y
1111010	122	z
1111011	123	{
1111100	124		
1111101	125	}
1111110	126	~
1111111	127	Rubout

APPENDIX B
GLOSSARY

Algorithm A detailed method of solving a problem. An algorithm includes each step that must be taken to solve the problem, including instructions about what to do in various situations that might arise during solution.

Argument A number sent by a program to a function for the function to act on; for example, in SQR(5), 5 is the argument. (*See also* Parameter.)

Array A collection of memory spaces in the computer that are used for storing numbers and that are referenced by a one-letter name followed by a single subscript. (*See also* Matrix.)

ASCII American Standard Code for Information Interchange. The set of patterns of 1's and 0's that are used to store characters in the computer and that are transmitted from the terminal to the computer and back.

Assembler A program that translates other programs from assembly language to machine code. Assembly languages differ from other languages in that any one of its instructions translates into only one machine code instruction.

BCD Binary Coded Decimal. A method of storing numbers in the computer in which each digit in base ten is separately translated into base two and stored.

Bit A single 1 or 0, either written on paper or stored in the circuitry of the computer.

Branch A place in a program or algorithm at which there is a choice of subsequent action; the action is decided by conditions that have arisen during the solution of the problem.

Bubble sort An algorithm for sorting a list of items by repeatedly interchanging adjacent pairs of items in the list.

Bug An error in a program that causes it to break down or give incorrect results. *Debugging* is the frustrating process of trying to find and eliminate bugs.

Call As a noun: a reference to a function or a program statement that transfers control to a subroutine; for example, a reference to SQR or FNY is a call, as is a GOSUB statement. As a verb: to execute a call.

Central memory The part of the computer that stores the programs and data that the computer works on. The fastest and most expensive type of computer memory, central memory is also called *core*.

Central processing unit The part of the computer that performs all operations on data and that controls the function of all other parts of the computer, including memory, teletypes, line printers, etc. The central processing unit is also called the *CPU*.

Code As a noun: a collection of program statements. As a verb: to write programs. Someone engaged in the act of coding is writing the actual computer instructions as opposed to doing anything else involved in programming such as staring at the wall figuring out how to do a problem, debugging, or cursing the computer.

Command   A computer instruction that is to be executed immediately.

Compiler   A program that translates other programs from the language in which they are written into machine code. Each instruction in the language that the compiler starts with may translate into many machine code instructions. (*See also* Interpreter and Assembler.)

Core   The central memory. The term *core* stems from the bygone era during which central memories were built from tiny donut-shaped iron castings called "cores." Cores have been superseded by faster, less bulky technologies. (*See also* Central memory.)

CPU   *See* Central processing unit.

Cycle time   The amount of time it takes the computer to retrieve one word of data from the central memory.

Debug   *See* Bug.

Disc   A memory device that stores numbers by making magnetic markings on a rapidly rotating disc.

Editor   A program whose purpose is to help its user modify other programs or data files stored in the computer.

Element   One of the memory spaces that constitute an array or a matrix.

End-of-file marker   A special symbol in a data file placed immediately after its last data entry to tell the computer that no more entries exist.

End-of-record marker   A special symbol in a data file placed immediately after the last data entry of a record to tell the computer that the next data entry is the first of a new record. (*See* Record.)

Error message   Output from a computer indicating that it doesn't understand what is going on and that it wants you to do something about it. An error message is a symptom of a bug.

Field   A collection of characters in an IMAGE statement indicating where and how the value of a variable should be printed on the line.

File   A collection of data stored in the computer somewhere other than in central memory. (*See* Serial file and Random-access file.)

Flowchart   A diagram depicting how an algorithm is to be carried out. Typically, flowcharts write out the steps of an algorithm in symbolically constructed boxes interconnected by arrows that indicate the order in which the steps are to be performed.

Hardware   The physical elements of a computer: wires, switches, lights, etc. The hardware consists of everything contained in the computer after manufacture but before anybody has programmed it.

Hard-wired   A term describing behavior of the computer (or other device) that is performed by the hardware alone. For example, a computer with a hard-wired multiply routine is one that knows how to multiply without someone programming it to do so.

Hash   To process a string in a way that will yield a number for use in searching a data file. One hashing algorithm might be to add the ASCII code of the first character, two times the ASCII code of the second character, three times the ASCII code of the third character, and so on, in order to find the remainder obtained when the final sum is divided by 17. The file is then searched in the location of the remainder.

High-level language   A language which the computer understands only after a compiler or interpreter has translated it into a more computer-digestible form. Instructions in a high-level language are too complicated for a computer to execute without this kind of help. BASIC is a high level language, as are FORTRAN, COBOL, SNOBOL, and LISP.

Histogram   A diagram depicting the relative frequency of events. For example,

Programs working first time	XXX
Programs working second time	XXXX
Programs working third time	XXXXXXXXXXXX
Programs working tenth time	XXXXXXXXXXXXXXXXXXXXXXXX
Programs never working	XXXXXXXXXX

Increment   As a verb: To increase the value of a variable by some small amount, typically by 1. As a noun: the small amount itself.

Infinite loop   *See* Loop.

Input   As a verb: To enter data or programs into a computer. As a noun: The data being entered in a computer.

Interpreter   A program to translate other programs into machine code. An interpreter differs from an assembler and a compiler in that it does not translate a whole program for the computer to execute but rather translates a single instruction and waits, before it translates the next, for the computer to execute that instruction. (*See also* Compiler and Assembler.)

I/O   Input and Output, the processes and devices involved in transmitting data into or out of the computer.

Iteration variable   A variable used to keep a count of the number of times that the computer has executed a process. The variable in a FOR statement is an iteration variable.

Iterative method/process   A method of solving a problem by repeating a set of steps until the solution or a good approximation of it has been achieved. Hammering a nail is a good example: (1) Pound once. (2) Is the nail flush or bent beyond repair? If so, that nail is done with. If not, go back to step (1) and repeat.

Key   A name given to a record in a date file.

List   A print-out or display of the statements of a program; also called a *listing*.

Long precision   An option offered in some programming languages that allows you to instruct the computer to carry out certain computations with greater accuracy than normal.

Loop   As a noun: a series of instructions so arranged that the computer executes them repeatedly. An *infinite loop* occurs when the programmer has neglected to tell the computer when to stop, thus leaving it to execute the instructions forever. As a verb: to execute a loop.

Machine code   The language that the computer understands without assistance from programs such as assemblers, compilers, and interpreters. Machine code consists entirely of 1's and 0's.

Matrix   A collection of computer memory spaces that are used for storing numbers and that are referenced by a one-letter name followed by two subscripts. (*See also* Array.)

Memory   *See* Central memory, Disc, and Tape drive.

Monitor   A perpetually running program that controls all facets of the computer's operation. The monitor controls what programs are running and when, who is using the computer, how central memory is allocated, and so on. If the monitor breaks down, no work can get done on the computer.

Output   As a verb: To send data out of a computer. As a noun: The data being sent out of a computer.

Overflow   A situation in which either (1) a number has become larger than the computer can handle, or (2) the overall volume of data has exceeded the size of the computer's memory (or the fraction thereof allocated by the monitor).

Parameter   A variable used by a program to communicate information to a function, subroutine, or other piece of code. An argument is an example of a parameter. (*See also* Argument.)

Parse   To hunt through a list, file, or string for one item or letter at a time by starting at the beginning to discover a particular item or letter or to determine the structure of the list, file, or string.

Pass   To transmit information to a function or subroutine, usually by setting the values of parameters prior to a call. (*See also* Return.)

Peripheral device   A piece of equipment attached to the central processing unit for the purpose of inputting or outputting data or for storing data not wanted in the central memory. Every piece of computer hardware is a peripheral device except the central processing unit, central memory, and the switches, lights, nuts, bolts, etc., that attach to the CPU.

Primitive   A fundamental unit of a language used in writing a syntax. (*See* Syntax.)

Procedure   *See* Subroutine.

Program   A sequence of instructions in computer language that the computer remembers and executes. The computer and the programmer hope that the instructions are written so that the computer can understand them. The programmer also hopes that the instructions accurately reflect the algorithm he wants the computer to follow.

Random-access file   A data file structured so that any piece of data may be written or retrieved at any time regardless of its position in the file. The data items in a random-access file are either numbered or named so that the programmer can tell the computer which one to work with. (*See* File and Serial file.)

Record   A subdivision of a file, a record usually contains several pieces of data about one common subject.

Return   (1) To finish a subroutine and resume execution of statements in the main program. (2) To transmit data from a function or subroutine to the main part of a program. *Returning* is the opposite of *passing*. (*See also* Pass.)

Routine   *See* Subroutine.

Scientific notation   A technique for expressing numbers by writing them as the product of a power of 10 and a number between 1 and 10. For example, 3,500,000 equals 3.5×10^6 in scientific notation, and .0000932 equals 9.32×10^{-5}.

Serial file   A data file in which pieces of data can only be accessed one after the other, starting at the beginning of the file. It is often impossible to write on such a file anywhere except at the end. To find an item, you must parse the file. (*See also* Random-access file, File, and Parse.)

Sign bit   A bit in the representation of a number reserved to indicate if the number is positive or negative. Usually, if the bit is 0, the number is positive; if 1, negative.

Software   All the programs of a computer. The monitor, the compiler, the assembler, and any programs you may write are equally part of the software of the computer.

Statement   A single instruction within a program. (*See also* Program.)

String   A sequence of letters stored in the computer. Words and sentences are examples of strings, which may also contain digits and other symbols among the letters. "XYZ%93W" is a possible string.

Subprogram   See Subroutine.

Subroutine   A self-contained piece of a program that does, in effect, a job within a job. A subroutine is sometimes called a *routine*, a *subprogram*, or a *procedure*.

Substring   A contiguous piece of a string. For example, XYZ and YZ%53 are substrings of 57XYZ%53.

Syntax   A formal description of the structure of a language; a grammar.

Tape drive   A memory device that store numbers on magnetic tape.

Time sharing   A method of making one computer serve many users by shifting its attention rapidly from the programs of one user to those of others and back.

Variable   A symbol in a user's program which refers to a particular memory space in the computer.

Word   A subdivision of computer memory. A word is the amount of data that a computer can write to, or fetch from, memory all at once. Word sizes range from just 8 bits up to 48 or more, depending on the computer.

Zero column   The elements of a matrix whose second subscripts are zero. The zero column of matrix C, for example, is comprised of $C(0,0)$, $C(1,0)$, $C(2,0)$, $C(\text{any number}, 0)$.

Zero row   The elements of a matrix whose first subscripts are zero. The zero row or matrix M, for example, is comprised of $M(0,0)$, $M(0,1)$, $M(0, \text{any number})$.

APPENDIX C
A SUMMARY OF BASIC

The following summary is a corrupted syntax of BASIC. It includes explanations of the statements and right and wrong examples of each, the latter being items that a syntax does not contain. Meant as a quick reference source, the first section is optional reading for those who wish to know just what a syntax is and how it works.

Syntaxes

A *syntax* of a language is a description of its structure. A syntax of English, for example, tells you how to assemble nouns, verbs, adverbs, prepositional phrases, and so on, into correct sentences. It does not tell you what the sentences mean, or even whether they mean anything. It only tells you whether your sentences are grammatically correct. Similarly, a syntax of BASIC tells you how to write and recognize correct BASIC statements, but it doesn't tell you what effect the statements will have inside the computer. Needless to say, learning BASIC using only a syntax would be difficult. However, if you already know one version of BASIC, studying the syntax of another version might be a fast way to learn that version since you will probably be able to figure out what the statements do, and the syntax will reveal the little differences between the versions. A complete syntax of any form of BASIC will fit into very few pages.

To see how a syntax works, let us look at the example below, which contains two versions of the LET statement:

LET ⟨numeric identifier⟩ = ⟨expression⟩
LET ⟨string variable⟩ = ⟨string expression⟩

Now consider the statement

LET R = 6 + S

If this is a correct LET statement, it must fit one of the two patterns above. The items in angled brackets in each syntax are called *primitives*. In a correct LET statement, each of the primitives is replaced by an example of that primitive. For example, to make a LET statement in the second pattern above, we would write the word LET, an actual string variable—say X$—an equals sign, and a string expression. If we don't know what a ⟨string variable⟩ or a ⟨string expression⟩ is, we can look them up in the list of primitives at the beginning of the syntax. In the statement,

LET R = 6 + S

R is clearly not a string variable, and therefore, if this is a correct LET statement, it must conform to the first pattern.

The first question, therefore, is whether R is a ⟨numeric identifier⟩. You might suspect that it is, since it does identify a number stored in the computer, but you should nevertheless look in the definitions of primitives, where you would find that a ⟨numeric identifier⟩ is an ⟨identifier⟩ that is not a string variable. The definition of *identifier* includes ⟨variable⟩ and the definition of ⟨variable⟩ includes R. Thus R is a ⟨numeric identifier⟩. The next question is whether 6 + S is an ⟨expression⟩. Clause 3 of the definition of ⟨expression⟩ says that two ⟨expression⟩s with a plus between them constitute an ⟨expression⟩. Thus we must find out if 6 and S are ⟨expression⟩s. With very little research you will find that S is a ⟨numeric identifier⟩, that 6 is a ⟨literal⟩, and hence that both are ⟨expression⟩s. Hence,

LET R = 6 + S

is a valid LET statement.

This procedure may seem tedious, and you may dread deciding whether the statement,

IF (R + 6) * S(9) = X↑4 + 79 THEN 9744

is correct, but there are obvious shortcuts. After all, with the LET statement just discussed, you probably would have asked, "Is R a ⟨numeric identifier⟩? Is 6 + S an ⟨expression⟩?" Then you would have answered yourself, "Obviously," and that would have been that. The meanings of many of the primitives are evident from their names. Their definitions are included only to help in borderline cases.

Most syntaxes of computer languages are quite formal, describing the language exclusively in symbolic terms. They tell the user just what is legal and what is not. The syntax in this Appendix is not that formal. Since it does not cover any specific BASIC version, it cannot draw a sharp line between the allowable and the disallowed. Since the purpose of the heavy dose of symbolic formality evident in most syntaxes is to draw that sharp line, it has been discarded here. In particular, the structures of the statements are sometimes vague but are bolstered by the short descriptions which follow them. In the PRINT statement, for example, it is explained that strings and numbers may be mixed in the list, whereas in a formal syntax, a new primitive meaning "mixed list of strings and numbers" would be carefully defined for the purpose. The discussion of the primitives is likewise informal. An expression is described, for example, as, among other things, "two ⟨expression⟩s with a +, −, *, /, or ↑ between them." In a formal syntax, this definition would probably be replaced by something like

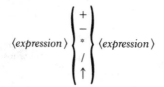

There are just three things which you might find confusing in what follows. First, the primitives ⟨*variable*⟩ and ⟨*expression*⟩ refer only to numeric variables and expressions. There are separate primitives for string variables and expressions. Second, "transfer control" to a statement means to go to that statement and continue execution from there. Third, the "next statement" refers to the one with the next higher number.

A Description of BASIC Functions

Functions are classified below according to whether they return a number, a string, or a matrix. The arguments that a function takes are shown by the argument enclosed in parentheses after the function name:

$$(N)\text{—numeric argument}$$
$$(S\$)\text{—string argument}$$
$$(M)\text{—matrix argument}$$

A function that has no argument shown takes no argument.

1. *Functions returning numeric values:*

ABS(N)	The absolute value
ASC(S$)	The ASCII code of the first character
EXP(N)	e raised to the power
INT(N)	The largest integer less than or equal to the argument
LOG(N)	The common (base 10) logarithm (*Note:* On some systems, this is the natural, or base e, logarithm)
LEN(S$)	The number of characters
LN(N)	The natural (base e) logarithm
NUM(S$)	The numeric value of the number represented by the argument
RND	Returns a different random number between zero and one each time it is called. (*Note:* Some RND functions must be sent a numeric argument, which they then ignore)
SQR(N)	The square root

Trigonometric functions (Note: The arguments must be expressed in radians)

SIN(N)
COS(N)
TAN(N)
SEC(N)
CSC(N)
CTN(N)
ATN(N)   (The arctangent)

2. *Functions returning string values:*

CHR(N)	A one character string whose ASCII code is the argument
LEFT(S$,N)	A substring of the string argument consisting of as many of the left-most characters as indicated by the numeric argument

MID(S$,N,N)	A substring of the string argument starting at the character indicated by the first numeric argument, with length indicated by the second numeric argument
RIGHT(S$,N)	A substring of the string argument consisting of as many of the right-most characters as indicated by the numeric argument
STR(N)	A string representing the number that is the value of the argument

3. *Functions returning matrix values:*

CON	A matrix filled with 1's
IDN	An identity matrix
INV(M)	The inverse
TRN(M)	The transpose
ZER	A matrix filled with 0's

Definition of Primitives

⟨array variable⟩	A single letter denoting an array: A, B, C, D, . . . , Y, and Z can be used as array variables.
⟨condition⟩	(1) Two ⟨expression⟩s separated by one of =, <, >, >=, <=, <> (2) Two ⟨string expression⟩s separated by one of =, <, >, <=, >=, <>
⟨expression⟩	(1) A ⟨literal⟩ (2) A ⟨numeric identifier⟩ (3) Two ⟨expression⟩s with +, −, *, /, or ↑ between them (4) an ⟨expression⟩ enclosed in parentheses (5) A function which returns a numeric value
⟨field⟩	(1) A group of contiguous number signs (#) (2) A group of contiguous number signs with one embedded decimal point (.) (3) a ⟨field⟩ of type (1) or (2) followed by four exclamation points (!!!!)
⟨file name⟩	A collection of letters, characters, and digits identifying a computer file, this collection being restricted by every system in its own way.
⟨file number⟩	Either a number sign (#) followed by an integer between 1 and 7 or an integer between 1 and 7 enclosed in parentheses, depending on the system. Possible file numbers are #1, #2, #3, #4, #5, #6, #7, (1), (2), (3), (4), (5), (6), and (7).
⟨function name⟩	The two letters FN followed by a third letter. The func-

tion names are FNA, FNB, FNC, . . . , FNY, and FNZ.

⟨*identifier*⟩

(1) A ⟨variable⟩
(2) A ⟨string variable⟩
(3) An ⟨array variable⟩ followed by an ⟨integer⟩ in parentheses denoting a valid element of the array
(4) A ⟨matrix variable⟩ followed by two ⟨integer⟩s separated by a comma and enclosed in parentheses denoting a valid element of the matrix

⟨*integer*⟩

One of the numbers 1, 2, 3, 4, . . .

⟨*literal*⟩

Any number expressed in a format the computer understands. Examples of literals include 3, −7, 4.179, 10972, 5.23E−17.

⟨*matrix expression*⟩

(1) A ⟨matrix variable⟩
(2) Two ⟨matrix variable⟩s separated by one of +, −, or *
(3) A ⟨numeric identifier⟩ enclosed in parentheses, followed by a * followed by a ⟨matrix variable⟩
(4) A function which returns a matrix value

⟨*matrix variable*⟩

A single letter denoting a matrix (A, B, C, . . . , Y, and Z can be used as matrix variables)

⟨*numeric identifier*⟩

An ⟨identifier⟩ that is not a string variable

⟨*statement*⟩

Any of the constructs shown in the statement section below

⟨*statement number*⟩

An ⟨integer⟩ between 1 and 9999, inclusive, that is used in a program to denote one of the statements

⟨*string literal*⟩

Any collection of letters, characters, digits, and blanks

⟨*string expression*⟩

(1) A ⟨string variable⟩
(2) A ⟨string literal⟩ enclosed in quotes
(3) Two ⟨string expression⟩s separated by a +
(4) Any function which returns a string value
(5) Any substring as legally expressed on your computer

⟨*string variable*⟩

A letter followed by a dollar sign ($). Valid string variables are A$, B$, C$, . . . , Y$, and Z$.

⟨*variable*⟩

A single letter or a single letter followed by a single digit. A, B, C, . . . , Y, Z, A0, B0, . . . , A1, B1, . . . , A2, . . . , Z9 are variables. Single letters are variables only if they are not used to denote either an array or a matrix in the program.

Summary of BASIC Statements

CLOSE statement

CLOSE ⟨*file number*⟩

This statement tells the computer that the file associated with this number will no longer be accessed. This file number can be used subsequently to open another file.

Correct Examples

CLOSE #3

CLOSE #6

CLOSE (4)

Incorrect Examples

CLOSE 1   (1 is not a file number)

CLOSE "ABC"   (Files must be closed by number, not by name)

DATA statement

DATA ⟨literal⟩, "⟨string literal⟩", ⟨literal⟩, . . .

This statement supplies items for READ statements. There is no effect when it is executed. Literals and string literals may be freely mixed.

Correct Examples

DATA 5, "XYZ", "ABC"

DATA 7E-09, 44

Incorrect Examples

DATA, 2, 4   (Extra comma inserted after the word DATA)

DATA 7 4 "XYZ"   (Commas missing)

DATA 5, 6, SEVEN   (Quote mark missing around SEVEN)

DEF statement

DEF ⟨function name⟩ (⟨variable⟩) = ⟨expression⟩

This statement connects the function named after DEF with the expression after the equal sign. When the function is subsequently used, the expression in this statement is evaluated.

Correct Examples

DEF FNA(M) = 2*M + N

DEF FNA(X1) = 31 + 4*Y

Incorrect Examples

DEF FNY(M$) = 89 + K   (M$ is not a variable)

DEF FNR(K(6)) = X9 + 3   (K(6) is not a variable)

DEF FUNC(X) = 49   (FUNC is not a legal function name)

FNA(Y1) = Y1↑3 + 48   (DEF is missing)

DIM statement

DIM ⟨*array variable*⟩(⟨*integer*⟩)
DIM ⟨*matrix variable*⟩(⟨*integer*⟩, ⟨*integer*⟩)
DIM ⟨*string variable*⟩(⟨*integer*⟩)

These statements serve only to tell the computer how large the arrays, matrices, and strings used in a program are. They have no effect on execution.

Correct Examples

DIM R(3)

DIM S(2,17)

DIM M$(44)

Incorrect Examples

DIM K$(4,1)   (String variable should have only one
                      subscript)
DIM R1(6)   (R1 is not a legal array name)

DIM L(1,2,3)   (Too many subscripts included)

DIM S   (Subscripts missing)

END statement

END

The computer stops executing program statements when it encounters this statement.

FILE statement

FILE ⟨*file number*⟩ "⟨*file name*⟩"

Some systems use:

OPEN ⟨*file number*⟩ "⟨*file name*⟩"

This statement connects the file named in the statement with the file number. Subsequently the file whose name appears may be accessed using the number. (*See also* Files statement.)

Correct Examples

FILE #3 "XYZ"

FILE (4) "MOPS"

OPEN #1 "BROOMS"

Incorrect Examples

FILE #1 DUST   (Quote marks around file name missing)

FILE 3 "LINT"   (3 not a valid file number)

OPEN #609 "DIRT"   (609 too large for a file number)

FILES statement

> FILES "⟨file name⟩", "⟨file name⟩", "⟨file name⟩", . . .

This statement is used on some systems instead of the FILE statement. The file named first on the list becomes file number one; the file named second is file number two; and so on. (*See also* FILE statement.)

> *Correct Example*
> ### FILES "RED", "WHITE", "BLUE"

> *Incorrect Examples*

FILES #2 "BIG", "BAD", "WOLF"   (No file number allowed in FILES statement)

FILES "OLD", "GREY" "MARE"   (Commas missing between GREY and MARE)

FILE "THREE", "BLIND", "MICE"   (FILES is misspelled)

FOR-NEXT statement

> FOR ⟨*variable*⟩ = ⟨*expression*⟩ TO ⟨*expression*⟩
> FOR ⟨*variable*⟩ = ⟨*expression*⟩ TO ⟨*expression*⟩ STEP ⟨*expression*⟩
> NEXT ⟨*variable*⟩

The statements between a FOR statement and a NEXT statement are executed repeatedly. The variable named in the FOR statement is initially assigned the value of the first expression; the statements between the FOR statement and the NEXT statement are executed; then the value of the expression following STEP is added to the variable, or, if there is no STEP, one is added. The statements are again executed and the variable value is again increased. This process continues until increasing the variable would result in its exceeding the value of the expression following TO. (If the expression following STEP is less than zero, the process continues until the value of the variable would be less than that of the expression following TO.) The variable in the NEXT statement must be the same as that in the FOR statement.

> *Correct Examples*
> ### FOR I = 4 TO 24
> ⟨*statement*⟩
> ⟨*statement*⟩
>
> .
> .
> .
>
> ⟨*statement*⟩
> **NEXT I**
>
> ### FOR J1 = 83.7 TO -11 STEP -6.1
> ⟨*statement*⟩
> ⟨*statement*⟩
>
> .
> .
> .
>
> ⟨*statement*
> **NEXT J1**

Incorrect Examples

FOR P = 1 TO 8   (Variables in FOR and NEXT statements
⟨*statement*⟩   must be the same)
⟨*statement*⟩
NEXT P1

FOR K$= 7 TO 22   (String variable is not allowed)

FOR S = 6 TO 100 STEP 6 - (96/16)   (STEP equal to 0 is not allowed)

FOR M = 5 STEP 1   (TO <expression> must be included)

NEXT   (Variable name missing)

GET statement

GET ⟨*file number*⟩ ⟨*identifier*⟩
GET ⟨*file number*⟩ ⟨*identifier*⟩, ⟨*identifier*⟩, ⟨*identifier*⟩, . . .

Some systems use

READ ⟨*file number*⟩ ⟨*identifier*⟩
READ ⟨*file number*⟩ ⟨*identifier*⟩, ⟨*identifier*⟩, ⟨*identifier*⟩, . . .

This statement fills the memory space(s) corresponding to the identifier(s) with the first available item(s) in the file whose number appears. The first available item is the earliest one in the file not yet accessed by a GET statement.

Correct Examples

GET #1 S

GET (3) M, N(6)

READ #4 K$, R(7, 9), L

Incorrect Examples

GET K, P1   (File number is missing)

GET #6 M, N, 4   (4 is not an identifier)

GOSUB statement

GOSUB ⟨*statement number*⟩

The computer transfers control to the statement whose number is in the GOSUB statement and continues execution from there. When the computer encounters a RETURN statement, it transfers control back to the statement immediately following the GOSUB statement.

Correct Examples

GOSUB 2000

GOSUB 7500

Incorrect Examples

GOSUB R	(Variable is not allowed as a statement number)
GOSUP 500	(GOSUB is misspelled)
GOSUB 60 + 70	(Expression is not allowed as a statement number)
GOSUB 14796210	(Statement number is too large to be legal)

GOTO statement

GOTO ⟨*statement number*⟩

The computer transfers control to the statement whose number appears in the GOTO statement and continues execution from there.

Correct Examples

GOTO 610

GOTO 793

GOTO 1

Incorrect Examples

GOTO	(Statement number is missing)
GOTO 170 + R	(Statement number may not be an expression)
GOTO M	(Variables are not allowed as statement numbers)

GOTO-OF statement (*see* ON-GOTO)

IF-THEN statements

IF ⟨*condition*⟩ THEN ⟨*statement number*⟩

Some systems also allow

IF ⟨*condition*⟩ THEN ⟨*statement*⟩

In the first form, if the condition is true, control is transferred to the statement whose number follows THEN. Otherwise execution continues with the next statement. In the second form, the statement following THEN is executed if the condition is true but not otherwise; execution then continues with the next statement.

Correct Examples

IF R = 6 THEN 900

IF M$ < "4MP9" THEN 113

IF K + 7 >= K↑4 + 19 THEN 1100

IF K <> 12 THEN LET R$ = "YES"

Incorrect Examples

IF R THEN 1200   (R is not a legal condition)

IF S = 7 GOTO 400   (GOTO cannot substitute for THEN)

IMAGE statement

: ⟨*string literal*⟩ ⟨*field*⟩ ⟨*string literal*⟩ ⟨*field*⟩ ⟨*string literal*⟩ . . .

This statement is used in conjunction with the PRINT USING statement to supply the format of the printed line. One value is printed in each field.

INPUT statement

INPUT ⟨*identifier*⟩
INPUT ⟨*identifier*⟩, ⟨*identifier*⟩, ⟨*identifier*⟩, . . .

This statement prints a question mark on the user's terminal and waits for the user to type a value or values to be stored in the memory spaces corresponding to the identifiers. Then execution is continued with the next statement.

Correct Examples

INPUT S

INPUT M(4,7)

INPUT K$,P,S(6)

Incorrect Examples

IMPUT R   (INPUT is misspelled)

INPUT 6   (6 is not an identifier)

INPUT R(5) R(6)   (Comma missing between identifiers)

LET statement

LET ⟨*numeric identifier*⟩ = ⟨*expression*⟩
LET ⟨*string variable*⟩ = ⟨*string expression*⟩

The computer evaluates the expression after the equal sign and places the value in the memory space corresponding to the string variable or numeric identifier after the LET. The word LET is often optional and can be omitted.

Correct Examples

LET K = 17 + P - K

LET M(6) = 6 + 44 + P

R$ = "AB" + "CD"

LET R$ = STR(P) + "Q"

Incorrect Examples

LET 6 + 7 = R   (6 + 7 is not an identifier)

LET R\$ = 73   (String variable may not be assigned
                          a numeric value)

MAT... =

MAT ⟨*matrix variable*⟩ = ⟨*matrix expression*⟩

The value of the expression after the equal sign is placed in the variable following MAT.
Note that a matrix expression evaluates to a matrix of values and that all these values are
stored in the spaces in the matrix after MAT.

Correct Examples

Suppose that A, B, and C are matrices and that they are the only matrices.

MAT C = B + A

MAT B = (2) * A

MAT A = INV(C)

Incorrect Examples

Suppose that A, B, and C are matrices and that they are the only matrices.

MAT C = M   (M is not a matrix; hence it is not
                       a matrix expression)
MAT A = B(5,5)   (B(5,5) is not a matrix)

MAT READ/WRITE/INPUT/GET/PRINT/PUT

MAT INPUT ⟨*matrix variable*⟩
MAT READ ⟨*matrix variable*⟩
MAT PRINT ⟨*matrix variable*⟩
MAT GET ⟨*matrix variable*⟩
MAT PUT ⟨*matrix variable*⟩
MAT WRITE ⟨*matrix variable*⟩

These statements have the effect of repeating INPUT, READ, PRINT, GET, PUT, and
WRITE statements, respectively, for each of the elements of the matrix except for those
elements in the zero row and zero column. First, the elements of the first row are treated
from left to right, then those in the second row are done, and so on. The MAT PRINT
statement formats the output in some special way. (*See also* INPUT, READ, PRINT,
GET, PUT, and WRITE statements.)

NEXT statement (*see* FOR-NEXT statement)

ON-GOTO statement

ON ⟨*expression*⟩ GOTO ⟨*statement number*⟩, ⟨*statement number*⟩, ⟨*statement number*⟩

Some systems use

GOTO ⟨expression⟩ OF ⟨statement number⟩, ⟨statement number⟩, ⟨statement number⟩

The computer evaluates the expression. If the value is 1, control is transferred to the statement whose number is first on the list; if it is 2, to the statement whose number is second on the list; and so on.

Correct Examples

ON R GOTO 100, 200, 300

ON K - 17 GOTO 93, 47, 196, 93

ON INT(L(4)*6) GOTO 98, 99

GOTO R OF 100, 200, 300

Incorrect Examples

ON M GOTO 30, 40, L   (L is not a statement number)

ON S$ GOTO 90, 100   (S$ is not an expression)

OPEN statement (*see* **FILE** statement)

PRINT statement

PRINT ⟨expression⟩
PRINT ⟨string expression⟩
PRINT ⟨expression⟩; ⟨expression⟩; ⟨string expression⟩;. . .
PRINT ⟨expression⟩, ⟨string expression⟩, ⟨expression⟩,. . .

This statement causes the value(s) of the expression(s) and string expression(s) to be printed on the terminal. Expressions and string expressions may be mixed indiscriminately, as may commas and semicolons. The result of commas among the expressions is the spacing of the expressions in columns across the page. Semicolons result in expressions being printed one right after the other on the line.

Correct Examples

PRINT R, S, T$

PRINT M(5), "HELLO"

PRINT 6 + 7; T$ + "XY", R↑5

Incorrect Examples

PRINT R, S T$ (Comma or semicolon is missing)

PRINT USING statement

PRINT USING ⟨statement number⟩ ⟨expression⟩, ⟨expression⟩, ⟨string expression⟩,. . .

This statement causes the value(s) of the expression(s) and string expression(s) to be printed on the terminal in the format of the IMAGE statement whose number follows USING. Expressions and string expressions may be mixed indiscriminately in the list. (*See* IMAGE.)

Correct Examples

PRINT USING 420 R$, S, T(6)

PRINT USING 1000 S$,16+R, T

PRINT USING 200 X

Incorrect Examples

PRINT USING S, T, U$ (Statement number for IMAGE statement missing. It may not be a variable)

PRINT USING 600, X   (Extra comma after statement number)

PUT statement

PUT ⟨file number⟩ ⟨expression⟩
PUT ⟨file number⟩ ⟨expression⟩, ⟨string expression⟩, ⟨expression⟩, ⟨expression⟩, . . .

Some systems use

WRITE ⟨file number⟩ ⟨string expression⟩
WRITE ⟨file number⟩ ⟨expression⟩, ⟨expression⟩, ⟨expression⟩, . . .

This statement outputs the value(s) of the expression(s) and string expression(s) to the file whose number appears. The output is written on the file immediately after the item that was most recently written by a PUT statement or retrieved by a GET statement.

Correct Examples

PUT #3 X, "YES", "NO", Y(4)

WRITE (2) K$+S$, 4↑9

PUT #6 S1, T(1) + U(1)

Incorrect Examples

PUT 4 M, N   (4 is not a valid file number)

PUT "XYZ" M, N   (A PUT statement needs a file number, not a file name)

RANDOMIZE statement

RANDOMIZE

The random numbers are scrambled on some systems when this statement is executed. Other systems do not have this statement and automatically scramble the random numbers at the start of every program.

READ statement (in relation to files, *see* GET)

READ ⟨identifier⟩
READ ⟨identifier⟩, ⟨identifier⟩, ⟨identifier⟩, . . .

This statement fills the memory space(s) corresponding to the identifier(s) with the first available item(s) in DATA statements. The first available item is the earliest item in the lowest numbered DATA statement that has not been accessed by a READ statement in the program. (See RESTORE)

Correct Examples

READ R

READ K(17)

READ M(1,4), S$, K

Incorrect Examples

READ 15 + 1   (15 + 1 is not an identifier)

READ R, S6, T7 U   (Comma is missing)

REM statement

REM ⟨string literal⟩

This statement has no effect on execution. The ⟨string literal⟩ may consist of anything the programmer wishes. The only possible error consists in misspelling REM.

RESET statement (*see* **REWIND statement**)

RESTORE statement (in relation to files, *see* **REWIND statement**)

RESTORE

Some systems allow

RESTORE ⟨statement number⟩

This statement resets the first available item in DATA statements. After a RESTORE statement, the computer considers all items in all DATA statements available even if they have been used in a READ statement. After a RESTORE ⟨statement number⟩, all items in DATA statements whose statement numbers are greater than or equal to the statement number after RESTORE are considered available.

RETURN statement

RETURN

The computer transfers control to the next statement after the most recently executed GOSUB statement not already used by a RETURN statement. If there have been no GOSUB statements, or if every GOSUB statement has been used by a RETURN statement, then execution of this statement results in an error.

REWIND statement

REWIND ⟨file number⟩

Some systems use one of the following:

RESTORE ⟨file number⟩

or

RESET ⟨file number⟩

This statement resets the first available item in the file whose number appears at the beginning of the file. After this statement, the next GET or PUT statement acts on the first item in the file.

STOP statement

STOP

The computer stops executing program statements when it encounters this statement.

THEN statement (*see* **IF-THEN statement**)

WRITE statement (*see* **PUT statement**)

INDEX